THE COLLECTED PLAYS OF
JOHN WHITING

Volume Two

In Volume One

THE COLLECTED PLAYS

OF

JOHN WHITING

VOLUME TWO

Edited by

Ronald Hayman

THEATRE ARTS BOOKS

NEW YORK

Library of Congress Catalogue Card Number 71-89993

Published by
Theatre Arts Books
333 Sixth Avenue, New York 10014
Printed in Great Britain by
Morrison & Gibb Ltd., London and Edinburgh

CONTENTS

CONTENTS

THE GATES OF SUMMER

INTRODUCTORY NOTE

WHITING started writing *The Gates of Summer* in 1953 and finished the first draft just before *Marching Song* was put on in 1954. It started a pre-London tour on 11 September 1956. Peter Hall directed, with James Donald as John Hogarth, Isabel Jeans as Sophie Faramond and Lionel Jeffries as Henry Bevis. Dorothy Tutin's understudy, Jocelyn James, played Caroline Traherne on the first night and subsequently when Dorothy Tutin had to go to hospital. There would have been time to replace her before bringing the play into London, but it closed in Leeds towards the end of October.

Norman Shrapnel reviewed it in Manchester for the *Manchester Guardian*:

> There are plays, as there are people, that one would particularly like to like, but which seem perversely bent on evading admiration. 'The Gates of Summer', John Whiting's new comedy, looks like one of these. It is a play of tone and mood. It appeals ambitiously enough to both nerves and emotions, and to strike them Mr Whiting has had to dig—the point of the archaeological excavations going on behind the scenes is not lost on us—assiduously into the past. . . . No ordinary comedy, certainly. What does it amount to? Precious little, if one had to answer in two precise words. A nice idea, if it were the idea, to set this nostalgic bit of misfiring pop-gun heroics against the holocaust to come. But the pattern is diffuse, the mood unstable, the lurking tears—for this critic at any rate—unrealised. As for the talk, it shifts with too little control through too many gears: desultory, direct, highfalutin, downright vulgar.

It had a German production in October 1959 at the Württembergisches Theater, Stuttgart.

PERSONS

SOPHIE FARAMOND

CRISTOS PAPADIAMANTIS

JOHN HOGARTH

HENRY BEVIS

CAROLINE TRAHERNE

SELWYN FARAMOND

PRINCE BASILIOS

*The action of the play takes place in and about a
country house in Greece a little way from Athens: the
time is the early summer of the year 1913.*

ACT ONE

The scene is a room in a country house in Greece, a little way from Athens.
The time is morning of a day in the early summer of the year 1913.
The house is built on two floors, and stands above a valley.
The room has several high windows which allow entrance from a stone terrace.
Through these windows can be seen part of an exterior wall which is washed in raspberry colour and contains a small window. A great vine surrounds the house. The floor of the room is stone partly covered by rugs. The ceiling, almost lost in shadow, is painted. There is a main door to the room which stands open showing the wide sweep of a stairway beyond. There is also a small arched entrance from a passage which leads to other parts of the house by way of a few shallow steps.
Within the room it remains cool as yet, and the shadows are only now beginning to shift. The sun strikes through the windows and brings to life in a vivid way several objects in the room—a scarlet shawl thrown over a chair, a piece of jewellery, a gold cross hanging on the egg-shell white wall—and the brilliance of these are marked in the quickening heat.
SOPHIE FARAMOND is standing at the window looking out across the terrace, and down the hill. She is fifty-four years old, and she can stare boldly into the morning sun for she is very beautiful. She has never feared the light: she has never feared anything except, perhaps, the consequences of her vanity.
In a far shadowed corner of the room is CRISTOS PAPADIAMANTIS, a Greek, sixty years of age. He is standing at a tall desk and holds a pen.
SOPHIE turns into the room.

SOPHIE: Put down the pen. (CRISTOS *does so.*) The man we have been trying to create is coming up the hill. (*She turns to the window.*) John.

    JOHN HOGARTH *has come up the hill, and on to the terrace. He now stands in the window. He has a top coat over his shoulders, and carries a hat and gloves.*

JOHN: The house stands alone above a wilderness. It's the colour

5

of fruit and looking up the traveller asks, Will it topple? I'll be at the windows on the south side, you said. And it's all true.

SOPHIE: There was a postscript to my letter. It said, Recognize me at once, please.

JOHN (*he kisses* SOPHIA): Haven't I?

SOPHIE: Yes.

JOHN: With the best will in the world I couldn't let you know when I'd be here. Have you been patient?

SOPHIE: For ten years. After such a time it would have been natural to send you false instructions.

JOHN: I left Alexandria three days ago and crossed in a boat with a party of olive green pilgrims. I stayed last night in Athens, but didn't sleep because of the song of the cats and the silent mischief of the bugs. So I hired a cart and set off at dawn with your letter in my hand. Here it is. It holds ten years of silence, Sophie. From the day you left England to come out here. Time to go, you said—and go you did. Why?

SOPHIE: I was becoming aware of my age. That's a reason. But you're young—shall I say thirty-six?—and you've left England, never to go back. Or have I misunderstood?

JOHN: No. Everything's been sold up.

SOPHIE: Then I imagine you must be burdened with a great deal of money. What have you done with it?

JOHN: Bought a state of exile.

SOPHIE: Shameful! Not a proper purpose.

JOHN: I'm free. Sophie.

SOPHIE: Again? For how long?

JOHN: Until the end. The first step into middle age did it.

SOPHIE: Who was she?

JOHN: Her name was Ada. You see I can speak of her in the past. She had very short legs, was a comfortable shape and the wife of a bishop. On the night of my thirty-fifth birthday her arms were round my neck, and she was whispering to me. The next morning I began the sale of everything I possessed. When it was done I felt remarkable. Sanctified. I had nothing in the world but money.

CRISTOS PAPADIAMANTIS *moves into the room.*

SOPHIE: This is Mr Cristos Papadiamantis, my secretary. Mr John Hogarth, from England.

CRISTOS *bows to* JOHN.

(*To* CRISTOS.) We won't do any more this morning. Go up, please, and make a fair copy as far as we've gone.

CRISTOS *goes from the room and up the stairs.*

I spend a few hours every day dictating to Cristos. I'm putting down some of my memories. You'll be able to sharpen my recollection on a number of incidents of the time in England we knew together.

JOHN: Are you writing the truth?

SOPHIE: Yes.

JOHN: Then you're not going to publish.

SOPHIE: Certainly I am. This autumn.

JOHN: That'll upset a lot of people. But I suppose this is a safe distance. The most they can do is hang your publisher.

SOPHIE: You escaped, I see.

JOHN: Without violence to my person, yes. The signal for my going was the baying of the newspapers. There were no tears. Except from that woman shut up in the country. She would be weeping, we can be sure of that, and in a lower room holding a holy book in one hand and biting the nails of the other would be her husband. They're probably still at it, God help them! She tried to lead me to the righteous life, Sophie. That was her only mistake. You know where such excursion must end. On this occasion it was an episcopal four-poster in a cathedral town. The rooks mourned over us through the night.

SOPHIE: I'd hoped he wasn't a provincial bishop.

JOHN: He forgave me like the good man he is, but that wasn't enough for Ada. She had to make a public confession to a national newspaper. Modesty prevents me saying why.

SOPHIE: Then I'll say it for you. She wanted everyone to know how lucky she had been. After all, John, I've always considered myself happy to know you in the drawing-room, so I can appreciate Ada's feelings. There, I'm already speaking of her as an old friend.

JOHN: In the end I took nothing but her teaching to heart and sold up my wordly goods. I've put the proceeds to an ungodly purpose. Which brings me here. Alone.

SOPHIE: The difficulty of exile for a woman is that she can't go unaccompanied. I had to provide myself with an escort at a small church in Kensington on the Tuesday before I sailed.

JOHN: Ah, yes. I'm sorry. How is Selwyn? Where is Selwyn?

SOPHIE: Buried alive at the dig below. You passed the place on the road. Selwyn has been working the excavation for eighteen months. He's found nothing.

JOHN: Is there anything to be found?

SOPHIE: Selwyn is sure of it. There have been several false alarms and then a most unpleasant man has hurried here from the Royal Museum in Berlin. They're putting up money.

JOHN: Has Selwyn found anything under the ground in these ten years of digging?

SOPHIE: Nothing important. For six years we dug over most of the North African desert. Excavations in Egypt rewarded us with a gold commode. And so we came to this place.

JOHN: What's he looking for here?

SOPHIE: He seems to think he may uncover some place of worship of great antiquity. Am I right, Henry? (*She speaks to* HENRY BEVIS, *who has come into the room.*)

HENRY: Quite right, Sophie.

SOPHIE: Henry Bevis is with us, John, as a Special Correspondent to 'The Times'. This is Mr Hogarth from London, Henry.

HENRY: From London! (*He shakes hands with* JOHN.) How is that beautiful country of ours?

JOHN: Have you been away from it a long time, Mr Bevis?

HENRY: Yes.

JOHN: I thought so. Well, it was looking very pretty in the spring.

HENRY: And the people?

JOHN: They've never been pretty at any time of year, have they? But I thought they were looking very fit.

SOPHIE: Henry's absence from England isn't voluntary, John. He was sent here to report on whatever is found in that great hole Selwyn is digging. How he's managed to fill a column of 'The Times', once every two weeks I've never understood. Surely, Henry, there must be a limit to the number of ways even you can describe such quantities of mud.

HENRY: It's the suspense, Sophie. No one knows exactly what Selwyn hopes to find.

SOPHIE: I'd have thought the flutter of anticipation even in those small archaeological circles about St James's Square must now be stilled after eighteen months.

HENRY: You musn't expect quick results in this kind of work, Sophie. Must she, Mr Hogarth?

JOHN: I've no idea.

HENRY: Selwyn has all the patience of an old soldier.

SOPHIE: Yes, I suppose those many years of quite undistinguished service must have taught him that.

HENRY: How unlike you are. Is that the basis for a successful marriage, I wonder?

SOPHIE: Don't brood over me, Henry?

JOHN: Sophie, I've remembered something. When I got out of the cart at the bottom of the hill I left a box at the side of the road.

SOPHIE: One of the men can bring it up later.

HENRY: I'll go down for it.

JOHN: You'll do nothing of the kind. It's very heavy, and that hill is very steep.

HENRY: I'm going down to the dig. I can bring the box back with me. I'll be pleased to do that, Mr Hogarth.

JOHN: Well, thank you.

HENRY: A word: very unwise to leave anything about here. (HENRY *goes out through the window.*)

SOPHIE: Such an old young man. And how the poor creature sweats in this climate. Why did you suddenly remember your box?

JOHN: It was the mention of marriage.

SOPHIE: I don't see any connection.

JOHN: We were on the edge of a discussion. I wanted to avoid it.

SOPHIE: You'll find when you get to know him that it's never difficult to knock Henry off a subject. But he's been meditating on marriage for some weeks now.

JOHN: Must I get to know him?

SOPHIE: Well, how long are you staying?

JOHN: I'll be here two days if everything goes well.

SOPHIE: Why should it go badly? Come here. Yes, there about your eyes—God help you, those are lines of thought. I'd say of recent contemplation.

JOHN: We're well into the twentieth century, Sophie. You're going to have to accustom yourself to a change in the faces of those you love.

SOPHIE: And a change in their habits, it seems. Where are you going from here?

JOHN: When I left Ada curled up and quilt covered for the last time and went back to my rooms I'd decided to sell out. Everything around me—except a bottle of gin—lay cowering beneath the hammer. I stayed alone for two days. The storm had broken about me and Ada. There were no letters except postcards with a single word, usually of a biblical nature. No one came near me but my ancient firelighter. Then, on the second night, there was a shout on the stairs. I thought at first the mob had come. I picked up the poker and went to meet it. Instead of the sansculottes I found an old man entangled in the curtains of the stairs—caught like a gigantic bat. I freed him. He embraced me. I freed myself. He went on and collapsed like a ruin before the fire and at once began to talk. He used none of the words recently associated with me. Indeed, he's never heard of Ada, he said. He talked and the words were as fresh to me as his friendliness. He loved me, he said, for I was a son of freedom. He, too, Basilios, was a son of freedom. I was again taken in his arms. He talked through the night. At half-past five I gave him my cheque for one hundred thousand pounds. At half-past seven I gave him my hand and the promise of my services. At half-past nine he left. But there remained on the table a document which made altogether too clear my future commitment to revolution.

SOPHIE: Revolution. So that's the news you've brought me. I think you've been ingenuous. You'll never see your friend again, and certainly not your money.

JOHN: Basilios is a man—the one sex I don't make mistakes about. He'll be here to fetch me as he promised within two days.

SOPHIE: You're very sure.

JOHN: I've reason to be. Basilios talked to me in a language I've known since childhood. Yet until that night I'd never heard it spoken.

SOPHIE: Do you mean Greek?

JOHN: I mean the language of action.

SOPHIE: Am I to expect barricades on my doorstep?

JOHN: No. I shall travel north four hundred miles to the trouble centre. The affair is small enough for me to play a big part. I shall be happy.

CAROLINE TRAHERNE *comes into the room by the windows. She is twenty-five years old. She carries a large bunch of wild flowers and herbs which are recently gathered.*

SOPHIE: Do you know John Hogarth, Caroline?

CAROLINE: Yes. ⎫
JOHN: No.   ⎬ *They speak together.*
               ⎭

SOPHIE: Well, yes, or no, this is he. Mrs Traherne, John. My daughter by Selwyn's first wife.

JOHN: How do you do. Have I met you before?

CAROLINE: No. But I know you from Sophie's book.

JOHN: That's very interesting. (*He at last gently disengaged his hand from* CAROLINE.)

SOPHIE: Those are most unsuitable flowers for the house.

CAROLINE: I brought them in to save them from the heat of the sun.

SOPHIE: Save them? But you've uprooted them.

CAROLINE: Well, then, their last hours can be cool and dignified. Unlike Henry, who is staggering about in the sun under an enormous box. (CAROLINE *goes from the room by the passageway*.)

JOHN: I'd no idea Selwyn had a daughter. Did you know when you married him?

SOPHIE: It was mentioned. She was a child then, of course. In the keeping of some nuns.

JOHN: What's she doing here?

SOPHIE: Recovering from a disastrous marriage contracted seven years ago when she was eighteen.

JOHN: Who was her mother?

SOPHIE: Nobody at all. She lies buried beneath a solitary tree in the Orient. A sacrifice to Selwyn's military career.

JOHN: What did the girl mean when she said that she knew me from your book?

SOPHIE: I didn't know she'd read it.

JOHN: It means, though, that you've written about me.

SOPHIE: Of course. Do you think I could write of those days and forget you? Without you there'd be no story to tell. Let's always remember there was nothing but the years between us then.

JOHN: There's more than age between us now, Sophie. There are the separate ways which brought us here. You came in resignation. I've come in affirmation. That day ten years ago, the day you married Selwyn. I mourned for you then, Sophie.

SOPHIE: You feel I made the one certificate serve for both marriage and death.

JOHN: Everyone does that. No, I mourned the end of an era which you had made so much your own. I think I could have borne it if you'd died—but you married! You became a woman, Sophie. Oh, Sophie!

SOPHIE: It was the morning of a birthday. I awoke very much

alone. You were in the country. What were you doing? I forget. No one came near me for hours, it seemed. Then your gift was brought to me. Ah! you were still young at that time to give me birthday presents without flinching. I took off the wrappings and there was the musical box. Something to be given to a child— or to me. I opened the lid and the music began. And with the music the tears. I knew then it was time to go. Selwyn had often called to tell me he was planning this exploration of the past. I'd known him for many years. I'd long admired his amazing spirit. We were of an age and both needed a companion in exile. I proposed marriage that evening, and was accepted.

JOHN: When I came back from the country you were married and gone without a word. No one knew why. All they said was that you seemed serious. I wouldn't believe it.

SOPHIE: Surely that was a time to take something seriously, even if it was only Selwyn. But you—here—now—what excuse have you? At the kindergarten age of thirty-five you're intending to take seriously—what?—a revolt, the rallying cries of manifestos and a mad old man.

JOHN: Yes, all those. And the reason is this: thirty-five—yes, I am— but how do I account for these grey hairs and the fact that I no longer make love without sadness? My contemporaries remain darkly pigmented and continue to go to bed laughing. So you must think of me, Sophie, as one who has also reached a time, if not an age, to be serious.

SOPHIE: Very well. But you mustn't expect me to talk about revolution and freedom. That's not my kind of seriousness.

JOHN: Once you had no seriousness at all.

SOPHIE: In those days. But was there so much to be serious about? No. You could always find something if you went looking for it Like trouble. Why should I have bothered? I was what is called happy. That's nothing to be solemn about. At least, it wasn't when I was young. Perhaps it is these days. I don't know. Now you've an occupation I expect you look back in horror on the years we spent in London. I think that's a pity.

JOHN: Not horror. This feeling of sadness for what I loved.

   CAROLINE *has come into the room.*

CAROLINE: I know very well what you mean. Age doesn't come into it, Sophie. That's a mistake you would make. You can be finished at twenty-four.

JOHN: How old are you?

CAROLINE: Twenty-five.

JOHN: And you're finished?

CAROLINE: Yes. Hasn't Sophie told you?

HENRY BEVIS *comes through the windows. He is bowed beneath a large box which he carries on his shoulders.*

JOHN: Many, many thanks. Are you all right? I feel we should get it up at once, Sophie. Where am I?

SOPHIE *points through the main windows to the small window set in the exterior wall.*

SOPHIE: You're there.

HENRY *moves towards the stairs with the box.*

JOHN: I'd better go with him, I think. (JOHN *follows* HENRY *from the room.*)

CAROLINE: Is he staying?

SOPHIE: John? For a while. He's on his way to a revolution. He seems to think it should begin the day after tomorrow.

CAROLINE: He's on every page of your book, you know. Even the pages where he's not mentioned. For he's the time you can't get out of your head.

SOPHIE: How do you come to have seen the book?

CAROLINE: I kissed Cristos and he showed it to me.

SOPHIE: You're corrupt in almost every way.

CAROLINE: Why do people put up with me?

SOPHIE: Your husband didn't.

CAROLINE: Don't be sentimental. You wouldn't have liked Boy Traherne, either.

SOPHIE: I dislike him intensely for one thing. That is, running off and making it necessary for you to be here at this time.

CAROLINE: Do you think he'd be interested in my tragic story?

SOPHIE: He? Call him by his name.

After a considerable pause CAROLINE *softly and tentatively says.*

CAROLINE: John. (*She laughs.*) Ouf! that first time you say a name as a name. Some cold bath, eh? But once you're in—hey! you're in—and it's fine and healthy. John. John! (*She raises her voice.*) John! John!

JOHN HOGARTH *appears at the window of his room and looks down.*

JOHN: Yes?

CAROLINE: Nothing. (JOHN *goes back into the room.*) The man in the book: the man in the bedroom. Now, then—I've to put them together, haven't I, to make sense?

SOPHIE: To make a man.

CAROLINE: Well, to start with he was born, like the rest. Somewhere in a drawer there'll be faded photographs of a naked baby, which he was, one time. It's always wise to remember that. So things went well, and he began to grow.

SOPHIE: He came to London when he was eighteen. Where did he come from? I've never bothered to ask. Where does love come from? He had money—his mother was an American. He had energy—his father was a Scot. Yet he had no pretentions. He didn't want to do anything with his money or himself.

CAROLINE: And he lived splendidly, at that time.

SOPHIE: Yes.

CAROLINE: What was the secret? The something you know. Tell me. I've an idea he was happy.

SOPHIE: I think he was. Although—

CAROLINE: That's not in your book.

SOPHIE: I shall come to it.

CAROLINE: Come to it now. With me. In your book you call him the first twentieth century man. What do you mean by that?

SOPHIE: He was the only man I knew who seemed perfectly unequipped to face the future. I knew he'd survive.

CAROLINE: Riddles. Good. He's not simple. Good.

SOPHIE: It's an unfortunate fact, Caroline, that the qualities needed for survival as a person are the same unsocial qualities which can destroy an individual, a community, or even a nation. So the lack of moral equipment of the genius and the great criminal are much the same. It's what you haven't got that matters. John's great strength was that he lacked seriousness.

CAROLINE: It's the answer. No unhappiness, in other words.

SOPHIE: And no love.

CAROLINE: Between the weak wail of arrival and the whimper of departure there is not cause for alarm but cause for laughter. Can I see it that way—with him—through him? Can I?

SOPHIE: Wait a minute. I'm speaking of John ten years ago. He's changed.

CAROLINE: A man who believed all that—why should he want to change? Looked at his way, it suddenly becomes worth doing—this hanging around. No one wants to play out the thing seriously, but if it's really a charade—well, then!—how d'you do. (*She looks up at the window.*)

SOPHIE: He left England in all seriousness. He left Ada—

CAROLINE: Ah! she was the great scandal, wasn't she? Ada, you say. Like that. And then tell me he left in all seriousness.

SOPHIE: He was very fond of her.

CAROLINE: Since my husband left me I've become attached to a hot water bottle on cold nights. Seriously? Not at all. A man doesn't give up a country for a flannel bound comforter.

SOPHIE: He didn't. He gave it up to start a revolution. That's the business in hand.

HENRY *has come down the stairs and is now in the room.*

CAROLINE: And that's a solemn fact, is it?

SOPHIE: So he says. Is it the heat, Henry?

HENRY: I've been talking to Hogarth.

CAROLINE: Did he make you laugh?

HENRY: Good God, no. He's been telling me the most terrible stories of the people he's going to in the north. I'd never have thought such injustice went on these days.

SOPHIE: He's impressed you, I see.

HENRY: Such sincerity must be impressive.

SOPHIE (*to* CAROLINE): You see what I mean? (SOPHIE *goes from the room and up the stairs.*)

HENRY: Caroline, would you say I'm a sensitive man?

CAROLINE: As a literary gent, Henry, you're a duck.

HENRY: I only ask because sometimes I seem to lack an appreciation of the suffering of others. The conversation with Hogarth made me understand that. It worries me. I know perfectly well that unhappiness exists, but I've never been able to think of a way to do anything about it. You, for example—now, I know you've been very unhappy. When you first came here I tried to help you with my companionship. But it wasn't any good, was it?

CAROLINE: No.

HENRY: I think your kind of unhappiness confused me. I'm very muddled about marriage.

CAROLINE: Who isn't?

HENRY: I am more than most people. What I'm trying to say is this: I don't think I'm big enough to take on a revolution as Hogarth's doing, but I think I could help you. I say, I think I could help you. To be happy—happier.

CAROLINE: All right. Go ahead.

HENRY: Now?

CAROLINE: Well, it depends on what sort of comfort you're thinking of giving me.

There is a pause.

HENRY: Do you read poetry? I mention this because when I was a boy I was lonely and unhappy and I found it a great help.

CAROLINE: Henry, I need more than a rhymed couplet.

HENRY: That's what I mean. I never seem to be able to suggest anything—helpful. It's this place, I think. Although most of us are English the values seem to be different.

CAROLINE: You miss London.

HENRY: Very much.

CAROLINE: Why don't you go back?

HENRY: I shall, as soon as your father's finished the excavation and I can put in my final article. If he finds something I can really write about—something to which I can do justice—well, it'll make my name. That's what I'm bargaining for. I think I'd better go down to the dig for my morning session now. Care to walk with me?

CAROLINE: No. What do you do down there?

HENRY: Sometimes I do a little sifting, but not often. I don't get on with the workmen. (JOHN *has come down the stairs and now enters the room.*) Anyway, that's where I'll be for a while, Caroline. (HENRY *goes out through the windows.*)

JOHN: Sophie tell me that you've been very unhappy.

CAROLINE: There was a time.

JOHN: You're getting over it.

CAROLINE: Yes. It was nothing. A marriage. He left me. Ran away.

JOHN: I see.

CAROLINE: Do you see it from his point of view or mine?

JOHN: His, I suppose. I'm also running away from a marriage. Not my own. Someone else's.

CAROLINE: He just went into hiding. From what I hear you're making for the open country.

JOHN: I hope so.

CAROLINE: You're looking for more than the heroism of love.

JOHN: I'd say the stoicism of love. Yes, more than that.

CAROLINE: Liberation.

JOHN: Of others. Not myself.

CAROLINE: Have you been talking to Sophie?

JOHN: For a moment. But she insisted on asking a lot of questions, so I came away.

CAROLINE: She thinks you've changed.

JOHN: She's quite right.

CAROLINE: I don't think so.

JOHN: How can you possibly know?

CAROLINE: By remembering what I've read about you. Not only in Sophie's book, but in the newspapers. All show the man you are. Why should you want to change.?

JOHN: What are you talking about?

CAROLINE: You. I'm talking about you.

JOHN: Have you been interested so long?

CAROLINE: As long as I can remember. I'm not concerned with the morality of your behaviour in the past. I'm concerned that you're here—now. Why won't you look at me? There. What do you see?

JOHN: I've had the last conversation of this kind in my life!

CAROLINE: Sophie told me her name. It was Ada.

JOHN: Very well, so it was Ada.

CAROLINE: And because of her the London mob threw stones at your windows. That was in the papers. Was she worth it?

JOHN: They'd got it into their heads that I was breaking up something very dear to their hearts: a home. You know how that country domesticates its idols. The main demonstration was a parade past my house of elderly women carrying banners. That went on for some hours. I felt compelled to send them out tea and sandwiches. They leant against the railings eating and drinking and booing whenever I passed a window.

CAROLINE: Women have always felt strongly about you.

JOHN: Women feel too much about everything. That is the dreadful inequality of sex. It was their reserve capacity for actively demonstrating emotion which at last defeated me. Poets are lucky. They can spin out the truth of their passion to at least the length of a sonnet. With my lesser talent I've had to content myself with a brisk action and one short word.

CAROLINE: Which so often led to broken windows.

JOHN: All the best games end in destruction.

CAROLINE: We never get out of the nursery where everything finishes broken up. You played the whole of your life in London that way, didn't you? Without seriousness, because you knew the time would come when you'd have to put your toys away. So better smash them! You were right. You were quite right.

JOHN: How would such behaviour help you?

CAROLINE: If I'd seen my marriage with Boysie—and the break-away—as you saw your love affairs, then I wouldn't have been unhappy. By the way, I'm not unhappy any more. Why should I be? Throughout my married life I believed that love—you know, the rubnose, softpaw kind—was calculable. It never entered my head not to take it seriously. You, on the other hand, saw it as an incidental. That seems to be reasonable.

JOHN: Is this reasonable? Dawn. London. I wake. It's night within the room until the curtains are drawn back. The bed-covers over my body are heavy as sin. Throw them off! Step freely— ha ha! boldly— to the window. Draw back the curtains. Stare at the sky for a sign. Hm. It's raining. The policeman at the corner is weeping. The cold strikes me like an unkind reminder. Last night's warrior becomes a goose-pimpled pudding. Cover the poor mockery with a gown. The day must be begun, it seems. Very well, then—good morning. Breakfast. The day's news beside the tray. So, there's energy to engage that still virgin for a start. She gives up her miserable secrets reluctantly, column by column, and the sign is not one of them. Go, light fires! Open the letters of the day. Will one hold the word, the news from another land, the call to action? No. They demand, beg, entreat, abuse—nothing more. Dress. Talk to myself in the looking-glass. Walk out. Meet a man. He complains of my treatment of his daughter. He threatens me with action. Action! Christ, if it were true. He means litigation, which is the English substitute. My interest in him has gone and so, I see, has the sun. Something must be done if only to put in my journal. Well, turn in here. It is a theatre where men knock each other about with wooden swords and die, get up, and bow. The curtain rattles down on the play and the day. Hohum! The sky remains inscrutable—positively unhelpful. Curtain it off with the rest. It is another room—another place. I'm welcome. There's no doubt about it. Here between the sheets there is something to be done with authority, if not with dignity. Let me look at the face before turning away. It smiles, so all's well. Goodnight. Good morning. Dawn. London. I wake. It's night within the room until the curtains are drawn back. The bed-covers over my body—and so on. Day by day by night-time. Reasonable?

CAROLINE: There is one thing.

JOHN: Tell me.

CAROLINE: The moment of happiness which was in the smiling face before you turned away.

JOHN: It was never a very intelligent face.

CAROLINE: Nothing to do with it. Always reasonable to make someone happy.

JOHN: I'm sorry. Not possible now. Sorry. My appointment is not with you, I'm afraid. It's with a man who took me by the hand and dragged me from childhood—all those broken toys, remember —to this present time. Basilios.

CAROLINE: It is a serious business, I see. Why did he chose you?

JOHN: Some years ago my friends wanted to get me settled. Before I knew what was happening I found myself to be a Member of Parliament. It seemed a good time to make a speech. The motion happened to concern the Government's attitude to this minority group under Basilios in the north. They had recently shot the British Minister, and subjected his wife and daughter to humiliating proposals which both had accepted before returning to England.

CAROLINE: One of the lesser perils of our Imperial policy.

JOHN: In a speech to the House opposing reprisals I suggested the country should be accepted into the British Empire. It seemed that at the moment of surrender both ladies had been wrapped in a Union Jack. No one agreed with me that it was the natives' way of honouring the flag and the speech was dismissed as an impertinence. Yet it was a report of that speech in an old newspaper which brought Basilios to me. The faded cutting was in his pocket. It remained the one call to unity and action his country had ever known. Spoken by me when I didn't know the place was on the map. How could I resist such an appeal to leadership?

CAROLINE: So the whole thing's a joke, after all. Just a joke, as it was in the past. You don't take it any more seriously than— Ada?—or perhaps me. You haven't changed.

JOHN: I don't want to be unreasonable about this. An incident which begins as a joke can have serious consequences. You've been unhappy, I know, but please don't ask me to console you. Anyway, there would hardly be time, for Basilios will be here before you can say, I love you.

CAROLINE: I love you.

SELWYN FARAMOND *and* HENRY BEVIS *come into the room by the windows. They stop on hearing John's last words to Caroline.*

SELWYN: Then marry her, my dear fellow. Congratulations. Good news. I've been worried about the child. How are you otherwise?

JOHN: Otherwise I'm very well. What on earth are you talking about, Selwyn?

SELWYN: Declaration of love. Made by you both as I came in. Bevis heard it. Yes?

HENRY: Yes.

SELWYN: Never mind. I shouldn't have come in at that moment.

CAROLINE: Why did you?

SELWYN: I want a bath. Be a daughter to me and tell the men to carry up hot water. (CAROLINE *goes out by the passageway.*) Dirty work, Hogarth.

JOHN: What?

SELWYN: This digging.

JOHN: Oh, I see what you mean. Yes, it must be.

SELWYN: But I think it will be worth it. I'm sure we're about to uncover something remarkable. (*He takes a small maquette of a human figure from his pocket and holds it out to* JOHN.) What do you make of that?

JOHN (*he takes the figure*): It's a woman, isn't it?

SELWYN: Yes. One of the workmen found it yesterday. Significant attitude of worship, don't you think?

JOHN: It seems familiar. I don't know why.

SELWYN: If we can get something from this site it will shake them up in London. I want to do the BM crowd in the eye. They've never shown any interest in my work. If it wasn't for the Germans we'd not be able to go on. England's done nothing for the expedition.

HENRY: Are you being quite fair, Selwyn? 'The Times' has kept the country informed. Through me.

SELWYN: Hogarth, what's this about you being on your way to some trouble in the north? Is it another of Bevis's fairy stories?

JOHN: No, it's true.

SELWYN: Then do be careful. The political situation in the Balkans has never been so confused. Why are you going? Have you been sent by the Crown?

JOHN: Good God, no! I wanted to leave England.

SELWYN: That's a substantial reason. Some woman, was it?

JOHN: All women. I wanted to get away from the whole business.

SELWYN: There was no need to go to the length of starting a revolution. You could have helped me. Nothing like digging and sifting for keeping the mind off sex.

JOHN: I suppose not.

SELWYN: Bevis has found it invaluable. Haven't you? When I was in the Army and it became troublesome I'd always call a church parade. Made the men rather unhappy turning out so late at night, but it always worked. Still, everyone has their own method.

JOHN: Well, it's a personal problem. Here. (*He gives the figure to* SELWYN.)

SELWYN: Sophie's pleased to see you, I expect.

JOHN: Yes. We've been talking.

SELWYN: About the old days? She pretends she doesn't miss them. And she pretends very well. Stay on for a while, my dear boy, and keep her amused as you did in the past. And Caroline. She had a bad time before she came here. Married a bastard. Stay. We're not much troubled by the nuisances of London. The weather's good, the local people are friendly to everyone except Bevis, and we don't have to be pleasant to each other if we don't want to. As for women—no worry about them here. They're a simple good people without the refinements which make life such hell in London. Stay on, do.

CAROLINE *comes back into the room.*

CAROLINE: They're getting your bath ready. The water will be in by the time you've undressed.

SELWYN: Thank you, Caro. Come up and talk to me, Hogarth. Have a bath if you like.

JOHN: I'll come and talk. Are you going back to England when you've finished here?

SELWYN: No. Sophie and I'll never go back. There's some very interesting work to be done in Asia Minor. I may join in. Different period, of course. Same digging. (SELWYN *and* JOHN *go out of the room and up the stairs.*)

HENRY: I try to make myself believe that I feel such an outsider because I'm here as an official observer. No more.

CAROLINE (*she is looking after* JOHN): He's only a visitor.

HENRY: Hogarth? Yes, but he seems to have the art of engaging himself at once. I heard enough of your conversation as I came in to know that he's given you more comfort in a few words than I've been able to give in months. I suppose it's the way he said it.

CAROLINE: It's not a matter of words, Henry. That's the mistake you're making. Read poetry, you said. There you were off the mark. I went through a poetical marriage. Boysie knew about every art except one. Life with him was never too damned beautiful for words. There were so many to be spoken, sung, whispered, written, rhymed, scratched on the window pane, carved into wood and stone—words for everyday use and casually slung at each other, words for public abuse and shouted from the housetops, words with single meaning and words with double meaning, good words, bad words, holy words and dirty words. And when the day was over and you'd think the talking would have to stop—no, there'd always be that dribble of stale words for explanation of failure, betrayal, misery and horror. Buried beneath, suffocated, dead, was love.

HENRY: Now you listen to Hogarth. Intently.

CAROLINE: Henry, couldn't you take an overwhelming interest in something?

HENRY: I think I could if I tried.

CAROLINE: I don't mean in me. I mean food or politics or God. Or something.

HENRY: Would that help you?

CAROLINE: Not at all. But why should you help me?

HENRY: I cling to that as the one definite purpose I have.

CAROLINE: Nonsense! You're a journalist put down in this place for quite another reason. You're probably the only person I know, Henry, for whom hard work is the solution.

HENRY: My work, yes. Is it shocking to you that the concern of my life is bread and butter?

CAROLINE: Less shocking than your ambitions: to be in love, to be somewhere else than here, to be someone. Think what you'll take on if you achieve all that.

HENRY: I'm not ashamed of my ambitions. And never forget, Caroline, that you can build palaces, even empires, on bread and butter.

CRISTOS *has come down the stairs and into the room.*

CAROLINE: What do you want?

CRISTOS: I thought you were alone.

CAROLINE: I can be. Can't I, Henry?

　　HENRY *walks out of the room by the windows.*

CRISTOS: That was unkind. I didn't mean to interrupt you.

CAROLINE: We were only talking about ourselves. Same subject as usual.

CRISTOS: What I'm obliged by custom to call your unhappiness.

CAROLINE: You don't believe it, do you?

CRISTOS: No. Do you?

CAROLINE: Not any more.

CRISTOS: I expect you were angry when your husband left you. Englishwomen are good losers in every game, except marriage.

CAROLINE: Oh damn! Where is he.

CRISTOS: Talking to Selwyn in his bath.

CAROLINE: You know who I mean.

CRISTOS: Apparently I do.

CAROLINE: Have you met him?

CRISTOS: For a moment. I've known a John Hogarth for some months, of course. Very well. (*He holds up two small notebooks he is carrying.*)

CAROLINE: From Sophie's book.

CRISTOS: I'm very interested. Is it the same man?

CAROLINE: Yes, he's the person Sophie's been writing about.

CRISTOS: I know that. Let me put it this way: is it the man in the book you're willing to come down those stairs?

CAROLINE: It's a question of identity. I see what you mean.

CRISTOS: I remember the morning you sat with me reading these books. You were smiling. I found it very disturbing. Sophie and I seemed to have done the job too well! Did you smile when you met the other Hogarth? Not the man Sophie and I put together, but the man of independent action. They're not the same.

CAROLINE: Why tell me that?

CRISTOS: You're English, and so you're likely to prefer a romantic fiction to the real thing. If you were Greek or French—or even German—I'd not be saying this to you.

CAROLINE: It sounds like a warning.

CRISTOS: I mean it to be that.

　　SOPHIE *comes down the stairs and into the room.*

CAROLINE: Can you really believe, Cristos, that I'm still young enough to be in love with a man in a book?

CRISTOS: I wanted to be sure that you're not.

SOPHIE: Now John Hogarth's here I hope I'm not going to find people standing in corners talking about him all the time.

CAROLINE: Cristos was giving me advice.

SOPHIE: Would you like to tell me what it was?

CAROLINE: He thinks that after my misery with Boysie I may be on the look out for an ideal. He's afraid that I've found it in your book under the name of Hogarth. He pointed out that there's a man of that name in the house at the moment. However, I'm not to confuse them. They're not the same. The man in the book's a fiction. According to Cristos.

SOPHIE: That's untrue. My memory's as clear as a spyglass.

    HENRY *comes in through the windows.*

HENRY: I say, I think somebody responsible should come down to the dig. Something's happened. I'm not quite sure what. One of the workmen has fallen through a hole and disappeared, but there seems to be far more to it than that.

CAROLINE: Selwyn's in his bath.

HENRY: If I could understand what those fellows are talking about it might help.

CRISTOS: I'll come down. I speak the same language as those fellows.

HENRY: So you do. But then you are Greek, aren't you?

CRISTOS: Yes. It's very helpful. (HENRY *and* CRISTOS *go out through the windows.*)

SOPHIE: How happy Henry will be if at last that excavation gives up its secret. He'll be able to write this final brilliant despatch we've heard do much about and return at once to London and honour. What will you do?

CAROLINE: By that time I hope to have found someone else to put up with me.

SOPHIE: I suppose you mean John. Will you make your intentions clear to him? In so many words.

CAROLINE: Are you jealous—Mummie?

SOPHIE: A little. Then again I don't think you're good enough for him. I never knew your husband—indeed, I've never met anyone who admitted to doing so—but from what you've told me I'd say he was tolerant and kind, if not very bright. And he left you.

CAROLINE: You, anyway, are not going to let me forget that.

SOPHIE: Not for a moment.

CAROLINE: Well, at least I had the nerve to get married when I was young. Unlike you, who'd never take the risk until you were old enough to enter into this arid married state with Father.

SOPHIE: That's a point. I suppose it does take courage when you're young. Especially when you intend to marry someone called Boysie Traherne.

CAROLINE: What about John Hogarth?

SOPHIE: Darling he'd never marry you. He might pop you under the covers for an hour or two.

CAROLINE: I wouldn't be lonely and unwanted for that little time at least.

SOPHIE: So that's what you're expecting. Have you forgotten? He's here for a different purpose. He's not travelling for pleasure this time. My dear child, it's a fact that men sometimes get sick of us; not individually or personally, but sick of our whole ravening sex. Then they take up soldiering or archaeology, throw themselves into politics or find other things to do which we don't understand—such as revolution. When that happens we haven't a chance. We can fight among ourselves for a man but when we have to get to grips with an idea a man believes to be right then we're beaten. All we can do is to sit back and meditate on past triumphs.

CAROLINE: You're lucky. I never loved anyone but Boysie. I can't meditate on him for the rest of my life.

SOPHIE: Well, Boysie could hardly be described as a triumph, I agree. But you'll find someone worthy of you, Caroline. Goodness knows where, and it won't be John. Remember why he's here. To do his part in something real. He believes in the liberation by revolt of these wretched people. It may seem absurd to us, but it's a fact. Accept it.

CAROLINE: Why start playing soldiers at his age?

SOPHIE: A man always wants to do something positive after a love affair. John's just left Ada, remember. What did Boysie do after he left you?

CAROLINE: He had a nervous collapse.

SOPHIE: That proves my point.

JOHN *comes down the stairs and into the room.*

JOHN: Selwyn's a most energetic bather, isn't he? The room's flooded and as a mere spectator I'm soaked to the skin. He saw Henry and the Greek gentleman running down the hill and wants to be told what it's all about.

SOPHIE: Nobody knows at the moment. Henry arrived up here with an account even more garbled than he sends to 'The Times'. Pay no attention. We've had such alarms before.

JOHN: I think you should have a word with Selwyn. He's at his bedroom window, stark naked, with a pair of field glasses and an improvised megaphone.

SOPHIE: I'll go up in a minute. John, when are you expecting your friend to come for you?

JOHN: Basilios? In two or three days. Why?

SOPHIE: Couldn't you travel north to meet him?

JOHN: Do you mean at once?

SOPHIE: Well, say tonight.

JOHN: I suppose I could. Are you trying to get rid of me?

CAROLINE: Yes, she is.

SOPHIE: John, we're old enough friends to be frank with each other.

JOHN: Certainly, Sophie. But no friends are old enough to be straightforwardly impolite to each other. (CAROLINE *laughs*.) I'd like to stay here for a few days. A little while ago you seemed happy about that. Why have you changed your mind?

SOPHIE: I haven't.

JOHN: Then what have we to be frank about?

CAROLINE: Me.

SOPHIE: I'm so very fond of you, John, and I wouldn't wish anything to take away from your affection for me. Certainly not this arrogant and impertinent child. In other words, I don't want to be blamed for what happens.

CAROLINE: Dear Sophie, always burning her bridges before I come to them.

SOPHIE: I'll go up to Selwyn. (SOPHIE *goes from the room and up the stairs.* JOHN, *in silence, moves to the windows.* CAROLINE *watches him*.)

CAROLINE: You were right to be firm with Sophie. Of course you can stay here as long as you wish.

JOHN: That wasn't the reason. It's not that I very much want to stay here. I just want to put off going north for a while.

CAROLINE: Why? (JOHN *does not answer*.) What's the matter?

JOHN: Selwyn seems to think I may get killed in this business.

CAROLINE: Well, don't sound so surprised. Had it not occurred to you?

JOHN: It had occurred to me but I didn't think it had to anyone else—not seriously.

CAROLINE: But surely that's the point. You can at last be taken seriously by others. Why else are you here?

JOHN: Here? This is a strange undisciplined country. A good place to be alive in.

CAROLINE: It seems that's not the reason you came.

JOHN: Why did you come? Was it only because your father happened to be here?

CAROLINE: Not only that. When I was shut up in a nunnery as a child one of my teachers was a Greek. She told me wild, unorthodox stories of the country. I remembered them when I was alone in London and I thought this might be the place to bring me alive again. It's done so.

JOHN: I know what you mean. You become aware. Yes? Am I right? Aware that you're taking up space and that the sun exists to strike down and enwrap you. Aware that you are here! Alive, wound up—more!—working, ticking, going. Registering something more than a mood. Yes. It's a discovery to be reckoned with, I agree. Life is not, after all, founded on the meal table, the privy and the bed.

CAROLINE: In this place even those things might take on a certain significance.

JOHN: You think it's the element of place?

CAROLINE: Not entirely. It's also because Selwyn talked to you. About being killed. With that in mind even the most commonplace objects can become charged with mystery.

JOHN: I should never have thought of you as a commonplace object.

CAROLINE: What did you say?

JOHN: You're confusing me. Are you doing it deliberately?

CAROLINE: I want you to see yourself in the proper light, that's all. As a man who hasn't got all his life before him I think you should.

JOHN: You talk as if I'm condemned.

CAROLINE: There's time for a reprieve. You've only to change your mind.

JOHN: Out of the question. I'm committed to action—on my honour.

CAROLINE In that case—(*She moves to* JOHN *and holds out her hand.*)

—goodbye. The world will surely go without you. (JOHN *takes her hand: he does not let it go.*) You're doing something which I don't understand, but I suppose is very fine.

JOHN: I'm not one of those men who have to love the country they're prepared to—

CAROLINE (*after a moment*): Say fight for. I didn't mean that. I meant it's supposed to be a good thing to give up so much. Everything you've known in such fullness in the past. Good food, sleep, the comfort of whom are gone in this spartan search for an absolute truth in a harsher reality. Great man—almost a saint, you are—yes—for the way of sanctity is the road to the north.

JOHN *is still holding her hand.*

JOHN: I think you've misunderstood. The pleasures you've talked about had become as bitter to me as any penance. Every one was the harshest reality which I couldn't stomach. For they're only tolerable when they're more than themselves. When the food feeds more than the body, when sleep is more than an escape to a dream and the comfort of women is more than a cushion.

CAROLINE: I see. But tell me something. Did you say to yourself, This is the last time? D'you see what I mean? Take the comfort of women. Did you say to yourself, This is the last kiss, the last embrace? This is not only farewell to whatshername—Ada—but farewell to all loving for all time. Did you say that? (JOHN *takes both her hands in his.*) Say it now. (JOHN *is silent.*) Let the day go. It gets cooler towards the evening. Then's the time for thought and decision. The smell of the baked earth comes up from the valley making the scent of the flowers sour and more understandable. Evening is the time for straight talking and straight thinking in this country. The sun goes down and rubs the gilt from the edges. The senses aren't treacherously attacked by every colour, shape and sound taking on a form of old happiness. The days in this place—the days under the sun have all been—have all happened before. But the nights are new in time—to newmet people— you'n'me—and they can be used in any way we—John—please. Please! put off, John—John, put off telling—to y'self—me— telling whether Ada—a dead love now—was last—very last time.

JOHN *pushes her hair back from over her ears and folds his hands about the back of her neck.*

JOHN: It was the last chance.

CAROLINE: How—chance?

JOHN: All my life I've treated every opportunity as the last chance. I've looked—oh, sadly—on each encounter as the last. But I was cheated. The sun came up and the sun went down and, damn it, life had to be lived. And opportunity didn't knock once. It beat a positive tattoo at my door.

CAROLINE: Which every time you opened.

JOHN: It was never shut. (*He kisses her on the forehead.*) But now the foot of time is edging it to. Soon there'll only be space in that doorway for the lightest and most frivolous opportunity to get through. The last—the smallest and least consequential—will have to stay, I suppose, to comfort my extreme age for there'll be no getting out.

CAROLINE: My God! Can't you—(JOHN *kisses her on the mouth.*)—see? Can't you see—that before you—haven't you eyes?—oh, yes! you've eyes—before you is not a quickly closing door. No, John—darling, my new found one: der—fool! there before you are the wide open gates of summer. You've lived only—nothing but—the early months of your year of life. Stay on. I'll not mind —never mind—if you go on from me to another—fairer, she may be—but be aware—be'ware—not old, not sleeping but now whilst young—of the fairest to hand. Stay. Go on from me—after all—if you want to go—on. Go on.

JOHN *puts his finger against her mouth.*

JOHN: You're lying. You're saying something you don't believe. That's not good. That's bad. You must—and of course you do— think that you are the last. No going on from you—Caroline— who hold the secret—Caroline—the true ending. So let's have no renunciation from—Caroline. You.

CAROLINE: I don't give up anything—ever. But there comes a time—secret: furtive: upon you before you—no!—know it and a decision has to be made. (*She kisses* JOHN. SELWYN *comes down the stairs, crosses the room, and goes out through the windows.*) You'll not find that in a day's march.

JOHN: I'll not find that in a lifetime's campaigning.

They are fast in each others arms.

CAROLINE: Ah! my revolutionary. I'll be your marching song. This can be a struggle for freedom worth fighting. So to the barricades which are down—down!—fallen before the uprising.

Take the law into your own hands and strike. The tormented are impatient of control.

JOHN: Be still.

CAROLINE: Yes. Yes. Yes.

CURTAIN

ACT TWO

The scene: part of the room of the first act remains showing the windows and the door leading to the stairway.

Now the terrace beyond the window is also revealed.

The time is two days later: evening.

The terrace is a compact area before the house and is enclosed by a low wall. The passage of slippered feet—it is a place of leisure—has given a mirror surface to the mosaic floor. At the centre several steps lead to the pathway going down to the road. The exterior wall containing the small window of John Hogarth's bedroom is now clearly seen.

A long table with food and drink has been taken out to the terrace.

The harshness of daylight has gone and with the sun low there is an incisive coolness which seems to etch the scene in a most unmisty twilight. It will not be night for some time.

JOHN HOGARTH *is alone on the terrace. He is holding a long-barrelled, single-shot practise pistol. A little way from him, and lined on the wall, are various objects: a drinking glass, an orange, a small bottle, a straw hat (Henry's) a playing card and a cigar.* JOHN *is using these as targets. He fires. Not one of the objects is disturbed.*

CAROLINE *appears at the small window above and looks out to the country-side.*

CAROLINE: The dancers! Don't frighten away the dancers. Do you see them? Under the hill. There's been a wedding. One of the workmen. Down there the men and women are making the bond. That slow and heavy circle will tread the pattern into the earth through the night. There's a tribute to love if ever there was one. Can you hear the music? It'll be a thin pipe. Listen. (JOHN *has reloaded the pistol: he fires.*) Ah! you don't want to hear. Does that sharp noise comfort you? Yet you'll not save your life with that kind of toy. Practise all you can, you'll never shoot your way out. (CRISTOS *has come down the stairs of the house and crossed the room.*

31

He now stands inside the windows unseen by JOHN *and* CAROLINE.) Do
you still believe the quickest way to someone's heart is with a
bullet? Will you never learn? They're dancing under the hill.
Set your sights a little higher, John, and you'll see them—dancing
the day into the earth—burying it for ever and ever. Doesn't that
mean something to you?

JOHN: No.

He fires again. CAROLINE *goes back into the room. After a moment*
CRISTOS *steps out on to the terrace.*

CRISTOS: I don't want to disturb you.

JOHN: I'm alone.

CRISTOS: I mean disturb your practise.

JOHN: The required number of rounds have been shot off. I can rest
now.

CRISTOS *pours some wine and takes a glass to* JOHN.

CRISTOS: I hope you're happy with our local wine.

JOHN: To be quite happy I'd need to be here a few weeks. It still
bites a little.

CRISTOS: You're not intrigued by it to stay on. No, I see you're not.
Unfortunately, it doesn't travel. Like myself.

JOHN: How do you come to speak English so well?

CRISTOS: I went to school in England, and afterwards lived there
for many years.

JOHN: From choice?

CRISTOS: Yes. The place fitted my temperament, for I think it
must be the saddest country in the world. I long for that perpetual
autumn where it is unnecessary—oh, impossible—to face reality:
where every leave-taking is performed with the grave courtesy of
an obsequy: where the houses look like tombs and the tombs
houses: where the mist of bravely unshed tears softens even the
harshest gesture. Beautiful!

JOHN: Why did you leave?

CRISTOS: My national characteristics failed me. Not being an
Englishman I craved something unworthy. I was ruined by a desire
for excitement.

JOHN: You mean you found it? In England? Just a minute. This is
extraordinary. What did you do? Start a political party? Not that?
Surely you were not mad enough to create a work of art.

CRISTOS: Of course not.

JOHN: Women? My dear fellow, you must have known from your

public schooldays that Englishwomen were made to purge us by pity and terror.

CRISTOS: Yes. I learnt that at an early age.

JOHN: Then I give up.

CRISTOS: Do you know Epsom Downs?

JOHN: Horse racing. Of course!

CRISTOS: I lost everything. The animal was called Homer II and its liquid eye avoided mine as it was led to the enclosure. It had carried my two thousand pounds into fourth place. I came back here to my only remaining property.

JOHN: I'm sorry. I didn't know this was your house.

CRISTOS: Selwyn rents it from me for the period of the excavation. Yes, it's my house. My position is difficult. I sometimes forget myself and behave very much as a host. Forgive me.

JOHN: It's a charming lapse. Please sit down. (HENRY *has come up the hill and now steps on to the terrace.* JOHN *speaks to him.*) What's happening?

HENRY: They're still trying to get through to the workman who fell into the hole. He seems to have dropped into an underground chamber. He's been there two and a half days now. Selwyn lowered food and wine and some candles to him. But the fellow makes no attempt to get out. All he does is wander about below and shout with laughter.

JOHN: Has he gone mad?

HENRY: We should know later tonight. Selwyn seems to think he can reach the place himself within a couple of hours. Of course, everything's been held up by this marriage of the foreman. About two hundred of his relations are down there at the dig roasting sheep. Have you notices the dancers?

JOHN: They've been pointed out to me.

HENRY: Queer music. Rather infectious, though. Even I found myself tapping my foot.

CRISTOS: That's because dancing's in your blood, Henry.

JOHN: Henry has dancing in his blood!

CRISTOS: From his mother. She's an actress.

JOHN: Really. Locally?

CRISTOS: No, no. In London.

JOHN: What's she doing at the moment?

HENRY: 'The Feather Duster Girl.'

JOHN: Bevis. You're not Bunny Bevis's boy?

HENRY: Yes.

JOHN: Little Bunny Bevis! You mean you're her flesh and blood?

HENRY: Yes.

JOHN: How extraordinary! I saw her before I left London.

HENRY: Oh?

JOHN: That ageless, bewitching creature! I looked in the night before I sailed. Bunny came on to a scene decorated with enormous flowers. You'd have been proud of her, Henry. The gentlemen of the chorus swep' off their toppers and Bunny came through them to the footlights with her eyelids working like shutters, and confided a song to us which must have been written by her worst enemy. (JOHN, *spinning an imaginary parasol, sings:*) I'm the wild wed wose/You didn't pluck fwom your garden/ On your way to your new sweetheart/You chose those silly lilies/And the fwilly daffodilies/To Cawwy on your way/For your wedding day bouquet./But you didn't seem to seeme,/Your only, lonely, dweamy,/Dainty, cherubeamy—ooh! (presto) Little wild wed wose.

    SELWYN *has come up the hill and on to the terrace.*

SELWYN: Bravo! The latest thing from London, eh?

JOHN: Henry's mother's new song.

SELWYN: Enchanting, ever young thing she is, too. I remember her when I was quite a boy. She's one of the few women, I'd say, who know exactly what qualities to bring into a man's life to make him happy. Equal parts of gaiety, silence, and plain damned silliness. Not an idea in her head, you know. So refreshing. Funny she's never married. (*He has poured himself some wine.*) This is very pleasant. Where are the women?

JOHN: Dressing.

HENRY: Shall I fetch them?

SELWYN: I think you've missed the point, Henry. My statement that this is very pleasant, and my query as to where the women happen to be are not unconnected. See what I mean?

JOHN: So you hope to get right into the excavation tonight, Selwyn.

SELWYN: Yes. I've left them working on the tunnel. We should know the result of eighteen months work by the morning. You'd better be there, Bevis, standing by with your adjectives when I go in. 'The Times' will want a full report.

HENRY: I'm ready for anything. What about the fellow already down there?

SELWYN: I can't get a word of sense from him. Damned fool!

HENRY: Is he still laughing?

SELWYN: Yes. With all respect to your countrymen, Cristos, I've found these workmen inclined to take the whole business rather lightly. I mean, this little fellow falls through a hole into a place where no man has set foot for over two thousand years, and all he does is to wander about giggling like a lunatic. Not only that, but the night we propose to enter the inner chamber the foreman decides to get married. It would have been churlish not to provide wine, but I can't say that I approve.

SOPHIE *has come down the stairs and into the room. She now comes out on to the terrace.*

SOPHIE: Will you take me down, Selwyn?

SELWYN: Down, my dear. Do you mean you want to see the digging?

SOPHIE: Certainly not. I want to join the wedding party for a while. I think we should all go. Is the girl pretty?

SELWYN: Not very. She has a heavy moustache.

SOPHIE: Come along, Cristos. You must interpret my best wishes. And John—how can I make you come along?

JOHN: You might drag me by the hair.

SOPHIE: I see. I'm sure I shan't have to persuade Henry with his morbid interest in marriage.

HENRY: I'll come down, certainly.

SOPHIE: We can all do with a little gaiety of this kind. And think how pleased they'll be to see that we're interested.

SELWYN: You'll find it very different, my dear, from the goings-on at Saint Margaret's.

SOPHIE: Nonsense, Selwyn! People the whole world over get married for the same thing.

JOHN: Tell us what it is, Sophie.

SOPHIE: I'd like to give the bride a small gift, Cristos. What do you think would be suitable? (SOPHIE, SELWYN *and* CRISTOS *go from the terrace.* HENRY *remains for a moment to pick up his hat from the wall.*)

JOHN: It's very strange. A simple ritual invented by lawyers and priests can make a woman like Sophie behave in this absurd way. Look out, Henry! In her present mood she might try to engage you to one of the local girls.

HENRY: I very much want to get married, Mr Hogarth. Not, of course, to a local girl, but to someone of my own class.

JOHN: Have you anyone in mind?

HENRY: I had. (*He starts to go.* JOHN *calls after him:*)

JOHN: Do you mean Caroline?

HENRY: Yes, I mean Caroline. (HENRY *goes from the terrace.* JOHN *stares after him and then sadly looks down the barrel of his pistol.* CAROLINE *has come into the room. She stands watching* JOHN, *silently. It is* JOHN *who speaks.*)

JOHN: I know you're there. Come out.

CAROLINE *stays in the room.*

CAROLINE: And I know you're there. Alone.

JOHN: Henry wants to marry you.

CAROLINE: He once got as far as telling me what his income is.

JOHN: What is it?

CAROLINE: Eight hundred.

JOHN: Not enough. Why didn't you tell me about him? I've made him unhappy.

CAROLINE: Well, someone had to be made unhappy in this affair. And that's what the Henrys are for. You've made me very happy.

JOHN: Oh, damn you. (CAROLINE *laughs.*) Come out here.

CAROLINE: Do you really find comfort in that little weapon? Are you expecting to be attacked?

JOHN: Yes.

CAROLINE: From this quarter? Ah! be brave and put it down.

JOHN *returns the pistol to its case. He walks through the windows into the room.* CAROLINE, *who is beside the window, quickly puts her arms around his neck. They kiss.*

JOHN: You're a pest.

CAROLINE: You shouldn't be doing this. But you've a good excuse. It's all anyone wants for such behaviour. For when you left London you didn't know I existed and neatly filled this space. I'll wait, you thought, safe with Sophie.

JOHN: That's what I am doing. Waiting in safety.

CAROLINE: Are you? You meant t'do it. No doubt about it. Wait for your friend before going off to war. You could no more've imagined me, eh, as a friend on the way. Don't look so cross. It's upsetting, I know, to be knocked off y'path to war'n'glory which you'd so carefully plotted, but it's something you've got to get used to. Please!

JOHN: You arrogant and designing—

CAROLINE: Call me names.

JOHN: Later. Why should you think this is any more than an interlude?

CAROLINE: How to pass a night or two in a waiting room without the boredom of loneliness?

JOHN: Just that. How do you know it's more?

CAROLINE: Shall I tell you? Because you've never known anything like this before.

JOHN: This! Each and every one is not only the last chance. It is the first time. And I'm not a man to be detained by novelty. Try again.

CAROLINE: All right. I'm better than any of the others.

JOHN: Who've gone before. Are you.

CAROLINE: I'm just putting the idea in your head. Am I?

JOHN: Yes.

CAROLINE: Then there's your reason for staying on.

JOHN: Oh, no. Not good enough. Unworthy of you, Caroline. I left the best horse I ever had in England. With regret, but I left it.

CAROLINE: Will you leave me—with regret?

JOHN: Of course.

CAROLINE: But you'll leave?

JOHN: I shall. (CAROLINE *breaks from across the room.*) Don't go.

CAROLINE: Well, now, you may go it seems yet I must stay. Very well. I've not the cruelty needed to leave you after what we've been through together.

JOHN: Put like that it sounds an ordeal.

CAROLINE: What else? A carrying on of the game? No.

JOHN: Stop answering your own questions and listen to me. I'm an innocent traveller. I mean I'm travelling in an innocent way. I break my journey. You say I didn't know you'd be here. That's true. But I've always been aware of the perils of travel and you're one of them. They attend us on the way.

CAROLINE: Have there been so many on this journey?

JOHN: Enough. I came through Rome: I might have changed my religion. A man on the boat had a scheme to make me a fortune: I might have invested. The maid who brought coffee to my bedside in Alexandria—she wasn't you, certainly, but she had— ah, well, the sun was already high. But y'see what I mean. None of these kept me so why should you? Tell me, squirrel, the ever so special reason why I should stay with you and not go north with Basilios.

CAROLINE: Stay with me and you can stay alive with honour.

JOHN: The word honour should never pass a woman's lips except in its narrowest and most personal sense. You've made a monstrous suggestion. If I don't lead this revolt and stay with you everyone will applaud my courage in exchanging the trials of revolution for the horrors of marriage. Is that what you mean?

CAROLINE: I've never spoken of marriage.

JOHN: You will.

CAROLINE: Have you ever been in love?

JOHN: When I was fifteen. She was—

CAROLINE: I don't want to know. What about the others?

JOHN: I've travelled a great deal, you must remember.

CAROLINE: And of all your travelling companions I was the best. Yes? There! you've a dear face when you relax your mouth. To smile or to kiss—me. (JOHN *does so: briefly.*) Will the man be here tonight to fetch you? I only ask because I must think what I've to do. What would you have me do? Travel on? Looking for the encounters you've tried to avoid. Oh, you—for you the world holds yourself and humanity. It's the same with everyone who wants to stir up trouble. Revolution is for men who can't love. You can, if you'll give yourself the chance.

JOHN: I gave myself every chance in the past. I presented myself well scrubbed and well dressed, sober and tactful for the pre-liminaries. If there was a husband I was good-natured. The early stages were distinguished by punctuality and discretion. The mutual pact was sealed—on my part, at least—with affection and firmness of purpose. Time, Caroline, and time again I was well on my way to being in love with a person.

CAROLINE: That's behaviour. Got no more to do with it than the angle of your hat. You speak of formalities. Didn't you suffer?

JOHN: Horribly. About the fourth week. Oh, to stop playing the dancing ape!

CAROLINE: Poor animal!

JOHN: Yes! You'd blubber over such lack of freedom for your doggies and birdies and dearly sweet gee-gees. But a man? Why, you only bite your finger to stop your laughter. Goad the beast and it will give tongue. Do you recognize human speech? What is it you want to hear? Surely not the beaten, desperate cry: Will you please go away and leave me alone!

CAROLINE: We always go. There's that to be said for us.

JOHN: Go? Yes, but you leave behind a long backward look.

CAROLINE: We have to fight with outdated weapons. We hope the dull edge of remorse stays sharp enough to penetrate the heart.

JOHN: And think of it as only the first thrust of the engagement. For, from longer range, the letters start coming. The small wound caused by remorse must be kept open by the pen. The first letter on parting—

CAROLINE: 'Dear John, Your cruelty to me last night—'

JOHN: Letters stay unanswered. What next?

CAROLINE: A telegram: 'If offended in any way—'

JOHN: At last in person on the doorstep day and night—veiled—or in a carriage across the street—watching. Once even disguised as a washerwoman to be met on the stairs. So it always ends one way. In flight. The last letter speaks to me over the many miles—

CAROLINE: 'Dear John, Your silence tells me that I have failed to please you. Now so far away I shall hope to be remembered as nothing more than a friend of whom in future times of trouble anything may be asked.'

JOHN: That's what it seems to say. It's hard to be sure with the page scarred and blistered by tears. Into the tin box with it. And on. No, Caroline, love can never stand up to the onslaught of your sex. Never.

CAROLINE: And so it has led from one to another until in headlong flight you pass this way.

JOHN: Pass. Yes. Good girl. Pass this way.

SOPHIE *has returned up the hill on* CRISTOS'S *arm. They come on to the terrace.*

SOPHIE: Who's in there? Why don't you light the lamps? (SOPHIE *and* CRISTOS *move from the terrace into the room.* CAROLINE *begins to light the lamps.*)

JOHN: Back so soon. What was it like?

SOPHIE: Very disappointing. Even at my age I'd have thought a peasant wedding would be sweetly idyllic. That is nothing of the kind. How could it be when the man is obviously a blackguard and the girl quite distressingly drunk—and ugly.

CAROLINE: You'll have to look elsewhere for your romance, Sophie.

SOPHIE: I shall. Far beyond this house, at least. Cristos, I'd intended to ask you to go to my room and fetch one of my handkerchiefs to give to that poor girl down there, but now I feel sure she'd only blow her great nose on it. Instead, will you go to the kitchen and find an old tablecloth to present with my compliments.

JOHN: You are in a bad temper.

　　CRISTOS *goes out.*

SOPHIE: It's the first time I've walked down that hill. Very tiring.

JOHN: It took a wedding to get you out and about.

CAROLINE: I suppose you insulted them. The wedding pair, I mean.

SOPHIE: Why should you suppose I'd do any such thing?

CAROLINE: Because you're always so damned rude to anyone who disappoints you.

SOPHIE: It would have been difficult, as everything I said had to be translated through Cristos. However, I can speak English and be understood by both of you. (CAROLINE *begins to go from the room.*) Where are you going?

CAROLINE: Kitchen. Oil for the lamp.

SOPHIE: The lamp's all right.

CAROLINE: It won't be in a moment. (*She goes out.*)

SOPHIE: So you're staying on with us. I'm very sorry. The sight of you being brought down by Caroline during the last two days has been very painful. I'd hoped it was only a matter of soldier's comfort, but it seems I have to watch your final humiliation. A tacit admission of love.

JOHN: What are you talking about?

SOPHIE: Ah! my dear boy, to be caught by love is one thing: to give it is another.

JOHN: You know, Sophie, you're becoming a contradictory old lady.

SOPHIE: John!

JOHN: You obviously see nothing odd in the fact that you should give your blessing to the lovers down the hill and immediately return to abuse Caroline and me—so much nearer to your heart— in the same situation.

SOPHIE: Then it is true. The night you arrived I saw the lamp in her irresponsible hand go bobbing towards your room. Even then I feared for your safety. Yet I believed you'd break free. We know, don't we, that there's no commitment made in the small hours. Dawn breaks most pacts and the sun burns up all vows. This time, however—well, you're older and you must at least come to rest in someone's bed. I was afraid it would be Caroline's and I was right, it seems. For your daytime behaviour with her has been most revealing. Tragic, I feel, that after all you've been and more important all you've avoided you should end up with that worthless girl.

JOHN: Must I remind you? In London you only knew of such things by letter and through conversation with me. Remember, Sophie, this is the first time you've actually seen the little lamp go bobbing down the corridor. This is no better—ha!—and no worse than those times in the past. And no more dangerous. I'm not staying.

SOPHIE: You're not? Then why are you letting me say all this?

JOHN: I like to hear you so concerned. You must still be very fond of me.

CRISTOS *comes in. He has a cloth folded over his arms.*

SOPHIE: It's not enough. A cloth. Give the girl a sum of money as well.

CRISTOS: Certainly. How much?

SOPHIE: All you have on you. Let Selwyn and Henry also contribute.

CRISTOS: Very well.

SOPHIE: I've been uncharitable. It's not the girl's fault she's so unpleasant. Come back at one, Cristos. I shall dictate a chapter at least tonight. (CRISTOS *goes out to the terrace and down the hill.*) I'm sorry I made a mistake about you and Caroline.

JOHN: Did you know Henry wants to marry her?

SOPHIE: That's because he's been out here such a long time. Nothing will come of it.

JOHN: What will happen to her? I'd like her to be happy. Some day.

SOPHIE: But not today. Not until you're far off. Let her be happy then.

JOHN: How?

SOPHIE: You're very concerned.

JOHN: Naturally.

SOPHIE: When are you expecting your friend?

JOHN: What? At any moment.

SOPHIE: Tonight?

JOHN: Perhaps. But about Caroline—

CAROLINE: Yes? (*She has come from the darkness of the passageway.*)

SOPHIE: We were speaking of your future happiness, my child.

CAROLINE: Were you, darling? What about my present happiness?

SOPHIE: We thought it problematic—(CAROLINE *has taken* JOHN'S *arm*.)—or merely affected. But we can be generous and admire you for putting a good face on your failure. I suppose you must have some qualities, Caroline, but I'm surprised that one of them should be to know when you've lost.

CAROLINE: You come of a different—and older—generation than John and I. We're made happy by smaller things of less duration that ever you could be. I suppose you were very beautiful when you were young but I never look at you—knowing you as I do —without thinking that you must have gone yah-yah! gobble— and then sat back emotionally stuffed and sleepy. (*To* JOHN.) Women eating. Do you hate it?

JOHN: Hate it.

CAROLINE: I'll starve. (*To* SOPHIE.) But for me—well, when I've been miserable a smile from a stranger has sometimes been enough. You don't understand that, do you?

SOPHIE: When I was a girl no stranger would have dared to smile at me.

CAROLINE: Poor thing. So what I've known with John is very wonderful. It's not f'rever. But what is? Over f'both of us— tonight?—perhaps we'll see the morning. But I believe not. There, I've taken away your cause for triumph, Sophie. Sorry. You were all ready, I know, to rub my nose in the fact that this man is also leaving me.

JOHN: Would you mind if I waited outside whilst this goes on?

SOPHIE: Not necessary. Please tell Cristos when he comes back that I'm in my room. I'd like you to knock on my door, John, for a moment before you go to shake my hand. That is, if your friend should arrive in the middle of the night. At that time Caroline will undoubtedly be in a position to wish you a long farewell. (SOPHIE *goes from the room and up the stairs*.)

JOHN: Let me look at you, Caroline. I'd have to know you longer before I could say you're serious.

CAROLINE: If ever there was a time to be serious this is it.

JOHN: I thought you were just maddening Sophie.

CAROLINE: No. You've taught me what you failed to teach the others. But I don't want Basilios to turn up before morning even now. How will he come? How does a man go off to war these days? What am I to look for? A group of silent horsemen on the hill. Is that it?

JOHN: Forgive me. After all that's happened it would be unbecoming for me to end in a bed.

CAROLINE: I understand perfectly. As a famous man you must finish up in glory.

JOHN: I'd like to confound my obituaries as they stand written at the moment.

CAROLINE: You may come through the whole affair untouched. I hadn't thought of that.

JOHN: I had. It would be just my luck.

CAROLINE: Let's behave as if it wasn't part of the day—as if it wasn't happening at all. Come on. Here's an opportunity you've never known. Always before you'd to be careful—wary—because a word meant being trapped. But there's no fear of committing yourself with me. You'll be gone by morning, and there'll be no letters following after you, I promise.

JOHN: I'm allowed to say honestly and without commitment that I love you.

CAROLINE: Yes, you're allowed to say that.

JOHN: And having said it—

CAROLINE: You haven't.

JOHN: Having said it I must at once get ready to go. I'm in an impossible situation.

CAROLINE: I know. (*She holds out her arms.*) Take refuge.

(JOHN *does so.*)

JOHN: I think aloud and you hear my thoughts. What would it have been? An abject return to England to carve legal indulgence and tell this story of ours in straight answers to misleading questions. Your hair smells of wood smoke: why is that? Marriage and retirement to the country to give us leisure to begin to hate each other—your hands are stained with fruit—for having dared to think we could make each other happy—quite bloodied over they are: see them—until the time would be when we'd only find true contentment in our hatred. I know: my mother and father married—we'd have children to take sides in our private war —your pulse: racing: oh dear, yes, it is!—children equally divided to carry on the battle when we were too old and tired to care. You've tears in your eyes.

CAROLINE: I know, you fool! Stay with me.

JOHN: What has it been? Discovery without the vulgar need to stake a claim. Mystery without fear of explanation. Silence without misunderstanding. We've not used up all our poetry on each other and been driven to counterfeit. Your lies amuse me —your unhappiness concerns me—and your most idiotic mannerisms enchant me. Leave it so. Be thankful for the horsemen on the hill.

CAROLINE: Stay with me.

JOHN: No.

    CAROLINE *turns away and goes out on to the terrace leaving* JOHN *alone in the room.* CRISTOS *has come up the hill and on to the terrace. He speaks to* CAROLINE.

CRISTOS: As a man long since unmarried I'm always amazed at the savagery attendant upon the simple union of two good people who are supposed to love each other. The families of the wedding party are engaged in a pitched battle. Someone made a comment on the bride's exact state of chastity, it seems. I'd not have thought it was a debatable point, as she had two children with her who cried, Momma, throughout the ceremony. (*He passes* CAROLINE *and enters the room.*)

JOHN: Sophie asked me to say that she's in her room waiting to dictate.

CRISTOS: Thank you. Her memory at this time of day is too accurate for comfort.

JOHN: Surely that's what you want.

CRISTOS: Accuracy about the past! Mr Hogarth, you speak like a scholar.

JOHN: Is there another value in reminiscence?

CRISTOS: Certainly. A record of what might have been.

JOHN: In that case, where does the truth get to?

CRISTOS: Now you speak, sir, as if the truth was a considerable detail. The book will only be read by the future.

JOHN: The Sophie's life in London is a myth.

CRISTOS: It will be by the time I've got it on paper.

JOHN: Until this moment I've looked on you as an historian.

CRISTOS: I'm sorry to have mislead you. How do you see me now?

JOHN: As an artist, you charlatan. I'm naturally concerned. I play a large part, I'm told, in your forthcoming work.

CRISTOS: You won't suffer, Mr Hogarth. Where in the past your behaviour has seemed irresponsible I've taken care to provide a motive even at the expense of libelling others. Where your actions have appeared cruel or selfish the reader will find an excuse—even if it's only in a footnote. In this work at least, sir, you will be represented beyond your wildest dreams.

JOHN: Thank you so much. (CRISTOS *goes from the room and up the stairs as* CAROLINE *returns to the room. Whilst on the terrace she has poured two glasses of wine. She carries on to* JOHN *and holds it out to him. He takes it.*) What's this?

CAROLINE: You're going. Let's drink to it.

JOHN: Not at all necessary.

CAROLINE: Now why should it embarrass you to have a woman see you as you see yourself? You are the last of the romantics and carry his accessories. Then you must damned well expect to be treated as such. You can't brood over your pistols and your past, your copy of Malory and your death in battle and have me see you as I see Henry. He's trying to make his way in the world. You're trying to make your way out of it.

JOHN: Very well, darling. If it's going to help you through these last hours by all means take part in my imaginary costume drama. (*He raises his glass*). To the freedom of man! (*He drinks.*)

CAROLINE: Oh, you did that beautifully! Anyone would've thought it was real. Let me try. (*She raises her glass.*) To the freedom of man! (*She drinks.*) How was that?

JOHN: Not at all bad. There was a note on your voice—militantly feminine—disturbing—might cause alarm in the liberal ranks. Try again.

CAROLINE: No. (*She takes the glass from John and with her own goes out to the terrace. She throws the glasses far out where they smash on the hillside. She comes back into the room. She speaks:*) That wine was poisonous.

JOHN: Yes. It wasn't very nice.

CAROLINE: I mean I put poison in it. The wine you've just drunk while we were fooling about. It was toxic.

JOHN: What?

CAROLINE: The wine, darling. I put poison in it.

JOHN: Are you serious?

CAROLINE: You'd have to know me longer before you could say that, so I'll tell you. Yes, I'm serious.

JOHN: Caroline: pull yourself together!

CAROLINE: I'm all right.

JOHN: And stop smiling!

CAROLINE: I'm happy.

JOHN: You're mad!

CAROLINE: No, I'm not. The stuff was in my drink, too.

JOHN: I'm not concerned with you at the moment.

CAROLINE: You must be. We were together in another way. We're together in this. That's right and proper. I'd not do anything for you alone. I love you.

JOHN: So much?

CAROLINE: Oh, so much! Just before we went to sleep last night I asked, How can I make this last for ever? And you said, That's only tomorrow. And suddenly I knew it could be.

JOHN: Give me the facts! The facts!

CAROLINE: Do they matter? Nothing to them. Walking on the hillside with Cristos one day I saw the scarlet berries. We'd been talking of the unhappiness of love, the impossibility of absolute oblivion. Then Cristos took a handful of the berries and told me that many people in this tragic country believed they held the secret. They call them Man's Friend. Cristos threw them away but the day you came I'd happened to be out on the hillside and gathered more.

JOHN: Just give me the facts!

CAROLINE: Do you mean the cook book facts? All right. Place whole in a pan. Cover with boiling water. Simmer on a wood fire. Drain. Keep to hand and when the horsemen on the hill approach use it.

JOHN: A wood fire—

CAROLINE:—yes, it stays in my hair. With the stain on my hands.

JOHN: I think you're lying.

CAROLINE: You'll know I'm not in about eight hours. When you fall asleep. Mild und leise.

JOHN: Don't whisper romantic German nonsense to me!

CAROLINE: Why not? Let's show them, John. Let's show this whole damned century with its passion for steam engines and plotting in cellars that there were two people who were unafraid to give themselves up to the oldest passion of all. The beauty and the sacrifices are all in the story books now. I want them as you do to be here in life. You must want it that way or you wouldn't have done the things you have and needed to go off to the north in further search. Sophie called you the first twentieth century man. Live up to it.

JOHN: Give me a chance!

CAROLINE: You'll live for ever in Sophie's book. As you really are. And I shall live with you in history as your last attachment. That makes me all at once want to cry. It's very wonderful.

JOHN: Splendid. Now listen to me, Caroline. I'm very very angry with you. A naughty girl, that's what you've been.

CAROLINE: I thought you'd behave so finely about this. And I'm sure Sophie would expect it, too.

JOHN: You mean I can't rush about the place screaming, Murder!

CAROLINE: Well, you can, but you're going to look silly and most unlike yourself if you make an uproar before Sophie and Henry and Selwyn.

JOHN: I'd certainly quite forfeit Sophie's respect. She'd probably begin to write her bloody book again from the beginning.

CAROLINE: It's a difficult position. I'd be brave and keep quiet.

JOHN: It's all a joke, isn't it, Caroline?

CAROLINE: Believe that, if you want to. It won't do any harm. You've always looked on everything as a joke, so why not this?

JOHN: Oh, my God!

CAROLINE: Everyone thought you'd leave me. As Boysie left me. Won't they be surprised? It's all so simple, too. Why didn't the others think of it, instead of writing you complaining letters?

JOHN: They didn't think of it because they were decent respectable women.

CAROLINE: Poor things! They'll be so mad when they hear about us. So many morning papers to tell them on so many breakfast tables, and so many tears of frustration falling in the porridge. God! I love you looking like that. Let's go upstairs. We've got eight hours or so.

JOHN: Certainly not! You're indecent. You should occupy the eight hours—

CAROLINE: How?

JOHN: I don't know. I don't know. (*He walks out to the terrace where he at once comes face to face with* HENRY *who has come up the hill.*)

HENRY: Selwyn's got through to the inner chamber of the dig. He's still there. I've been sent up for some drawing things. He wants to make some sketches.

JOHN: Has he found something interesting?

HENRY: I think it must be. I've not been in yet. Why don't you go down? They've enlarged the entrance. You've only to lower your head.

JOHN: Perhaps tomorrow.

HENRY: Will you forgive me? I must think about my column for 'The Times'.

JOHN: Tell me, you're very fond of Caroline, aren't you?

HENRY: I was hoping that matter wouldn't come up again. Do you think it's fair a question, Mr Hogarth?

JOHN: I think so. What do you know about her, that's the point?

HENRY: She makes mistakes.

JOHN: Such as?

HENRY: Believing herself to be emotionally attached to unsuitable men.

JOHN: I suppose you mean in love with me. Has she ever threatened you?

HENRY: With violence? You can't mean that.

JOHN: I do.

HENRY: She's always been most sympathetic.

JOHN: She's never been cruel to be kind.

HENRY: There have been times when she's said or done something she's regretted later.

JOHN: Too late sometimes, I expect. She's mad.

HENRY: Wild? I suppose she is. Yet we'd always forgive her, wouldn't we? Soon after she came here and I suppose I was pestering her she played a joke on me.

JOHN: A joke!

HENRY: It was really nothing—although I might have been killed. We were out riding together. Caroline used to wear boy's clothes for convenience. As an English journalist I was naturally interested in local habits and customs. On this ride we were going down a narrow defile near the coast when we came on a group of men. I wanted to speak to them and Caroline kindly offered to translate. I asked them various questions about their way of life. As I went on I saw the men's attitude become surly and then threatening. I did the best I knew. I held out a sum of money to them. At that they set on me. They dragged me from my horse. Luckily they were unarmed and had only their fists. I called to Caroline to ride off, which she did. I made my way back alone and very much the worse for wear.

JOHN: Hired assassins, I suppose.

HENRY: No, no. Cristos put the police on the case and a few days later they arrested two of the men. They both swore that Caroline had told them I was a wealthy Turk travelling the country buying up young girls—in this case their daughters—for immoral purposes. Caroline admitted that it was true. My innocent questions had been translated into damning demands. Poor child, she cried a little when she asked me to forgive her foolishness.

JOHN: Did you cry, too?

HENRY: I found it very touching that she should have thought those Greeks to have a sense of humour. She quite expected them to join in the joke. (JOHN *laughs: after a moment.*) I must get the drawing board.

JOHN: I'd like to speak to Cristos. He's with Sophie. Will you ask him to come down?

HENRY: Of course. (*He goes into the room leaving* JOHN *on the terrace and sees* CAROLINE *sitting alone smoking a cigarette.*) Hullo, you're there. Can't stop. Must go to my room. They've found something down at the dig, so I must start my last article. Then it will be goodbye, Caroline.

CAROLINE: Goodbye, Henry.

HENRY: I mean when I've finished the article.

CAROLINE: Well, get on with it, my dear. (*She goes to the window and out to the terrace and speaks to* JOHN *as* HENRY *leaves the room and goes up the stairs.*) Not a satisfactory conversation for you, I'm afraid. Even you could never convince Henry that such a thing as treachery exists. If you shot him dead on the spot his last thought would be, A most unfortunate mishap.

JOHN: The juice of a few berries in a glass of wine can't have any effect.

CAROLINE: Can't they? Look at the effect a few words to some strangers had on Henry when he was being boring.

JOHN: You're a monster.

CAROLINE: There's something you insist on forgetting. I'm with you in this. We'll always be together now. For people to remember.

JOHN: You'll soon convince me that everyone's going to benefit.

CAROLINE: Well, this revolution was a mistake, wasn't it? Things would have gone wrong and you'd have made a fool of yourself and it would have got into the papers and—oh, no, no, it would never have done at all.

SOPHIE *has come down the stairs and into the room. She calls.*

SOPHIE: John! Are you there?

JOHN: Yes. (*He moves into the room leaving* CAROLINE *on the terrace.*)

SOPHIE: Why do you want to speak to Cristos?

JOHN: I need his advice on a local custom I've just encountered. A matter of hospitality.

SOPHIE: He's gone out. Left in quite a temper. About you.

JOHN: Have I upset him?

SOPHIE: No. He was championing you. When he came to my room and picked up his pen I said, Now I shall begin to tell the truth about John Hogarth. He at once put down the pen and said, I'll not be a party to the destruction of a legend which the world will badly need in a few years. A destruction brought about, moreover, by your momentary pique. I answered him sharply. We were about to have a scene when fortunately he left the room. And the house.

JOHN: Can he be found?

SOPHIE: I see no reason for it. I'm capable of writing in my own hand.

JOHN: I meant for myself.

SOPHIE: It's very strange. I once described you as—

JOHN: —the first twentieth century man. I know.

SOPHIE: Yet Cristos sees you as the true representative of an age which is passing, if not past. He thinks you'll be swallowed up by a world which is going to regret the action and then find its comfort in fairy stories about the man it destroyed. That is your place in history, according to Cristos. A kind of Saint Jack of the Beanstalk. Interesting, isn't it?

JOHN: Very. But at the moment, Sophie, I'm unconcerned with my part in history and deeply interested in my part in the present. So tell me, why did Caroline's husband leave her?

SOPHIE: For none of the usual reasons. They say he was terrified of her. He became very strange towards the end.

JOHN: Go on.

SOPHIE: Is there any more to be said?

JOHN: Nothing, I suppose.

SOPHIE: Then let's change the subject.

JOHN: Certainly. How do you think I'll face up to the enemy.

SOPHIE: In the past you've made your own enemies and been very careful in doing so. You were wise. Friends don't matter, but it's most necessary to have the right enemies one can face with dignity and restraint.

JOHN: I'm speaking of physical danger.

SOPHIE: Oh, that, Well, I hope you won't make a fool of yourself.

JOHN: You feel I should pass into history silent and uncomplaining.

SOPHIE: Of course. You're keeping me in suspense as to what the final chapter of my book is going to be, but under no circumstances can I allow it to be a farce. That's Henry's part.

JOHN: The wealthy Turk.

SOPHIE: Ah! such a disgraceful incident. Lacerated and bruised mercifully beyond recognition for several days. She knew what she was doing. He might have been killed. And the fool still believes it was a joke.

JOHN: The fool!

SELWYN *has come up the hill and on to the terrace. He speaks to* CAROLINE.

SELWYN: Success! (JOHN *and* SOPHIE *stand listening within the room.*) Success, my dear child, after all these months. Go down and see your old Daddie's crowning triumph. The find that will put our names in the history books. Go down!

CAROLINE *leaves the terrace to go down the hill.* SELWYN *enters the room to* JOHN *and* SOPHIE.

SOPHIE: You've found something.

SELWYN: The most astonishing state of preservation.

SOPHIE: Of what?

SELWYN: An inner room—sixteen feet square or so. Hogarth, my dear fellow, we spoke of a place of worship, remember? Dedicated, we said. It's very much that. A bas-relief runs round the four walls from floor to ceiling.

SOPHIE: What does it represent?

SELWYN: Ostensibly man and woman's progress from the cradle to the grave, with overwhelming emphasis on a certain aspect.

SOPHIE: Come, Selwyn. Be brief: be lucid.

SELWYN: A strange experience. I climbed down into the darkness. The little idiot man already there had gone to sleep surrounded by his burnt out candles. The lamps were handed through to me and in their dancing light the still figures on the wall seemed to be animate. For two thousand years they'd remained until I brought them the light which set them performing again their endless love rites. A great moment. To hear a poem of Anacreon spoken by a voice of the time. The young sun-hot bodies joined by the freshly poured wine and playing their games forever to the silent music.

SOPHIE: Selwyn my dear. Selwyn, pay attention. Somehow I feel this is not the correct academic attitude towards what seems to be an important archaeological find.

SELWYN: There was a disturbing impression of youth. Even at that depth the place is warmed by the heat of the sun and there seems to remain the echo of a cry and of laughter and of the last deep silence. All in the inspired graffiti. My God, I'd no idea what I was looking for. Remember the little figure I showed you, Hogarth? Significant attitude, we said, but it meant little. My dear fellow, we were holding the poor creature upside down. Forgive me but you look quite shaken.

JOHN: It's surprising, Selwyn, that you should come all this way and spend all this time and then be pleased to verify a fact of human behaviour which could be observed at ease by visiting any one of a dozen houses in London.

SELWYN: I'm not an anthropologist. I know why you're upset. You left London to free yourself only to come so far and find material proof that the formal pattern of behaviour you wanted to escape was fully developed perhaps beyond your experience over two thousand years ago.

JOHN: I never thought I invented such goings-on.

SELWYN: Distressing. all the same. Now where's that fool Bevis? I sent him up for a drawing board. I must get some of this down on paper for the people in Berlin. My word, the Bloomsbury crowd are going to be mad when they hear about this. (*He has reached the foot of the stairs. He calls:*) Bevis, come down! Come down at once, man! (SELWYN *returns to the room and speaks to* JOHN.) I must set him to work on this article for 'The Times'. A detailed and poetic account is what's wanted. Something that will carry a breath of fresh air into a hundred reading rooms. I'm sure the boy can do it if he puts his mind to it.

SOPHIE: He'll do his best.

SELWYN: Why don't you go down, my dear? You'll find it interesting.

SOPHIE: Not tonight. I'm afraid of the path in the dark.

SELWYN: What about you, Hogarth?

JOHN: I'll go tomorrow.

SELWYN: Caroline couldn't wait so long. From the way she ran down the hill you'd have thought there was to be no tomorrow for her.

JOHN: What's that? She's gone?

SELWYN: Like a bird.

JOHN: Selwyn, could you spare me a moment on another matter?

SELWYN: Certainly. What is it?

JOHN: Your family.

SELWYN: What about it?

JOHN: Any insanity?

SELWYN: Hogarth, my excitement and enthusiasm are only natural to a man who's been working in the dark for eighteen months.

JOHN: I don't mean you. Have you—oh, really, this is very delicate —have you observed Caroline?

SELWYN: In passing. Is her behaviour eccentric? The girl has been unhappy in the past, but I don't think there's cause to fear for her mind. You mustn't worry that she'll do herself harm.

JOHN: What about others?

SELWYN: There she resembles her mother: more likely to kill with kindness.

JOHN: Thank you, Selwyn.

SELWYN: Anything more I can tell you?

JOHN: Nothing.

HENRY *has come down the stairs and he now enters the room carrying a drawing board and a handful of pencils.*

SELWYN: There you are. What've you been doing?

HENRY: Sharpening the pencils.

SELWYN: Look to your wits. I want a masterpiece from you.

HENRY: Shall we go down?

SELWYN: At once. (SELWYN *and* HENRY *go from the room, cross the terrace, and begin the descent of the hill.*)

SOPHIE: John, piece touchée, piece jouée.

JOHN: What do you mean?

SOPHIE: You know very well. Did you really think the game with her could be ended by knocking over the board?

JOHN: She's coming back. (*He is standing at the window looking down the hill.*)

SOPHIE: When you first came here you wagged your head and talked of my marriage to Selwyn. You made use of your gravest indictment: you said I'd become a woman. Oh, Sophie! Now we have the problem. What am I to gather from your present behaviour? That you've become a man? Oh, John!

JOHN: She speaks to her father. Kisses him. Claps Henry on the shoulder in a comradely way. And laughs. Laughs!

SOPHIE: Why not? She obviously has you for one at a disadvantage. No, no, John, this lack of decision won't do at all. You tell me that you're not staying, yet every word—all those questions!—indicate that you've given up hope of going. Now come along, what's it to be.

JOHN: She's very beautiful—carelessly so—as she walks—sure footed—sure of herself—sure of me—oh, God!

SOPHIE: The game's up, is it? Then let's have the post-mortem.

CAROLINE *comes on to the terrace from below.* JOHN *stays at the window between the two women:* CAROLINE *on the terrace and* SOPHIE *in the room.*

CAROLINE: Come out here. The ground under my feet is still warm from the sun.

JOHN: Your father's just told me that you'd not harm anyone.

CAROLINE: I wish I could put you out of your misery.

JOHN: Haven't you?

CAROLINE: I mean by making you understand that it's not a joke.

JOHN: You're beginning to regret it.

CAROLINE: Only when I look directly at you. Look away—like this—to the country and the naked hill waiting for the horsemen —then I don't regret it for a moment. Have you told the old lady?

JOHN: She knows nothing.

SOPHIE: The old lady knows nothing.

CAROLINE: Tell her what's happened. See if you get any sympathy. Go on, have a moment of panic.

SOPHIE: Why don't you walk down and confide in the men, John?

JOHN: Henry Bevis? I don't think so. Did you see the excavation, Caroline?

CAROLINE: Yes. Nothing more than a little dark secret hole in the ground. I looked at it closely. The figures of the men and women are very seriously happy. But, darling, you and I've learnt nothing new in over two thousand years. Mind you, we've forgotten nothing—that's clear enough. So lets' be content. (*A moments silence.*) There! did you feel that? The whole land took a deep breath and settled down for the night.

JOHN: I'll take advantage of it. Sophie, earlier this evening in a moment of nineteenth century romantic ardour Caroline put poison in my wine.

SOPHIE: Poison?

JOHN: From the scarlet berries on the hill. Man's Friend, as they're called.

SOPHIE: Oh, you silly girl! Yet it makes a much better ending.

JOHN: For me?

SOPHIE: No. The book, dear boy. Better than the battlefield. Less confusion.

JOHN: Sophie, I love you, but—

SOPHIE: And I love you, John. You're looking quite upset.

JOHN: Is that foolish of me?

SOPHIE: It's surprising. I don't understand. I mean, you came out here with the idea of ending your life on some sordid battlefield among complete strangers. You know how I felt about that. I thought it unwise. But this, John—this fits. Yes, I feel it's much the best way considering your early life. It has a tidiness which is most appealing.

JOHN: I'm glad your pleased.

SOPHIE: Not pleased, exactly. But there's a feeling of satisfaction.

JOHN: Good. Caroline took the stuff as well.

SOPHIE: That's not important. She'll hardly be mentioned.

CAROLINE *comes quickly into the room.*

CAROLINE: Now, look here, Sophie, you've been pretty filthy to me, but that's the dirtiest trick yet. I'm going to be in that book.

SOPHIE: I'll do my best to cram you into an appendix.

CAROLINE: I want the whole story. Nothing less. And I want a portrait. The Sargent, I think. Done when I was sixteen. Don't you dare monkey about with the facts. I loved him more than anyone.

SOPHIE: No, no, Caroline. Your agitated personality would ruin the dying fall of the last chapter. You must be muted.

CAROLINE: I won't be muted!

SOPHIE: Well, at least, dear, don't shout.

JOHN: May I just speak?

The two women attend him. There is a long silence.

CURTAIN

ACT THREE

The scene is John Hogarth's bedroom.
The time is later the same night.
The room is almost entirely occupied by a bed which is Byzantine in size and splendour. At the four corners gilded columns whirl giddily to the great canopy above. All around hang damasked curtains of extreme weight. There is a light burning directly over the bed beneath the canopy. The rest of the room is barely furnished by one chair and a small dressing table. John's box is open in a corner. His possessions are spilling out, giving the impression of flight suddenly abandoned.
There is one door to the room and one window.
JOHN is lying on the bed. He is in a state of undress, being only in his shirt and trousers.
There is a knock on the door.

JOHN: Go away!
    HENRY *comes into the room.*
HENRY: May I come in?
JOHN: What d'you want?
HENRY: Your advice. How are you feeling? Caroline told me that you've taken something which disagreed with you.
JOHN: Yes. I'm in no state to give advice on any subject.
HENRY: That's a pity. It's really help I need. I'm very worried.
JOHN: I've something on my mind, Bevis, as well as on my stomach and I'd like to be alone.
HENRY: You want me to go away. You mustn't worry. Problems seem so frightening at this time of night. So often they're solved by morning. That's been my experience. But after the sun's down what can you do? I've been walking about the hillside trying to get my mind in order.
JOHN: Have you managed that?
HENRY: No. You see, I've been in the dig with Selwyn.

56

JOHN: Instructive, I'm told.

HENRY: Mr Hogarth, what on earth am I going to say?

JOHN: Say?

HENRY: About Selwyn's discovery. For 'The Times'.

JOHN: I don't know.

HENRY: That's my problem. Shall we deal with it first and then come to you. From the moment I met you I felt there was a sympathetic understanding between us, and that this situation might well come up. When we could be of help to each other.

JOHN: What do you want me to do? I've not seen the place.

HENRY: Well, look at these. They're rough sketches made by Selwyn of the images. (*He unrolls a bundle of drawings and gives them to* JOHN.) You see my difficulty.

JOHN: Yes. (*He laughs.*) I see your difficulty. Having to describe these golden children.

HENRY: What line do you think I should take?

JOHN: Ignore them.

HENRY: That's bad journalism.

JOHN: What else is down there?

HENRY: Nothing. It's really too bad! I've waited for this discovery to give me material for my last article, and now look what turns up. If I don't make a success of it I can see myself being stuck in this wretched country for the rest of my life. I've been walking about at my wit's end.

JOHN: You'd best give a straightforward description, I'd think.

HENRY: Look at the drawings!

JOHN: Yes.

HENRY: Help me, Hogarth!

JOHN: Athens: Monday. (Have you a pencil?) The expedition led by Colonel S. F. Faramond (well, come on, man: take it down!) today reached an inner chamber of the excavation. (Shorthand, eh?) The work of eighteen months, as observed by Your Correspondent (that's you) has been successful. The find will disappoint many who had hoped for some revelation of the Periclean age, but will be of interest to those who have never before had any sympathy with archaeological science. (Stop sucking the pencil, Henry. Get it down. Here we go!)
This place—(have you a picture of your ideal reader? I have)—a room stamped down by time under the earth holds, sir, your youth. This place, dedicated to the sparrow and the swan, the

rose, the poppy and the lime tree, sacred to Aphrodite, keeps safe
the dark girl, the gay brave one in the language of the time, who
loved you (so she said) most. Your correspondent has no wish to
use these columns for confession or reminiscence but yes, she was
known to him.

For she was born to many of us among the raspberry bushes on a
hot afternoon in the garden when the younger children laughed
and played, but you and I, sir, older (at least fourteen), silent,
horribly wiser stayed out of sight: (I speak personally, Henry.
You were probably curled up in a theatrical basket) born in the
fevered heat on that torrid day with the sun falling out of the sky.
She stayed with you growing in beauty and experience as your
imagination and longing swept you into manhood. (Were you
swept into manhood, Henry? I was. It entailed swimming the
length of an ornamental lake at four o'clock in the morning
You're right. Another story). She was so nearly met. There was
always the chance of absolute discovery in so many encounters.
And yet. And yet.

Where was she? The dark girl with the wit of the sparrow, the
viciousness of the swan, the arrogance of the rose, the vulgarity
of the poppy and the contentment of the lime tree. Shall we say
she was with you until you lost your ambition? Yes, sir, age is
responsible for too much. That's agreed. It's responsible, you'll
remember, for the loneliness which made you do with that angel
in tweeds across the breakfast table. She's kind to dogs, that one.
At the moment she's patting a flat head and believes you to be
reading the financial page. Soon she'll go from the room and pat
you on the head as she passes. If you're lucky.

Your Correspondent wishes to send a message of hope to the
unloved.

The dark girl, the ideal born in the garden, has been protected
after all. Here, sir, are your boyish scribblings on the wall, the
formal patterns of desire scratched on the end papers of your
Liddell and Scott, the undergraduate poems and the solitary
drinking of your thirties, all translated to beauty and (God help
us, Henry! Look here) truth. (I'd no idea Selwyn could draw so
well. See that with the hands—so). How foolish you were, dear
reader of 'The Times', to think she was lost. She was here in every
way. Playing the games, laughing, lying, acting all the scenes and
being a woman. She was in this place. Waiting.

So put the dogs in kennels and send the angel in tweeds to the committee meeting.

Trains leave daily. From Tunbridge Wells and Leamington Spa, from Cheltenham and all university cities, from Baden, Monte Carlo, Venice, Aix, Calais, and all the places of loveless exile. Bags can be packed. The pilgrimage can begin.

Yet wait! before you blow the dust from your Gladstone. With the message of hope must come a warning.

Ah! sir, in two thousand years she has not aged. Her bed is still a jousting ground: yours is now a place of rest. Her way of adoration has become a goodnight kiss pecked into the forehead. There are other differences too painful for this journal to print. Wait!

The breath you used to blow the dust from your travelling bags has left you giddy and confused. Let the train go. That whistle is the signal for departure, not an impertinence.

In the Indian night which shrouds all love in seemly oblivion now, another traces the anagram with an enfranchised hand.

(Suddenly). Turn to page Six for reproductions of the find in detail.

HENRY: No, no!

There is a knock on the door.

JOHN: Nobody here! (CRISTOS *comes into the room.*) Hullo. I thought it might be—well, almost anyone else in this damned house.

CRISTOS: I've only just come in. The place seemed deserted. I felt you must have gone. What are you doing?

JOHN: Henry's article for 'The Times'.

HENRY: Hogarth, when I'm asked for my help I treat the matter seriously. That is, I've always done so until now. I don't know what your particular problem is, but if you told me you were in the most horrible dilemma known to man I think I'd laugh. Laugh in your face! (HENRY *goes out of the room.*)

CRISTOS: What have you done to upset him?

JOHN: What are we always doing to upset people? You've had a difference of opinion with Sophie, I understand.

CRISTOS: I wouldn't take down the dictation she was giving about you. She meant to rewrite certain passages in the light of her present knowledge.

JOHN: You think that's cheating.

CRISTOS: Oh, the whole thing's a swindle. It depends on who's to be the victim. I don't want it to be you.

JOHN: Why should you try to defend my reputation?

CRISTOS: Forgive me. I'm not. I'm trying to save my own creation.

JOHN: How does it come to be your creation when Sophie dictates?

CRISTOS: I'm making the book from her notes, certainly. You might say that I'm creating a work of fiction from certain established facts.

JOHN: Why doesn't Sophie protest?

CRISTOS: She'd only do that, I think, if she took the trouble to read it. She's not done so yet.

JOHN: At the moment she's in her room writing herself.

CRISTOS: I'm sure she's not. She's too lazy to write in her own hand. Half a line, perhaps. Nothing more. That won't scratch the surface of my central figure.

JOHN: I see. So whatever happens to me can't really affect your legend.

CRISTOS: No. I'll have to observe the practical details, of course. I'm hoping that from the time Basilios arrives you'll begin to live up to the book. That should make my work much easier. I've always preferred the truth.

JOHN: I'd like to help you in that. But I can't. I can only give you the facts and hope that your imagination can translate them to something worthy of your early chapters. I don't think it's possible, for the one end you can't have foreseen is domestic tragedy.

CRISTOS: Not marriage!

JOHN: No, no. Not that. Sometime ago you were walking with Caroline. You were talking of the unhappiness of love.

CRISTOS: We've done that many times.

JOHN: But on this occasion you pointed out a solution. The scarlet berries growing on the hillside.

CRISTOS: As a joke I believe I said—

JOHN: Many people in this tragic country believe those to be the answer. Am I right?

CRISTOS: Something like that.

JOHN: You've been taken at your word. Caroline distilled some of those berries this evening and put the stuff in my wine. And in hers.

CRISTOS: Oh, my God!

JOHN: So it seems as if the story will end here.

CRISTOS: You can't let that happen.

JOHN: Surely it's out of my hands.

CRISTOS: Keep away from her.

JOHN: I am. Too late.

CRISTOS: Your mind must be elevated. Make an effort.

JOHN: There's no point. She says it takes effect in eight hours.

CRISTOS: Less than that.

JOHN: Less? Then I'm dying before your eyes.

CRISTOS: Dying, Mr Hogarth?

JOHN: Yes. From the effect of the poison. Don't distress yourself. I'm calm. What's that noise? Are you laughing?

CRISTOS: Yes. I said to Caroline when she spoke of love, those— the berries—are believed by many to be the answer. Obviously our minds were not in accord.

JOHN: Meaning?

CRISTOS: The effect is mild. Romantic fiction calls it a love potion.

JOHN: An aphrodisiac. (*He looks at the drawings which he holds and then he throws them out of the window.*)

CRISTOS: That's what I meant. I should have remembered that Caroline is apt to see everything in terms of morality. She thought it was poison. Oh dear, I must tell the poor child at once.

JOHN: No! I'll do that. Later.

CRISTOS: Be gentle. An unexpected return to life can be disturbing.

JOHN: Yes. Yes, I'm understanding that at the moment. Here's the damned thing on my hands again. What do I do with it? Finish packing.

SOPHIE *comes into the room.*

SOPHIE: I thought it would do you no harm to have to think on a serious subject for a while. Especially after your frivolous behaviour of the last two days. But I've relented and come to tell you. The wine Caroline gave you was harmless; it has no effect which a day's forced march won't cure.

CRISTOS: Mr Hogarth has already confided in me, and I've put him right on that point.

SOPHIE: Have you, indeed? You're extending your meddling activities beyond his written life now.

JOHN: You knew all the time, Sophie.

SOPHIE: Yes, my dear. The cook has a most comprehensive recipe book. I knew the moment you spoke of Man's Friend. The berries from the hill.

JOHN: That's why you called Caroline a silly girl.

SOPHIE: Well, so she is. The place is overgrown with dangerous herbs which would have polished you off in an instant. But she chose that.

JOHN: Have you thought that it might have been intentional? That she knew what she was doing and lied to me.

SOPHIE: I don't think that's so.

JOHN: I'd like to believe that she meant it.

SOPHIE: Why?

JOHN: Because I'm in love with her.

SOPHIE: You mean you'd like to believe she meant no harm.

JOHN: No, no. I'd like to believe she tried to kill me. It shows a degree of attachment I've never known before.

SOPHIE: Surely there have been several who tried to kill themselves.

JOHN: Oh, yes, several. But only themselves. That was mere selfishness.

SOPHIE: Then the news that you are what everyone else would call all right is not very welcome.

JOHN: Not at all welcome. It makes flight imperative.

CRISTOS: Ah! you're an Englishman. How shall I ever get you truly down on paper for posterity to marvel at?

SOPHIE: You are now writing *my* book.

CRISTOS: My dear Sophie, read it.

SOPHIE: That's what I've been doing for the last two hours. I wasn't able to concentrate myself, so I picked up the manuscript.

CRISTOS: Well?

SOPHIE: You've done a good job of transcription. Nothing more.

CRISTOS: You think the John Hogarth in that book is the man you've been remembering aloud to me?

SOPHIE: Of course. What else? Do you mean I don't know what I've been talking about?

CRISTOS: If you think the man in the book and the man you told me about are the same then yes, I do. (CRISTOS *goes out of the room.*)

SOPHIE: Don't let me stop you from going on with your packing. I take it you're not waiting for Basilios.

JOHN: No, I must get out of here. It's a very dangerous situation.

SOPHIE: It is, if you've fallen in love with the girl. I was afraid it would happen, but you seemed so sure.

JOHN: I can't go until morning. There's no way of transport.

SOPHIE: Selwyn's been using some mules. You might take one of them.

JOHN: What's the time?

SOPHIE: A little past midnight.

JOHN: Only one person can save me now. Basilios. Why doesn't he come? To be under way through the night rolled in a blanket with the smell of the road dust and weapon oil for company could save me. If he's not here by morning I shall go to meet him.

SOPHIE: I think perhaps that's best. You know I'm not in favour of this insurrection, but I can see it's the only way out.

JOHN: I haven't lost my taste for it. Don't think that. It's not a mere expedient. My affections may now be here in this place but—how can I say this to you?—my duty and my honour are under the open sky in the north.

SOPHIE: Did you hanker after all that during the years in London?

JOHN: I think I must have done.

SOPHIE: You gave no sign of it.

JOHN: Didn't I? But even in those days the American in me wanted to be loved and the Scot in me wanted to be safe, and so began this everlasting and headlong flight.

CAROLINE *has come into the room.*

CAROLINE: You've always known what you've been running away from, but have you ever paused to think what it is you're running towards? No, for I'm the first person to check you.

SOPHIE: You want him to think about it now?

CAROLINE: Why not? There's the rest of the night.

SOPHIE: Then try, John, try to be all Scot. (SOPHIE *goes out of the room.*)

CAROLINE: I found these lying on the terrace. (*She is carrying Selwyn's drawings.*) Is this what you've been doing up here alone?

JOHN: It is not. They're your father's drawings of the figures in the dig.

CAROLINE: I thought you might have been remembering past triumphs.

JOHN: Caroline, why did you do it?

CAROLINE: Put the stuff in the wine?

JOHN: Yes.

CAROLINE: Because I can't weather another storm.

JOHN: Another?

CAROLINE: There would have been someone else, darling, somewhere, sometime, after you. You'd have gone and—well, you'd have gone and whatever I'd pretended I'd have been in clear calm water again with no excuse in the world for not sailing on. Yes, I'd have been on my way again smartly answering the helm when—look! it's nothing but a cloud. The sky's full of them. Natural things, like men. What's to be afraid of? That friendly little cloud's to be afraid of. And once again I'm trying to get through the deep waters. Exciting? Yes, it's exciting enough trying to steer a course. But there's panic aboard and Reason, the only unpaying passenger I have, is the first to go over the side. It's frightening when you can't see the sky, and there's no landmark in your past to go by. All swept away, they are. The tempest blows itself out. Nothing lasts for ever, not even bad weather. Some dawn or other it clears and you find yourself a long way out. You're safe. But you're drifting. And you're alone. Reason, the poor soaked fool, humble and ashamed, is fished out, hauled aboard, restored to its seat and at once starts giving advice. You take it and paddle on. This time I wanted to go down with all hands. And with you.

JOHN: It's not going to happen.

CAROLINE: Oh, yes, it is.

JOHN: No, you made a mistake. The berries are harmless.

CAROLINE: But Cristos said—

JOHN: You misunderstood. The stuff has a certain effect.

CAROLINE: What effect?

JOHN: Well, shall we say it strikes at a more private part than the immortal soul.

CAROLINE: I didn't know.

JOHN: Are you sure?

CAROLINE: Of course I'm sure.

JOHN: I'm glad.

CAROLINE: You're glad I thought we'd both be finished?

JOHN: Yes. No one's ever balanced my life so precisely with their own before.

CAROLINE: My God! You love me, don't you?

JOHN: Very much.

CAROLINE: Wait a minute. Have you forgotten? There's going to be a tomorrow after all. Can you say it knowing that?

JOHN: Yes.

CAROLINE: But, John, It's going to be for quite a while. Now say it.

JOHN: A man takes leave of a woman he's loved and an art he's practised in much the same spirit. He loves but he goes. That's what I'm doing now. Both are taken up in a moment of abandon which may occur in the best ordered life. It's difficult to believe that you who occupy little space as a person and the trivial act of writing a poem could in time crowd out the many necessary and amusing ways of living. But it's common knowledge that such is the case. Yet too many men end up as husbands or artists. Sometimes even the ultimate subjection: both.

CAROLINE: So I'm wrong again. It's not to be for quite a while. What's the matter with marriage?

JOHN: I don't know. Ask Boysie.

CAROLINE: He at least tried to make it work. You've never done that.

JOHN: I could make it work perfectly well. But as an arrangement it would be an impossible demand on the genius of the woman.

CAROLINE: Will you marry me, please? So forget Sophie. Go on. Be all Yankee. Will you?

SOPHIE *has come into the room.*

SOPHIE: If you delay your answer for a moment, John, there's some business you should attend to. (*She turns to the door.*) Will you come in, please. I found this gentleman waiting below.

PRINCE BASILIOS *comes into the room: he carries a large black iron bicycle.*

BASILIOS: Hogarth, my dear child! (*He casts aside the bicycle and embraces* JOHN.)

JOHN: I'm very pleased to see you, sir. Did you have a good journey?

BASILIOS: No. We feared an ambush of our person.

JOHN: Has your machine brought you all the way?

BASILIOS: No, no. We came by train. Our machine was bought nearby for the emergency.

JOHN: You must tell me about that. First, may I present to Your Highness Mrs Faramond and Mrs Traherne.

BASILIOS: Basilios! We are made happy, Mrs Traherne. The beautiful Sophie engaged our attention and our affection below.

JOHN: Did she, indeed?

BASILIOS: You, Mrs Traherne, are beloved of our great Archistrategos?

CAROLINE: I hope to be, if you mean John.

BASILIOS: Bring him comfort, Madam. Prepare your breasts for his tears. God sent us such little animals for our sorrow. Where shall I find comfort? It is a question which must be settled later.

SOPHIE: Infected with John's enthusiasm we've all waited your coming with impatience, Prince Basilios. When does the revolution begin?

BASILIOS: We are disturbed, shocked to hear such a word come from the mouth of a woman.

SOPHIE: You mean our sex should concern itself only with the status quo ante.

BASILIOS: If you please. When all seems to be lost the world may yet find its salvation in the conservatism of the great regiment of women.

SOPHIE: That sounds strange coming from a famous leader of the people. I must say that remembering your charming conversation and manner downstairs I find it difficult to see you leading a mob of peasants to storm a palace.

BASILIOS: Hogarth, I think, has the same feeling about a lovely woman touched by the mud and blood of politics. He's told you nothing. Have you, my dear?

JOHN: Very little

BASILIOS: So it seems. Do not think ill of us, Sophie. We do not rise at the head of the people. They have many leaders. No, my darling simpleton. The revolt is to restore the impoverished and unhappy aristocracy of my country. We are a few brothers bound by a belief in a former way of life. When so many today look forward we look back. But such things must not—no, never!— concern you. Now, shoo-shoo, little ones! Hogarth and I must talk in secret. So, shoo! to your prattle and gossip, your novels and embroidery frames. Shoo!

CAROLINE: I think he wants us to go.

SOPHIE: For the first time in my life, Caroline, I feel you're on my side against something. (SOPHIE *and* CAROLINE *go out of the room.*)

BASILIOS: No cause to give way to despair before them.

JOHN: You've come with bad news.

BASILIOS: You see it in my face. Yes, my beloved boy, there is bad news.

JOHN: May I be told?

BASILIOS: I left London when I had converted your cheque into gold. There was too much to carry about my person, and so I stored it in a strong box bound with iron. I hired two Germans for my bodyguard.

JOHN: Yet you were robbed.

BASILIOS: Wait! We made the journey across Europe safely. We arrived in my country. At once I called a meeting of the Committee. I spoke to them. I told them of your promises. Many wept. I told them of your donation and the hundred thousand golden pounds were brought in. They were silent. Each man with his own thoughts.

JOHN: This is very moving. Please go on.

BASILIOS: The Archbishop spoke first. Where, he wanted to know, was the money to be kept? He at once suggested the cathedral. I countered this. It was to be kept, I said, under my bed. Hogarth, my dear, I will not even let my bicycle out of my sight in this country. On my way here I stopped by the roadside to perform a natural function. A matter of a moment, but when I returned the machine had been stripped of its pneumatic tyres, as you see.

JOHN: So the money found its way under your bed. Preparatory, I hope, to its original purpose of paying soldiers for the revolt.

BASILIOS: Of course. Yet no sooner was it beneath the bed than I began to receive petitioners. All my old friends. The Archbishop came to ask for a new roof on the cathedral, an aged general wanted new colours for a long disbanded regiment and my brother needed money for his gambling debts.

JOHN: I hope you reminded them of the true purpose of the funds.

BASILIOS: I did, my son. All of them. Except one.

JOHN: A woman.

BASILIOS: So beautiful. So unlike the others. Modest, she came with no demands, but with a proposition. Not for love of politics. For love of me. Precise and smiling she proposed that your money should be spent on a great reception. She told me it was the English way. It is known as charity. Admission would be charged. Your money would be doubled. The Committee of Freedom could sweep to victory. The idea was mad, yes! But I loved her, Hogarth! I listened to her talk but I didn't hear what she said. Before I could bring myself to my senses I found the grounds of my house to be transformed. All had become the setting for an English garden party. Marquees had arrived from the Army and

Navy Stores, cakes were sent from Buzzards', a military band was playing Gilbert and Sullivan and my darling was in white organdie with English roses on her arm. I wept, my dear Hogarth. I wept for unutterable joy. The affair cost a fortune.

JOHN: Yet. Yet it was not a success.

BASILIOS: No one came except my beloved. She was heartbroken. Can I say that I was sad? No, I cannot, for it became my duty to console her. We walked the gardens in silence until the sun went down and the Chinese lanterns were lit. The river pageant moved past in splendour for my lady. My God! Hogarth, never have I loved in such a way. Her face was to the stars as the firework display was set off. Later in the ballroom we danced for the first and last time. The thousand empty drinking glasses rang a lament for the guests who had never come. But for us the fiddles sang— and sang until their voices were faint to us through the empty corridors of the house which led us dancing to our further sport. When I took her in my arms the diamonds fell from her hair, her throat and wonder from her fell down the gown. At that moment, unknown to me, the mob led by the Committee of Freedom—the Archbishop, the General and my brother—had stormed through the gates of the house. Well known to me, alas, was the fact that the box beneath the bed on which we played held no more than fifty golden pounds.

JOHN: Just enough to pay your fare here and buy a bicycle.

BASILIOS: Immediate flight was necessary the moment they broke down the door. Treachery at cock-crow, Hogarth. It was dawn as I went on foot over the hills to the south. They may still be at my heels. That's why I bought the machine. (JOHN *is sitting at the window in silence*.) You're angry with me, my son.

JOHN: No. What happened to the lady?

BASILIOS: Being Russian she pleaded diplomatic immunity. She was kneeling before the Archbishop as I left. Don't be angry with an old man, Hogarth.

JOHN: Was she beautiful, and were you truly happy?

BASILIOS: She was beautiful, yes, and for the last time I was truly happy. The last time. For with her hands she closed the gates of love behind me.

JOHN: I wanted to be sure the money wasn't wasted, that's all.

BASILIOS: Don't forgive me, Hogarth, or I shall weep!

JOHN: Nonsense! There's nothing to forgive.

BASILIOS: Ah! my wonderful boy, you came to bring freedom to a country, and instead you're content to bring happiness to an old man. (*He is beside* JOHN *at the window and he kisses him.*) Call back the women. See, there they walk. Let's be brave before them. Let's show we're not unmanned. (*He calls.*) Come up, my children! Come up, my darlings!

JOHN: Shall I be honest with you, Basilios? I wasn't concerned with the freedom of the country. I wanted freedom for myself. I'd have died in your cause, Basilios, whatever it was.

BASILIOS: My dear boy, you come from a country which has always spoken lightly of dying for the cause. Your great predecessor, Noel Byron, said you remember, If thou regret'st thy youth, why live?/The land of honourable death/Is here:—up to the field and give/Away thy breath! God took him at his word, though, and fetched him off here.

JOHN: Even Englishmen must expect God to take them at their word sometimes.

BASILIOS: He must love them as he loves all his children. I think more than most for he gave them a special duty. To provide the legends of our time. But a day is coming, Hogarth, when the single man of vision will need more than God on his side. He will also need a party organization.

JOHN: You were to provide that in the Committee of Freedom.

BASILIOS: I was only a weak instrument. I failed, Hogarth. Have you anything at all to thank me for?

JOHN: Yes, I think so. You trusted me. That may not seem much to be thankful for at the moment, but it will tell in time. Also you brought me here.

BASILIOS: To the beautiful Mrs Traherne? Shall I be content, my dear? (SOPHIE *and* CAROLINE *come into the room.*) We called you to us as we wish to take our leave. Our conference is done. I can go away content, he tells me.

SOPHIE: It's very late. Won't you stay tonight and go on in the morning?

BASILIOS: As things are it is wiser to travel at night.

CAROLINE Is John going with you?

BASILIOS: Answer her yourself, Hogarth. See how much happiness can be given in one small word.

CAROLINE: Well? Either yes or no will do.

SOPHIE: I take it there's been some upset in your plans.

BASILIOS: To explain I'd have to talk politics, and you don't want me to do that.

SOPHIE: I don't mind.

BASILIOS: From deep experience I've found that women as beautiful as you, Sophie, should not be allowed even to speak of politics. A woman will always try to do right, and such a philosophy has nothing to do with political life.

SOPHIE: Very well. If the matter is only domestic I'd like to know how much longer we'll have John as a house guest.

BASILIOS: Cherish him. He's a great man. I wish I could tell you of the magnificent part he's played, but I must leave it to history. Now I shall go. Dear Hogarth. Pray don't think me a foolish old man in all things. When we're young it's possible to control the affairs of the state and the affairs of the heart at the same time. Older, one of them must be relinquished. Dear Hogarth. (*He embraces John.*) I shall make for the coast. The fishermen are still friendly, they tell me. So a little boat shall carry me off.

JOHN: What will happen to you, sir? Where will you go?

BASILIOS: Where can I go? There is only one place. To Ithaca. To my wife's family.

JOHN: God help you.

BASILIOS: And you, my son. (BASILIOS, *who has picked up the bicycle, and* SOPHIE *go out of the room.*)

CAROLINE: I'd say there's nothing left for you but to be happy. Sad, isn't it?

JOHN: And what is there left for you?

CAROLINE: You. Or have you some other commitment of honour to fulfil?

JOHN: No. I've nothing at all. Not even money now. What do you say to that? People always thought I was a rich man. I was not. I had an indulgent mother.

CAROLINE: Could you work?

JOHN: That's unkind.

CAROLINE: I didn't mean it.

JOHN: Yes, you did. You were looking at me as if I'm a pack horse you're about to load. You're not going to send me out to work Caroline. That's one thing nobody's ever suggested.

CAROLINE: Don't get so excited. We shall have to eat.

JOHN: There it is! The voice of the new century. We shall have to eat!

CAROLINE: Sorry. Boysie always left the practical details to me.

JOHN: You talk like a housekeeper.

CAROLINE: Won't that be my position?

JOHN: Now listen to me. For one moment listen to me. When I say that I love you I love you. Why when you hear it you should also hear the clatter of saucepans, the rattle of teacups and the rustle of bills I don't know. For God's sake, why should the mystical union of two souls be celebrated in a kitchen? Is the act of desire now dependent on the price of bedding? Caroline, Caroline, it's too soon to live happy ever after. Too soon.

CRISTOS *comes into the room.*

CRISTOS: Sophie's standing on the terrace kissing a strange old man with a bicycle.

JOHN: Never mind. Now that Selwyn's finished at the excavation you'll be seeing the last of her.

CRISTOS: I've been talking to Selwyn about that. It leaves me with a domestic problem.

JOHN: Well, now!

CRISTOS: You see, Selwyn's lease of the house runs only to the end of the excavation. I shall have the place to myself again.

CAROLINE: How much does Selwyn pay?

CRISTOS: Only a nominal sum. It's not that which worries me. I like having people around me. English speaking people. I've explained why to Mr Hogarth.

CAROLINE: Surely the excavation would be of interest great to tourists. It's your land. A small sum for admission. A guide. Me.

JOHN: No, Caroline, no! You're a monster, a fiend! First you domesticate love. Now you're trading it. There is a name for that sort of thing, my girl.

CAROLINE: What are you talking about? I'm only advising Cristos on how not to be lonely.

JOHN: If you can't leave me in peace at least leave those young everlasting lovers down the hill their privacy.

CAROLINE: Now you're talking romantic nonsense.

CRISTOS: Aren't you going to the revolution, Mr Hogarth?

JOHN: No.

CRISTOS: I'm sorry to hear that. What are you doing instead?

CAROLINE: Well, what are you doing?

JOHN: I'll wait for some decision to be made for me.

CRISTOS: That reminds me. Where's Henry? A cable's come for

him. From England. A boy brought it from Athens tonight. (*He has taken a cable from his pocket.*)

CAROLINE: What does it say?

CRISTOS: I've not read it.

CAROLINE: Give it to me. (*She takes the cable from* CRISTOS *and opens it. She reads:*) 'Cancel further articles on digging stop Proceed incognito to expected trouble centre Bosina stop Membership of secret society taken out for you signed Northcliffe repeat Northcliffe.'

CRISTOS: I don't want that back. (CAROLINE *is holding the cable out to him.*) I'll never have enough courage to give it to the poor boy.

CAROLINE: Somebody will have to give it to him.

CRISTOS: He's very fond of you.

CAROLINE: All right. Send him in when he comes back.

JOHN: Are you off to work on your book?

CRISTOS: No, I'm going to bed. Goodnight. (CRISTOS *goes out of the room.*)

JOHN: There's another person who won't forgive me for not living up to his ideals.

CAROLINE: Forget all that. Just be yourself.

JOHN: I've never been anything else. Come here. Don't stand so far away.

CAROLINE: But I'm so near I can—(*She kisses him.*)

JOHN: What on earth's going to happen to us? Without the benefit of clergy, the sanctity of wealth and even the solace of age. No one will receive, respect or love us. Worst of all, they'll laugh at us. There's nothing so absurd as a man who's given up the world for love. They'll look at you and think. Is that it? And you'll have to admit it is. Don't go away. I want you where I can lay hands on you at a moment's notice.

CAROLINE: I've not moved. I'm in your pocket. This is a beautiful house. Sophie, Selwyn and Henry will soon be gone. No one would find us here.

JOHN: In a few days the place will be overrun by German professors with little trowels. They'd nose out why we were here.

CAROLINE: We can lie to them. I can lie in any language. Then we'll stay for ever. Cristos will accept the situation in no time, and be so proud to have you living there.

JOHN: He's proud to say I've stopped here on my way, but he won't be happy if I stay here permanently.

CAROLINE: Every moment makes it obvious that I put the wrong stuff in the wine. Tonight could have been so simple. Now we shall sit up talking.

JOHN: Caroline, a way has got to be found. You don't seem to understand my position. I left England saying that I was going to fight for a glorious cause. I made a great deal of it. The papers were full of it. A cartoon in 'Punch' showed me going aboard a ship called 'The Rake's Progress'. A question was asked in the Upper House; in the Lower House there were cheers and counter-cheers. From the fuss no one would have thought that I was trying to get *out* of the country. But I did. Only to find the cause is lost before I arrive. Now, I'm very sensitive to public opinion. How shall I feel when the news gets back to England that there was nothing but pillow fighting with you in a villa near Athens?

SOPHIE *comes into the room.*

SOPHIE: I'm on my way to bed.

CAROLINE: Have you seen Basilios off?

SOPHIE: Yes, poor man. From what he told me he won't see a bed for weeks. He was insistent, John, on the fine part you've played in the revolution. You passed through it, apparently, untarnished and burning bright. His words.

JOHN: You got on well with the old man.

SOPHIE: He has a natural sympathy. I'd be a fool if I didn't see that his sorrow is caused by more than the failure of a revolt. When a man looks into your face, kisses you and whispers, So dies my ambition, he's not referring to a political party. Ah, well, he's gone. But you're still here.

JOHN: Don't let that be a problem any longer.

SOPHIE: I won't. For it's I who'll be leaving now that Selwyn's finished at this dig. Somewhere in Asia there's another piece of innocent ground waiting to be molested by him. Soon he'll be at work again digging up a day that was a thousand years ago, and I, nearby, less fortunate, at work on a mere decade. Yes, the future definitely seems to lie in the past.

CAROLINE: I don't believe that. For you, if you like. But you meant all of us, didn't you?

SOPHIE: Yes. Except, perhaps, Henry.

CAROLINE: Well, as a matter of fact we were talking about our future when you came in.

SOPHIE: You're planning it together?

CAROLINE: Yes. ⎫
JOHN: No. ⎭ *They speak together.*

SOPHIE: You've both been staggering under the past. You'll double the burden for each other if you share it. Not, as you think, halve it.

JOHN: The problem's not arithmetical, Sophie. It is how I can decently continue after what's happened. If you've any suggestions please tell me. If not, go to bed.

SOPHIE: I've been thinking about it since Basilios left.

JOHN: Any conclusion? For example, how are you going to end your book now?

SOPHIE: About that I could wait no longer. Some decision had to be taken. You'll die on the battlefield, as you wished.

JOHN: How can you? I thought you loved me.

SOPHIE: I do. So I shall end the book that way. It had to be arranged for another reason. You must know that modern readers like the end of a book to be sanctified by marriage. They call it, rather strangely, the happy ending. I've known from the first, of course, that such a resolution would be impossible with you as the main character. So I shall use the best alternative for the lending libraries. You'll die in battle.

JOHN: When?

SOPHIE: Tomorrow morning. I've sent a cable to the Editor of the London 'Times'. It says reports from the mountains speak of you falling gallantly at the head of your native troops led in a lost cause. Naturally, I signed myself Henry Bevis. (SOPHIE *goes out of the room.*)

CAROLINE: How sad! How terribly sad!

JOHN: Is it? I wonder.

CAROLINE: I mean because no one will believe me now when I say we were here together.

JOHN: No, not a soul will believe you.

CAROLINE: Unless, of course, you turn up in London as yourself. With me.

JOHN: I'll not do that.

CAROLINE: I feel as if I've never seen you before. Damn, oh damn and damn! This is what Cristos warned me about. Falling in love with a legend. You're a man. Just a man. Two a penny. That's what you are.

JOHN: Seeing me that way is the penalty of winning, Caro. You've never been anything but a woman to me. I've never asked that anyone I've loved should be more. (*He lifts* CAROLINE *in his arms and puts her on the bed.*)

CAROLINE: You mean, however splendid the pursuit, and however corrupt the trickery, I'll end up with a man. Just a man.

JOHN: That's all. (JOHN *gently pulls on the heavy silken cord and draws the curtains which quite surround the bed. There is a knock on the door.*) Yes.

HENRY *comes into the room.*

HENRY: I want to apologize. I'm afraid the worry about the article made me lose my sense of humour and then my temper.

JOHN: All forgotten.

HENRY: I took another long walk and came to a decision. (*He is a little wild-eyed.*) I'm going to tell the truth about Selwyn's discovery.

JOHN: That's brave of you.

HENRY: Then I shall be called home in disgrace.

JOHN: Yes. Home! Wait a minute. (*He looks in his pockets. Whilst he is doing so* CAROLINE'S *bare arm comes through the curtains of the bed. She is holding out the cablegram to Henry. He takes it, staring at the bed. He pulls the cablegram from the envelope. He reads it. Slowly, his face crumples. John has moved to Henry and now puts an arm round his shoulders. Together, in silence, the two men stand staring down at the cablegram. Then, quietly, John speaks.*)

JOHN: Do you have a little badge, or something? (HENRY *shakes his head.*) Go home. To mother, Incognito. Keep your mouth shut. Your articles will go on arriving. I shall also sign every one Henry Bevis. (JOHN *gently takes the cablegram from* HENRY, *and begins to move to the door.* CAROLINE *speaks from the obscurity of the bed.*)

CAROLINE: May I ask one question? Just one.

JOHN: Yes.

CAROLINE: I want to know. Do we all get what we deserve?

JOHN: Yes. (*He is at the door.*)

CAROLINE: Every time?

JOHN: Yes. (JOHN *gives a sad smile to* HENRY *and quietly goes from the room.* CAROLINE'S *arm is still extended between the curtains of the bed. Suddenly, imperiously, she snaps her fingers. Slowly,* HENRY *moves to the bed and takes her hand in his.*)

There is a pause.

CURTAIN

NO WHY

INTRODUCTORY NOTE

WHEN Peter Hall commissioned *No Why* in the summer of 1957, he intended it to be a curtain-raiser for Whiting's translation of Anouilh's *The Traveller without Luggage,* but instead of using it when he finally produced the Anouilh at the Arts in January 1959, he got Whiting to translate Anouilh's *Madame de* . . . *No Why* was published in the *London Magazine* and produced as a radio play by Martin Esslin but it didn't get staged until July 1964 when John Schlesinger directed it as part of a programme of one-act plays, *Expeditions One,* at the Aldwych. Tony Church played Henry, June Jago Eleanor and Elizabeth Spriggs Sarah.

PERSONS

(in order of their appearance)

JACOB, *a child*
HENRY, *his father*
ELEANOR, *his mother*
MAX, *his cousin*
SARAH
AMY } *his aunts*
GREGORY, *his grandfather*
FIRST SERVANT
SECOND SERVANT

The action of the play passes in an unfurnished attic.

Time—the present.

ACT ONE

Die Ros' ist ohn' Warum, sie blühet, weil sie blühet,
Sie acht't nicht ihrer selbst, fragt nicht, ob man sie siehet.
ANGELUS SILESIUS

SCENE—*An unfurnished attic room. Night.*
*The roof is beamed. There is no window, and the only light comes from a single
unshaded electric lamp. There is one door, up* C. *The only furniture is an
upright chair placed down* RC. *The lamp is on a small wood shelf* R.
When the CURTAIN *rises, a small boy is sitting on the chair. He is in
pyjamas. His name is* JACOB. *Throughout the play, except when indicated
otherwise, he looks in front of him, appearing neither to see nor hear anything which occurs.*
After a moment the door is unlocked from outside. HENRY, *Jacob's father,
enters and comes down to* L *of the boy.*

HENRY: You know why you're here.
      JACOB *appears to be about to speak.*
Shut up. You know why, don't you? Bad boy. I want you to
understand. Naughty boy. Say you're sorry. Come on, tell me
you're sorry. We all do things we're sorry for. Ask to be forgiven.
So much better. For you. For everybody. Makes them happy.
Make you happy, too. (*He crosses slowly above the chair to* R *of it.*)
You know you've done a bad thing. A bad thing. Mischief. You've
hurt me very much. You've hurt your mother. Yes, your mother,
Jake. You've hurt her very much. Make it better, will you? (*He
kneels beside Jacob.*) Will you? Say you've done wrong. Look at me,
Jake. Say you've been a bad boy.
      ELEANOR, *Jacob's mother, enters. She cries out.*
ELEANOR: No! (*She crosses to* L *of the chair.*)
HENRY: I'm not touching him. (*He gets up.*) I haven't touched him.
ELEANOR: Don't hurt him.
HENRY: I won't hurt him. I'm being very reasonable. Christ's sake,

81

Eleanor, when have I ever hurt him? I've always been fair. I want him to admit that he's been naughty. Done a bad thing. That's all.

ELEANOR (*to* JACOB): Say you're sorry, Jake. Tell Mother you're sorry.

HENRY: It's pride. (*He moves away to down* R.)

ELEANOR: Not in a little boy.

HENRY: Stuffed. Up to here.

ELEANOR (*to* JACOB; *kneeling by him*): Listen, Jake. You've done a bad thing. Wicked. No, not wicked.

HENRY: Yes, wicked. (*He returns to the boy.*) We had a nice day today, didn't we, Jake? All of us, together. You enjoyed yourself. Yes, you did. I know you did. I saw you laughing. You were happy. Yes, you were. Quite right. We all wanted it to be a good day. One to remember. For grandfather's sake. And it was. A very good day. (*He pauses.*) Until you did such a bad thing. As your mother says, a wicked thing. Well, it's done. Day's spoilt. Nothing can make it good. No, nothing can make it good now. Pity. Nothing. But you can say you're sorry, Jake. Say you're sorry.
      Silence.

ELEANOR (*rising and moving away to* LC): He doesn't understand what he's done. He just doesn't understand.

HENRY: (*crossing above the chair to* R *of* ELEANOR): He may not understand what he's done, but he must understand, I've made it perfectly clear to him, that it was wrong.

ELEANOR: It's not enough. You must understand. You must. I know.

HENRY: You're a fool.

ELEANOR: I want you to explain to him, that's all.

HENRY: You want me to pretend. You want me to end up in the wrong. End up by admitting that I'm the one who's done wrong. Have me confess. Have me on my knees. I know you. Anything for a quiet life. A quiet life. That's what you want.

ELEANOR: No. I just want you to explain to him.
      Silence.

HENRY (*returning to* L *of* JACOB): Jake, it's easy to go wrong. As you grow up you'll find it's very easy. We can do harm. We can hurt people. But we don't do these things. As you did today. We don't do them because . . . (*He breaks off and pauses.*)
      Silence.
(*Suddenly shouting.*) Who the hell do you think you are!

Silence.

(*More calmly.*) Why did you do it? I don't understand. Tell me why you did it.

ELEANOR: He doesn't know.

HENRY: Well, he knows he's shut up. (*To* JACOB, *crossing above to* R *of him.*) You know that, don't you? You know you're being punished.

ELEANOR: We want you to have time to think over what you've done.

HENRY: That's right. Because we love you. We love you very much. We want to forgive you. Let's do that. Say you're sorry.

ELEANOR: You haven't explained. You haven't.

HENRY: I know. You want me down on my knees. To him.

ELEANOR: No, I want—

HENRY: Have I done wrong? Well, have I? You want me to say so. I know. I know what you want.

ELEANOR (*moving to* L *of* JACOB): —I want him to understand, that's all.

HENRY: There are prisons. (*He crouches down by the chair.*) Jake, listen. Men are shut up all over the world. In prisons. Bad men, wicked men. Men who have done harm. As you did today. They sit by themselves. In little rooms. They walk in circles. In yards. Outside —(*pointing to the door*) out there!—are the others. We are the others. We are free. We live good lives. We don't destroy. We're good. We're good, Jake. Those shut up are bad. They're bad, Jake. So bad, some of them, so bad they never get free. They die shut up. Die. Never seen again. No. (*He pauses.*) Say you're sorry, Jake.

Silence. HENRY *rises and moves a pace to* R.

ELEANOR: Do you know what I'm thinking about, Jake? (*She smiles.*) I'm thinking about you grown up.

HENRY: Have you forgotten what he's done?

ELEANOR: No. No.

HENRY: Then why are you smiling? Why are you talking about the future?

ELEANOR: Because I want him with me. (*She kneels beside the chair.*) I want you with me, Jake. I shall need you. Always. Never away from me. So please your father. Be a good boy.

MAX *enters up* C. *He is a young man.*

MAX (*moving to* L *of* HENRY): Uncle Henry, Mummy wants to know how long you're going to be?

HENRY (*taking Max's arm*): Look, Jake, here's your cousin Max.

MAX (*to* ELEANOR): Mummy says you could be done with this in no time.

ELEANOR *rises.*

HENRY: Now you've always liked Max. Or so it seemed. Aren't you disappointed? Max was going to play the piano and sing some songs. And you were going to be allowed down, Jake. You were going to be allowed down to listen. With the grown-ups.

MAX (*to* ELEANOR; *moving above the chair to her*): Fancy. I'd never have got away with it when I was a kid.

ELEANOR: He doesn't understand.

HENRY: Max will sing some funny songs for us. And you can come down, Jake. When you've said you're sorry. Say you're sorry.

Silence. MAX *squats beside* JACOB, *looking up at him.*

MAX: Come on, Jakey boy. Don't spoil the party. Gramp doesn't get much pleasure in life. His fun's over. But you've got it all, boy. If you're good. If you say you're sorry. Because you've got to be good in some things so's you can be bad in others. Follow? Say you're sorry, you bad lad. Then everything's in front of you. See? Let Max teach you. If you knew what it's all about you wouldn't want to throw it away like this. Come on, you want to grow up, don't you? Then say: I'm sorry.

Silence.

HENRY: He doesn't care.

MAX: Who does? Let's be honest.

HENRY: He must be made to care.

MAX: Up to you. (*He rises and moves above* ELEANOR *to up* L.)

HENRY (*to* JACOB): You can't win! Not now! Save what you can, you little fool!

Silence.

(*Loudly; moving in to* JACOB.) I'll put you through hell!

Silence.

ELEANOR (*kneeling* L *of the chair*): Remember when you were a little boy.

HENRY: That's it. Remember how I taught you your prayers?

MAX *moves down* L.

ELEANOR: You remember how they go.

HENRY: Of course you do.

ELEANOR (*to* HENRY): Oh, darling, I'm so happy.

HENRY (*crouching down*): Let's try it, Jake. Just a little one to please me. I'll give you a start. Gentle Jesus, meek and mild. Go on from there. (*He waits.*) Well, anyway, you once said them. You said them once. I remember, if you don't. Down on your knees. Now look at you. Look at you now. Breaking a promise to Jesus, that's what you're doing. (*He rises.*) Think of it, Jake. Oh, Jake! To Jesus. How can you do it? How can you?

    Silence. SARAH *enters up* C *and moves down to* R *of* MAX.

MAX: Mammy, Jake's being such a naughty boy. Won't say he's sorry for dreadful things he's done. He's damned, sure enough. His daddy promised him to come downstairs and hear me sing and play if he'll confess. But no, he's mum, Mammy. Oh, he's damned.

SARAH (*putting her hand on Max's arm*): You're a good boy, Max. You never disobeyed your father. When he was alive.

MAX: Oh, Mammy, I loved Daddy with all my heart.

HENRY: This child loves no one. (*He moves away down* R.)

ELEANOR: He loves me!

HENRY (*turning*): You?

ELEANOR: He loves me!

HENRY (*to* JACOB): Do you?

ELEANOR: Yes.

HENRY (*to* JACOB): Love your mother?

    Silence. HENRY *laughs.*

ELEANOR: It doesn't need to be said. (*She rises and moves above the chair.*)

HENRY: Which is lucky for you. It never will be.

SARAH (*moving a pace to* C): Ah, this child doesn't understand the beauty of love. Pretty pretty. Doesn't understand the pleasure of giving in. I knew it so well! Until my hubbie was taken from me. To wake and find no one to submit to was a terrible thing.

MAX: You've still got me, Mammy.

SARAH (*moving back to* MAX): Yes, darling, I've still got you. (*She fondles him in a disgusting way.*)

MAX: Oo, Mammy, I love you, I love you so.

HENRY (*to* JACOB): See that, Jake? Hear that? Ashamed of yourself?

SARAH: Darling.

MAX: Oo.

SARAH: Sweet.

MAX: Oo.

SARAH: Kisskiss.

MAX: Oo, loveee.

MAX *and* SARAH *kiss.* HENRY *looks down at* JACOB.

HENRY: I had hopes of you. Even from the start. It was all so romantic. Soft lights and sweet music. Dancing cheek to cheek. I was young. When I think of that I could cry. True, I could cry. (*He moves to* ELEANOR *above the chair, groping for her hand. To her.*) Remember how we planned for him? What should he be like, our son? Should he walk on two legs or on four? We decided two, remember? So his head should be nearer the clouds. You wanted that with your love of pansy poetry. The more feet on the ground the more realistic his outlook, I thought. But you kissed me and I gave in. And he turned out just as our conception of him. All seemed right. Remember how happy we were? Remember the long winter evenings as we sat reading the school year-book and careers for boys and he lay farting in his cot? And we laughed and loved him so much. (*He stares down at* JACOB.) That was this little criminal.

ELEANOR: You forget. You exaggerate. We had him in the same way everyone has their boy. More or less. It was late. You were tired. I was nearly asleep. There was nothing strange or wonderful about it. Of course we talked about his school when he was little, and what he might be when he grew up. But only because you worry about money so much. It was all from the very start for our sake, not for his.

HENRY *lets go of Eleanor's hand, and moves away* R.

HENRY: You're taking his part again. This is not the time. If I was as soft as you are you'd have broken my heart long ago. Stand up to the boy!

ELEANOR (*to* JACOB; *standing above the chair*): Are you sorry for what you've done?

HENRY (*to* ELEANOR): Are you?

Silence. ELEANOR *turns slightly up stage.*

MAX: Mammy, when I was little was I sweet?

SARAH: You were adorable.

MAX: Did you ever have to shut me up like this?

SARAH: Never.

MAX: Not ever?

SARAH: No.

MAX: Did you ever have to give me a little smack?

SARAH (*after a pause*): Once.

MAX: Oo, Mammy!

AMY *enters and comes down* C.

AMY: I've had to leave Father down there. It doesn't seem right.

MAX (*crossing below* SARAH *to* AMY): Does he want to come up?

JACOB *looks at* AMY.

AMY: Well, you know what he's like. Hates to miss any fun that may be going. But I can't get the wheelchair up the stairs.

MAX (*moving up* C): I love Gramp very much. I won't let him be lonely. I won't.

MAX *goes out.*

SARAH: That's right, Jake. Look at your Aunt Amy. She's a really good woman.

ELEANOR, *above the chair, turns downstage again.* JACOB *looks out front.*

AMY: No, Sarah.

SARAH: Yes, Amy. A good woman.

AMY: No, Sarah, like little Jake here, I'm a wicked sinner. But I repent. Every time.

SARAH (*putting her hand on Amy's arm*): Oh, you serene and beautiful person. You're wonderful, like—like treacle.

HENRY: No.

AMY: Perhaps I can help. (*She kneels* L *of the chair.*) When I was a little girl, Jake, about your age, I wanted everything in the world for myself. I thought I was beautiful—

SARAH: You were, Amy.

AMY: —talented—

SARAH: You were.

AMY: —and lovable.

SARAH: Wasn't she, Henry?

AMY: And I thought I had a right to everything. I was lost in a dream—

SARAH: Cut it short, Amy. Get to the point. Tell him about your prison visiting. How you tramp the hospital wards. And how you love the lunatics.

AMY: I go to see the prisoners, Jake. Sometimes the condemned men. They often take my hand and ask forgiveness. As you can. Now. Will you?

Silence. JACOB *does not move.*

I go into the hospital wards. No sudden death there. A florid growth back to nature. There's a man who is nothing but an enormous mouth, and he always asks my blessing. Will you? (*She pauses.*) In the asylums they run to me. Their darling childish faces are shining with love. Their trust is so great. One night a young girl lay still. Moths settled on her open eyes and drowned there. The insane can learn nothing from me of faith and serenity. But will you?

Silence.

HENRY: Don't you understand what your Aunt Amy gave up to bring comfort to all these people? Haven't you any respect? She's offering her love to you and you won't accept it.

AMY: It doesn't matter, Henry. (*She rises.*)

HENRY: It does matter, Amy. Is he so proud that he thinks himself better than the condemned, the sick and the mad? At least he should recognize the sacrifices you've made. Oh, Amy, you were such a lovely girl when we were children. Has it been worth it? Living your life for others?

AMY: Always, Henry, when others accept it. Not like this bloody little bastard of yours. This filth.

SARAH: I don't know how you and Eleanor came to have such a child. How does our lovely, adorable brother come to have such a child, Amy?

AMY: Perhaps as a curse.

SARAH: From God, darling? They come from God, you know.

AMY: Of course, Henry, there is the criminal who doesn't repent. The sick man who dies in silence. The madman who laughs and turns away. Some don't need others. To hell with them! (*She moves away up* L.)

HENRY (*he kneels in front of* JACOB): Say you're sorry. I'll do anything. I'll give you anything. Jacob. Listen. You heard what Amy said. Come back to the family party before it's too late. Come with me. Please. Darling. Come back. Come back.

Silence. ELEANOR *cries out and moves away a pace up stage. A long silence.*

Come back.

Two SERVANTS *enter. They carry* GREGORY, *Jacob's grandfather, on a kitchen chair. He is old, a thrown-away doll of a man. The* SERVANTS *set him down* C, *facing the child.* MAX *has followed them into the room.*

MAX: Just as you said. He couldn't bear to miss the fun. (*He crosses above* SARAH *to down* L *of her.*)

SARAH: Father! Jake won't say he's sorry.

GREGORY: Does it matter?

The SERVANTS *stand up* C.

ELEANOR: What do you mean? Doesn't it matter? Needn't he say it? Can he come down without saying it?

GREGORY: No. It doesn't matter because it's too late.

ELEANOR: Too late?

GREGORY: Yes. If all criminals got away with saying they're sorry, where should we be?

JACOB *looks at* GREGORY.

ELEANOR: He doesn't understand what he's done.

GREGORY: Nobody understands what they do. You sound as if you think that's an excuse. You're a fool. You always were a fool.

HENRY: So I tell her, Father.

ELEANOR (*to* GREGORY): Please try and make him say he's sorry.

GREGORY *and* JACOB *stare at each other.*

GREGORY: Why should I? It doesn't matter now. Not when you get to my age. It's not important, I tell you. All that matters is something called—(*he hesitates*) justice.

JACOB *looks out front again.*

MAX (*to* SARAH): Oh, he's right. That matters lots. Where'd we be without it?

GREGORY: Has anybody got anything good to say about the boy? No matter how insignificant. Come on, speak up.

ELEANOR: He's always been very sweet to me. Loved me very much.

MAX (*as if declaiming newspaper headlines*): *Mother's love fails to save child.*

AMY (*coming down to above* L *of Gregory's chair*): They all love their mother. They cling to the idea. On the scaffold, under the knife. I love Mummy.

GREGORY: Remorse. Any sign of it?

HENRY: I'm afraid not. After discovering the crime I went to see him. He was sitting up in bed eating jelly and drinking milk.

GREGORY: Seemed unconcerned?

HENRY: Yes.

MAX: *Distressing scene. Father in box. Admit's sons guilt.*

GREGORY: Has he been in trouble before?

HENRY: He used to wet his bed. He's over it now.

MAX: *Medical evidence causes stir.*

GREGORY: Let's come to the actual crime. Sarah, did you see it?

SARAH: Certainly not. I wouldn't look. I'm not used to such things. Ask Max. I always keep things nice.

MAX: She does, Gramp.

SARAH: I keep off the nasty. So I wouldn't look at what Jake did.

ELEANOR: Then how did you know it was so bad?

SARAH (*shouting*): I read the newspapers, don't I? I know what a man is! (*She points at* JACOB.) That! It ought not to be allowed!

    MAX *protects her, putting his arm round her.*

GREGORY: Amy, you're used to everything. The whole bag of tricks. Lunacy, sickness, the lot. What's your opinion? How bad was this?

AMY (L *of Gregory's chair*): It was unforgivable. In my experience. A crime. An atrocity.

GREGORY (*to* JACOB): You hear that? What do you expect us to do? Take you back as our little boy? Our hope and our future. You can't expect that.

MAX: *Judge sums up.*

HENRY: I've tried to explain to him how we live, Father.

GREGORY: Does he understand?

HENRY: I think he understands that the road back is long and hard.

GREGORY: I'm too old to go back, Henry.

HENRY (*gently*): We're talking about Jacob, Father.

GREGORY: Little Jacob. What's he done?

AMY (*shortly*): He exists, Father. Look at him, there in front of your face. He is, Father.

    GREGORY *turns and stares at the child.*

GREGORY (*laughing loudly*): Jesus Christ. I don't have to find any punishment for you. Take me away.

MAX: *Sensation. Child condemned.*

GREGORY: Take me away.

    The two SERVANTS *lift* GREGORY *in his chair.* AMY *moves up* LC.

SARAH: You will let Max sing his song, won't you? The one about the commercial traveller's mother-in-law. He's learnt it specially.

GREGORY: Yes, let Max sing his song.

MAX: Oo, thank you, Gramp.

SARAH (*turning to* MAX): If I get a bit tiddly, Max, promise to tuck me up, sweet.

MAX: 'Course, Mummeee.

    The SERVANTS *carry* GREGORY *from the room.* SARAH *and* AMY *exit after them.* MAX *moves up to the door.*

ELEANOR (*to* HENRY): Let me stay with him.

HENRY: No.

MAX: *Last appeal fails.*

> MAX *goes out.* ELEANOR *follows him, shutting the door.* HENRY *and* JACOB *are left alone.*

HENRY: When all's said and done there are only two left face to face. The executioner and the victim. And when it comes to that, Jake, when it comes to us, left alone, together, like this, what is there between us? (*He moves slowly above the chair and round to* C.) There's no hate. There's no love. There's nothing. Because we recognize each other for what we are. But the executioner comes out of the shed alive. Unfair. Poor devil.

> *Silence. When* HENRY *speaks again, a second voice is heard. It is Henry's, amplified and independent. It speaks the following words.* HENRY *also speaks these words, and he is aware of the voice. Glancing about, he tries to shout it down. He hesitates, falters, catches up again to speak in unison, is borne inexorably along until the last moment.*

It has to be this way. Because we are good. Out there. (*He indicates the door.*) Good people. Living good lives. We've repented our existence. We're truly sorry that we are. We're on our knees for being. So we're allowed to go free. We're allowed to go wherever we like all over this little, tiny world. We're not confined. Oh, no. (*He moves down* L.) First of all there's the secure freedom of the womb. There's the freedom of the family. The freedom of loving someone. And more, being loved. And at the end there's the liberty of the tomb. (*Returning to* C.) All this could have been yours, Jake, if you'd said you were sorry. Don't you see what you were being offered? How could you be so stubborn? You were being offered what everybody wants. And you refused.

> *Silence. The second voice begins.* HENRY *stumbles after it.*

You brought it on yourself. Look at us now. No feeling, as there should be between father and son. Not even feeling as between two human beings. You in here. And I'm . . .

HENRY'S VOICE (*alone*): Out here.

HENRY: You did it. You did it. First. By the enormity of your crime. Second. By refusing to confess. Confess. You did it. You did it. I wanted to love you so much. I wanted us to be together. I wanted to love you. Now . . .

HENRY'S VOICE: I wish you'd never been born!

HENRY: No!

HENRY'S VOICE: I wish you'd never been born!

HENRY (*in a whisper*): I wish you'd never been born!

Silence. A piano begins to play below: a popular tune. There is the sound of laughter.

(*Alone*) I'm going down, now. (*He moves above the chair to the shelf* R.) I'm going back to the party. You'll stay up here tonight. You've been a very naughty boy, Jake. You must be punished. I'll come up in the morning. And then I shall hope to find my real little boy. (*He unplugs the electric lamp and moves with it to the door.*) The boy I want to love.

HENRY *goes out. The door is locked. The piano is being played downstairs.* JACOB *gets up from the chair. He comes forward and stares into the theatre. He waits, as if for a word. Do any of us speak? No. And if we did, what would we say?* JACOB *turns and goes up stage into the darkness. The piano plays. The chair falls.*

We get used to the darkness. We see. The CHILD *has hanged himself from one of the roof-beams. He swings on the cord of his pyjamas, and the trousers have fallen about his ankles. He looks a useless object: a bag of bones. Cheap meat on a butcher's hook.*

The piano and the laughter continue, as—

the CURTAIN *falls*

A WALK IN THE DESERT

INTRODUCTORY NOTE

A WALK IN THE DESERT was written in 1959 and televised by the BBC on 25 September 1960 in a production by Naomi Capon with Kenneth Haigh as Peter and Nigel Stock as Tony. Tracey Lloyd was Shirley, with Lawrence Hardy and Joyce Heron as Mr and Mrs Sharp.

PERSONS

PETER SHARPE
LAURA SHARPE, *his mother*
CHARLES SHARPE, *his father*
TONY COLEMAN, *his friend*
SHIRLEY FLANDERS, *his enemy*

The action of the play takes place in a house in a provincial town in England. The time is the early part of the year.

ACT ONE

A small town in the English Midlands.

Distant gasworks seen across polluted meadows. It is winter, early evening. Sunday.

A public park. Goalposts. The statue of some forgotten liberal reformer: bird-stained. Childrens' swings are tied to the posts in a puritan way. The bandstand drips with recent rain. Puddles.

Distant church bells: evensong.

A canal. It borders the park. Trees overhang. The water is black, reflecting the street lamps which are beginning to show against the sky. The canal is spanned by an iron bridge. Ornate for such a simple crossing, it must be a memorial to someone or something.

Facing the canal, beyond a road, is a row of houses. They are in pairs. They have the solid ugly faces of nineteenth-century prosperity looking into the twentieth century without forgiveness. Steps go up to the front doors: the basement windows have kept their heavy grilles. The brown stone of the houses is stained. The plants in the narrow gardens seem to be dying, although evergreen.

The church bells can be heard. They fade.

A drawing-room in one of the houses. Nothing 'contemporary' here. Haute bourgeoisie: 1930. And for nearly thirty years, until the present day, it has stayed so. Furniture: mahogany. Curtains: velvet. Books behind glass. A wood fire. Winter flowers. Everyone goes soft-footed over the heavy carpets. The clock has a musical strike, hardly audible.

PETER SHARPE is lying on a sofa. He is reading a Sunday newspaper. In a moment he will lower the paper and can be seen to be a young man of twenty-four.

97

His mother, LAURA, *stands at the foot of the sofa looking down at him. She is wearing a hat and coat and is
pulling on some gloves.*

LAURA: Will you be all right, Peter?

PETER: Yes.

LAURA: We shan't be long, dear.

PETER: Where are you going? Church?

LAURA: No, darling. We're going to the rehearsal. I've told you.

> PETER *drops the paper to the floor: puts his hands
> behind his head: stares up at his mother.*

PETER: Of course. The amateur dramatics. Father's self-expression.

LAURA: You mustn't laugh at Daddie. He takes it very seriously.

PETER: What's he acting this time? Hamlet?

LAURA: No. It's a thriller. A whodunnit, as Daddie says. He comes
in right at the end. As a detective.

PETER: Does he speak?

LAURA: One line. He makes an arrest.

PETER: Good. Well, it passes the time.

LAURA: What are you going to do?

PETER: Do?

LAURA: This evening.

PETER: I don't know. Tony's coming round.

LAURA: Oh, that'll be nice. I'm so glad that you've got him as a
friend. Of course, he's quite a bit older than you.

PETER: Yes.

LAURA: Well, I expect he'll have some idea of what he wants to do.

PETER: I expect so.

> CHARLES SHARPE, *Peter's father, has come into the
> room. He is carrying a raincoat, a book and a clothes-brush.
> He holds out the brush to* LAURA.

CHARLES: Give me a brush down, my dear.

> LAURA *takes the brush and begins to do so.* PETER *has
> not moved.*

PETER: Can I hear your line for you, Father?

CHARLES: My what?

PETER: Your line in the play.

LAURA: Now don't tease him, Peter. He's very impressive when he
comes in through the french windows and arrests the murderer.

PETER: What happens then?

LAURA: The curtain comes down. It's the end, you see.

PETER: I see.

> CHARLES *has been slowly turning round as his neat dark suit has been brushed. Now he stands staring down at* PETER.

CHARLES: Well, at least I do something on my Sunday evening, Peter. I know you find our little amateur dramatic club funny, but it's sociable. I meet people. And we have a few laughs.

PETER: And there's the exercise walking to the church hall and back for rehearsals.

CHARLES: Certainly.

PETER: I'm sure there's lots to be said for it.

CHARLES: There's more to be said for it than sticking in the house all day. I don't think you've been off that sofa since the papers came this morning.

> LAURA *has put down the clothes-brush and now comes forward to help* CHARLES *on with his raincoat.*

LAURA: Now, Charles, remember . . . he gets very tired.

CHARLES: I know. But I'm sure there are things you could do, Peter. A hobby of some kind.

PETER: What do you suggest?

CHARLES: I can't suggest. A hobby is a personal thing.

PETER: Like a woman. For the hours when you're alone. Go to your rehearsal, Father.

LAURA: But you're not going to be left alone, darling. (*To* CHARLES.) Tony Coleman's coming round.

> CHARLES *is into his coat: he pushes the book into a pocket.*

CHARLES: That's all right, then. Come on, Laura, we shall be late. We'll want an umbrella. It was spitting with rain.

> CHARLES *goes out of the room.* PETER *glances up at* LAURA. *She is about to speak, when* PETER *interrupts:*

PETER: Have you got any cigarettes?

> LAURA *opens a bag she is holding and begins to look anxiously through it.*

PETER: Oh, not if you've got them in there. They'll stink of powder. I'll smoke Tony's when he comes. You look very nice.

LAURA: Thank you, darling.

PETER: You look absolutely right for a rehearsal of a thrilling play in the church hall on a Sunday night. How do you manage it?

LAURA: Well, Daddie likes me to be properly dressed.

PETER: How would he like me, I wonder?

LAURA: He loves you very much, Peter. I know he still thinks of you as his little boy.

PETER: What?

LAURA: Daddie does. He's disappointed, of course. . . . (*She suddenly cries out.*) Don't open it in the house!

> CHARLES *can be seen through the open door struggling with an umbrella in the hall. He looks up, irritably.*

CHARLES: What do you say?

LAURA: Don't open it in the house. It brings bad luck.

> CHARLES *crosses the hall and goes from sight towards the front door.* PETER *looks up at his mother.*

PETER: Do you really believe that?

LAURA: Of course.

PETER: Well, it may explain quite a lot. . . .

> *In the open front doorway of the house:*
>
> CHARLES *is holding the umbrella open before him. He snaps it shut and reveals* TONY COLEMAN, *who has come up the steps.*

TONY: Good evening, Mr Sharpe.

CHARLES: Hullo, Tony.

TONY: What on earth are you doing?

CHARLES: My umbrella's broken. Mustn't open it in the house, you know.

TONY: Bad luck.

CHARLES: Come along in.

> CHARLES *and* TONY *move into the hall,* CHARLES *shutting the door.*
>
> *In the hall:*
>
> TONY COLEMAN *is thirty-six years old. He takes off his army-type raincoat and shows himself to be dressed in a tweed jacket, cord trousers, suede boots, club tie, signet ring: things like that.*
>
> *As* CHARLES *is taking Tony's coat from him and putting it over a chair he says quietly:*

CHARLES: It's very good of you to come round, Tony. My wife and I appreciate it very much.

TONY: You make it sound as if I'm doing a duty, Mr Sharpe.

CHARLES: Well, in the circumstances . . .

TONY: You mustn't think of Peter in terms of people visiting him,

or being sorry for him. He just wants what we all want. A bit of
company, a laugh, some way of passing the time.

CHARLES: Your friendship means a lot to him.

TONY: I'm glad. (*He smiles.*) Can I go in?

CHARLES: Of course.

> *In the drawing-room:*
>
> PETER *looks up. He waves.* TONY *is standing in the
> doorway.*

PETER: Hullo, Tony.

> TONY *comes into the room. He stands at the foot of the
> sofa looking down at* PETER.

TONY: How's the boy?

PETER (*smiling*): I'm all right.

> CHARLES *has come into the room after* TONY.
> LAURA *is at a looking-glass letting down a silly little
> veil from her hat. She can see* PETER *and* TONY *in
> reflection.*

LAURA: Why don't you both go out, Peter?

TONY: Why not? I've got the car.

> PETER *still stares up into Tony's face.* TONY, *smiling,
> stares back with confidence, not shy.* LAURA *has turned and
> looks from one to the other. Shut out from the secret under-
> standing between the two men she speaks a little too sharply:*

LAURA: The air will do you good. Peter, listen! I said . . .

PETER: I heard what you said. Give me a cigarette, Tony.

> TONY *takes a packet of cigarettes from his pocket and
> throws it into Peter's lap.* CHARLES *has come forward.*

CHARLES: Let them settle their own amusements, Laura. And we
must go. (*To* TONY.) I have a rehearsal. The amateurs, you know.

TONY: I often see your name in the paper.

CHARLES: Yes, they're very kind to us. But I shan't be mentioned
this time. I've got a very small part.

TONY: Oh, bad luck.

CHARLES: It's the way it goes. Sometimes a big part; sometimes
small. Turn and turn about.

TONY: That's the spirit.

CHARLES: Exactly. It's the spirit that counts. The getting together.
The—yes, the mucking in.

> CHARLES *stares down at* PETER, *who is inhaling the
> cigarette, hand over mouth.*

CHARLES: I wish I could get Peter to see that.

> *Silence.* LAURA *has gone to the door.* CHARLES *turns away and joins her. For a moment they stand together in the doorway.* PETER, *drawing on the cigarette, stares at them. Charles's voice is heard:*

CHARLES: There's some whisky in the cupboard.

PETER (*distinctly*): Goodbye.

> *Peter's face is seen closely as he watches his mother and father go. The front door is heard to shut.* PETER *exhales the cigarette: it is a sigh, a release. He is holding out the packet to* TONY, *who takes it.*

PETER: You're so nice to them.

TONY: Your mother and father? Why not?

PETER: You take them seriously. You don't seem to think the acting, all that make-believe in the church hall, is silly . . . or sad.

TONY: Is it, old boy?

PETER: Yes.

TONY: Sorry. Don't quite see what you mean. What shall we do tonight?

PETER: Astonish me with a suggestion, Tony.

TONY: What? (*He laughs.*) I say, the Sunday hell's got you, hasn't it?

PETER: No more than usual. No more than any other day of the week. Of course, on Sundays I have to suffer Father. I have to search my conscience. Why don't I *do* something? That question comes up every seven days.

TONY: Well, I expect he worries. He wants you to be happy.

PETER: Happy? Don't be silly. Father doesn't know anything about happiness. He wants me to meet people and chatter, get about best I can, join in, muck in, so that he doesn't have to be ashamed of me. Did he say something about whisky? Give me a hand.

> TONY *holds out both hands to* PETER, *who takes them.* PETER *swings his legs down from the sofa. It is apparent that he is crippled in some way. It may very well be that his right leg is artificial from above the knee. The disability is very noticeable as he releases himself from* TONY *and moves across the room.*

TONY: Do you want this?

> TONY *is holding out a walking-stick which was underneath the sofa.*

PETER: No.

> PETER *goes to a cupboard. He opens it and takes out a
> bottle of whisky. He holds it up to* TONY.

PETER: Feel like it?

TONY: Why not? Let's make it for the road and drive out to the
Black Bull. Harold's always good for a laugh on a Sunday night.

PETER: Harold's jokes are like his pub. Dirty, without being gay.

TONY: There's nothing wrong with old Harold. But if you don't
want to go. . . .

> PETER *holds up a glass with about an inch of whisky
> in it.*

PETER: I never know how much of this stuff it's decent to offer.

TONY: That'll do.

> TONY *takes the glass and adds some soda water which is
> on the cupboard.*

TONY: I don't see why you should have it in for Harold.

PETER: He's a drunk.

TONY: Well, maybe he does take a bit more than he should, but he's
made The Bull the only amusing place to go to for miles around
this bitch of a town. You're always saying you hate the place. Why
go for somebody who's trying to break it up a bit?

PETER (*he is drinking: making a face*): That's not the answer, Tony.
It's not an escape to sit in that horrible little bar with Harold
breathing over you, and telling you for the hundredth time how
he had the local tennis champion in the sports pavilion after winning the mixed doubles ten years ago. The place isn't even an oasis
of sin. It's just dull, that's all. But you go, if you want to. I'll be
all right.

TONY: I don't really want to go. I just thought it would be somewhere to make for. A sort of place.

> TONY *has wandered away across the room. As he goes he
> picks up a local newspaper: folds it.* PETER *is leaning
> against the cupboard watching* TONY *with the same intent-
> ness with which he looked at his parents.*

PETER: Tony—

TONY: Um?

PETER: Why do you come here?

TONY: Would you like to see a Western? (*He is reading the advertise-
ments.*) It's called 'End of the Trail'. Starts at seven. At the Regal.

PETER: No. I'd rather sit here and have you read 'David Copperfield'
to me.

TONY: What? Oh, I see, you're being funny.

PETER: Yes. Why do you come?

> TONY *throws down the newspaper and turns to* PETER.

TONY: Look, old boy, we're what's known as friends. Perhaps I'm a bit innocent in such matters but I've never thought friends needed a reason to see each other.

PETER: You're ducking the question. Go on, answer it. I'm interested.

TONY: I have answered it.

PETER: Then I don't understand. You're very popular in this tonw. We must ask good old Tony Coleman. I'm sure they're always saying that. If there's any amusement in this God-forsaken place I bet you know where to find it. And . . . what's the matter?

TONY: Nothing. Go on.

PETER: And yet you come to see me. What about the girls, Tony? You make money out of that estate business of yours. You can afford to take the girls around. Out to the Black Bull. Why don't you?

TONY: Finished?

PETER: Yes.

TONY: I was born in this town. Like you. I grew up in it. Like you. I went to the Grammar School when it was a grammar school, and not the local louts' reformatory. I've always accepted the place as it is. . . .

PETER: Not like me.

TONY: No, not like you. The war took me away, but when it was over I was quite glad to get back and go into the business. And when I was back . . . yes, there were the girls. I did my share of walking over the Common to the woods past the sports ground, and for the really serious business down to the meadows behind the gasworks. And there were the evenings with the boys, with Harold before he married and took the Black Bull, when we went drinking. Nice uncomplicated times.

PETER: Well then, what are you doing here?

TONY: I'm thirty-six, Peter. The girls I went with have mostly married by now. Those that haven't . . . well, they'd probably catch a nasty chill if they went walking by the gasworks today. As for the chaps . . . they settled down. Home comforts, you know. Do it yourself. That sort of thing. And I'm left.

PETER: Are you . . . are you trying to tell me . . . are you trying to tell me that you're lonely?

TONY: I wandered in to a dance at the Town Hall the other Saturday night. They've been going on as long as I can remember. They were always good for a pick-up. But this time . . . I was out of my depth. I couldn't have danced that stuff. And they were drinking soft drinks. Didn't seem interested in sex as such. Anyway, the girls were awful. Then one of them asked me if I was a welfare officer. I could have hit her fat pasty little face. (*He laughs.*) No, but really . . . a welfare officer. I was after creating the social problem that night, not solving it. (*Pause.*) Yes, I suppose I am.

PETER: Lonely?

TONY: It's such a word. Let's say middle-aged, and leave it at that. What shall we do?

PETER: I don't know. I don't know.

> PETER *is sitting on the sofa again, his right leg stuck awkwardly before him.* TONY *has his whisky glass cradled in his hands and is looking down into it.*

PETER (*very quietly*): I thought you knew people. People as they are today, I mean. I thought you got about.

TONY: Are you disappointed?

PETER: A bit.

TONY: You must ask someone of your own age. Someone like Brian Dickinson. Does he still live next door?

PETER: Yes, he's home again. After all the success and shouting he's come back to Mummie, the bloody fool.

TONY: Just thought of this. Why do you want someone to tell you? You could go about on your own, if you wanted to. Find out for yourself.

PETER: Yes, I could. But, you know, you get more than a sense of embarrassment with this sort of thing. (*He strikes his leg.*) You get a sense of shame.

TONY: Why? It wasn't your fault.

PETER: No, it was what they call bad luck. Did I open an umbrella indoors? Or walk under a ladder? Or smash a mirror? I was brought up to look out for such things.

TONY: It was chance.

PETER: Yes. You happen to be standing in a certain place at a certain time. And all the shut umbrellas and unbroken mirrors can't prevent that. I'd only been in the army a week, you know. I suppose

I was the typical National Service idiot, but I was quite enjoying it.
I never saw the truck backing towards me. It knocked me flat on
my face with the tailboard. I wasn't hurt. Just angry. Then the
wheel went over my legs. And the pain . . . Jesus, that took the
anger out of me. I wanted to cry. I passed out.

TONY: Forget it.

PETER: Chance. A summer morning. Two fools in badly fitting uniforms. One learning to drive a truck. The other dreaming. To this
day I can't remember what it was so occupied me that I never saw
the truck coming. It would be nice to think that it was something
important. For I had a lot of time to fill in later on. Nearly a
year in hospital. Everybody was very kind. So kind that I came
to hate the word. And the act. That wasn't chance. That was
deliberate.

TONY: You suspect kindness. You don't hate it. And you mix it up
with pity. Like your father.

PETER: Perhaps.

TONY: You should accept it. Along with the unlucky chance.

PETER: Why should I?

TONY: Because that's the way things go, my dear old boy.

PETER: Why do they go that way?

TONY: Don't ask me. But you see it all the time.

PETER: So I accept it. Now where am I?

TONY: Oh hell. You're just one of the unlucky ones, I suppose.

PETER: And Brian next door is one of the other kind.

TONY: That's right.

PETER: He and I used to play together when we were small. We
were born on the same day. That gave a sense of mystery to our
friendship which was very satisfying to little boys. And our lives
were much the same until our call-up. You know what happened
to me. Brian got through untouched. He never even caught a cold
in the head. And when he came out he wrote his book. His *funny*
book about army life. With its comic sergeant-majors and fatuous
officers.

TONY: Yes, I've read it.

PETER: Everybody's read it. And seen the film. And laughed and
laughed. Brian's rich and famous. I'm . . .

PETER holds up his glass. He looks at TONY.

PETER: Shall I have some more of this?

TONY: Why not?

> TONY *takes Peter's glass and his own over to the cup-board to pour the whisky.*

PETER: I'm left here. Things go on. But how they go on . . . I don't know about that. And you're no help, it seems. I read magazines and newspapers, and there are the people. Some of them up to no end of strange things. I pass them in the street. But I don't *know* anybody. News from the World, Tony, that's what you should bring me on Sundays. How the Young Live and Think.

TONY: Damn the young.

PETER: Our Special Correspondent. The Man on the Spot.

TONY: Shut up. Take this.

> PETER *takes the glass of whisky. Drinks.*

PETER: And every one of them . . . all the people in the news . . . are at a certain place at a certain time. Just as I was. Headline! Man Killed in Car Smash. He should have been a moment ahead or a moment behind, in more or less of a hurry. Headline! Old Woman Coshed on Common. She should never have taken the short cut home. Never. Headline! . . .

> *The doorbell rings. Silence. The two men glance at each other.*

PETER: See what I mean?

TONY: Who is it?

PETER: I don't know. Let's find out.

TONY: I'll go.

PETER: No, no.

> PETER *pulls himself up from the sofa and begins to move towards the door.*
> *In the hall:*
> PETER *comes from the drawing-room into the hall. From somewhere in the room behind him a small clock is striking rapidly.* TONY *can be seen, glass in hand.*
> *When* PETER *is in the hall the front-door bell rings again. Very strident here.* PETER *looks up at the bell: it is above the door. Silence.* PETER *goes to the front door.*
> *He opens it.*
> *In the open front doorway of the house:*
> *A young girl is standing on the steps of the house. She is about twenty. No hat. A raincoat. A handbag held against her body. The street light is behind her casting her face in shadow for the moment.*

GIRL: I've come about the advertisement.

> *She holds out a slip of newspaper to* PETER, *who takes it. He steps back into the light of the hall and reads the cutting through. He looks up.*

PETER: Yes, of course. Come in.

> *The girl comes into the hall. Her pretty tilted face can now be seen. Thin, tense body under the neat clothes. Small, red hands.*
>
> *She turns in the middle of the hall as* PETER *shuts the front door.*
>
> *In the hall:*

GIRL: Through here?

> *She means into the drawing-room.* PETER *comes forward, shaking his head.*

PETER: No. Let's go in here.

> *In a darkened room:*
>
> *There is a little light from the street lamp, for the curtains are not drawn.*
>
> *The door opens.* PETER *comes into the room. He switches on the light. It is one of a pair of small crystal chandelier lights.*
>
> *This is a dining-room, little used. It has the desolation of an unwanted room. A long table, with eight chairs round it like mourners. A gilt-framed mirror over the fireplace. A sideboard set out with silver pieces.*
>
> *The girl has followed* PETER *into the room. She stands just inside the doorway. Almost imperceptibly she shivers as the cold of the room strikes her.*

PETER: Shut the door.

> *The girl does this, and then moves to the end of the long table, standing beneath the light.* PETER *has gone to the far end of the room: there is less light here.*

GIRL: You are Mr Brian Dickinson, I suppose.

PETER (*after a moment*): Yes.

GIRL: The writer.

PETER (*he has been staring down at the newspaper cutting: now he looks up*): Yes, of course. Have you read my book?

GIRL: No. But I saw the picture. I thought it was ever so funny.

> *A pause. The girl looks down at her distorted reflection in the table top: she traces it with her finger.*

GIRL: Well . . . you say there you want a secretary . . . temporary . . . typing and shorthand . . . apply Sunday, 7 o'clock . . . here I am. I suppose you're waiting to tell me you've already got somebody.

PETER: No.

GIRL: I don't know if I'd suit. I last worked in a coal office. This'd be different.

PETER: Yes.

GIRL: I thought you'd have lots of people applying.

PETER: What's your name?

GIRL: Flanders. Shirley Flanders.

PETER: How old are you?

> *The girl is looking across the table directly at* PETER.

SHIRLEY: Twenty. What's the matter?

PETER: Nothing. Why?

SHIRLEY: You were looking at me as if . . . well, I don't know . . . as if there's something pretty strange about me. Look, you must ask me any questions you want. I've never gone after this sort of job before.

PETER: I've never had a secretary before.

SHIRLEY: Then we both start flat.

> *In the drawing-room:*
>
> TONY *is seen. He is standing in the room, smoking a cigarette and drinking whisky. He looks across the room through the open door at the shut dining-room door. He slightly turns his head: there is only a murmur of voices from the other room.*
>
> *In the dining-room:*
>
> SHIRLEY *is speaking.*

SHIRLEY: . . . so, you see, that's the only thing. What hours would you want me?

PETER: It's hard to say. Probably mornings.

SHIRLEY: That'd be all right.

PETER (*after a moment: quietly*): Yes, you'll do.

SHIRLEY: But you haven't asked me anything proper.

PETER: What? No. Will you wait here a minute?

> PETER *comes up the room.* SHIRLEY *watches him.*
>
> *In the drawing-room:*
>
> TONY *looks up as the dining-room door opens.* PETER *comes from the room and crosses the hall into the drawing-*

room. For a moment SHIRLEY *can be seen standing alone, but almost at once the two men move from her line of sight.*

PETER *holds out the newspaper cutting to* TONY, *who takes it.* TONY *reads it: looks up.*

TONY: Well? She's come to the wrong house.

PETER: Yes

TONY: She wants next door. Have you told her?

PETER: No.

TONY: Why not?

PETER: What?

TONY: Why not?

PETER: You're scared of young people, aren't you, Tony? It showed when you told me about the Town Hall dance. And I don't know anything about people of my own age. Not in the last five years. Well, there's one. Aren't you curious?

TONY: No.

PETER: I am. Come on, you wanted something to do. Something for a laugh. Let's interview her.

TONY: How can you?

PETER: She thinks I'm Brian Dickinson. She thinks I write funny books. She thinks I want a secretary. (*He calls.*) Miss Flanders!

TONY: Look here, Peter, what . . .

SHIRLEY *can be seen in the dining-room across the hall.*

SHIRLEY: Shall I put the light out?

PETER: If you like.

SHIRLEY *reaches out to the switch: darkness beyond her. She comes forward across the hall and into the drawing-room. She stands facing the two men.*

PETER: This is Mr Tony Coleman, a friend of mine. He's a business man. Knows all about secretaries. What did you say your first name is?

SHIRLEY: Shirley.

PETER: This is Shirley Flanders, Tony.

TONY: How do you do.

SHIRLEY *nods her head. She is looking from one man to the other, unsure.*

PETER (*smiling*): Sit down.

SHIRLEY: Mr Dickinson, I don't think I'll suit you at all. Much better if I . . .

She half turns to the door.

PETER (*interrupting her*): Don't you need the job?
> *The girl stops, turns back, looking at* PETER.

SHIRLEY: Well, yes . . . yes, I do.

PETER: Then sit down.
> SHIRLEY *looks around: then goes to an armchair and sits.*

SHIRLEY: What exactly would you want me to do?

PETER: Well, my working day . . . let's see. I get up at eight and before breakfast I go for a brisk walk. (*Almost involuntarily* SHIRLEY *looks down at Peter's leg: he sees this: pause.*) I come back, and after breakfast I start work which goes on until lunchtime. It would be very nice if you could come in about nine.

SHIRLEY: Yes, but what would you want me to do?

PETER: Type. Take some dictation. Don't look so worried. It wouldn't be difficult. There'd be letters to answer, of course. Film companies, the publishers, magazine people, and letters from admirers. Fan letters, you'd call them.

SHIRLEY: Well, I could try. I'd do my best. There's just one thing . . . . (*pause*)

PETER: What's that?

SHIRLEY: Perhaps it's a bit early . . . I mean, I don't want you to think . . .

PETER: Money?
> SHIRLEY *nods her head.*

PETER: I'm prepared to pay you fourteen pounds a week.

SHIRLEY: How much?

PETER: Fourteen. Is that fair?

SHIRLEY: Fair? Why, I didn't expect . . .

PETER: Would that make you happy?

SHIRLEY: Oh, yes.
> *She suddenly looks like a child. Leans forward, brushes back her hair: intent, smiling.*

PETER: Good. Well, let's hear something about you. (*To* TONY.) That's what we're waiting for, isn't it?
> TONY *turns away. After a glance at him* PETER *looks down at* SHIRLEY.

PETER: Go on.

SHIRLEY: I left school when I was fifteen. For a little while I worked in a shop. Woolworths, actually. But I wanted to better myself, so evenings I went to a secretarial course. Clayton's Commercial

College. Opposite the station. Know it? I did quite well, all considered. So when I was seventeen I took this job in a coal office. I was there for about eighteen months. Then I had to leave.

PETER: Why?

SHIRLEY: Personal reasons, if you understand me. But you don't want to hear this sort of stuff. You want to know how many words a minute I can do.

PETER: Not at all. This is just what we want to hear. Carry on.

SHIRLEY: Well, that's all, really. I haven't worked since the coal office.

PETER: Where do you live?

SHIRLEY: Tukehurst Road.

PETER: That's the other end of the town.

SHIRLEY: Yes, the new estate.

PETER: Do you like it?

SHIRLEY: It's all right.

PETER: Surely you don't live alone.

SHIRLEY: Oh no. I live with my Mum and Dad.

PETER (*sudden smile*): Like me.

> SHIRLEY *smiles back at* PETER: *a moment approaching sympathy between them.*
>
> TONY *has come forward.*

TONY: I say, you don't need me here for this. I'll push off.

PETER: No! (*He holds* TONY *by the arm.*) You mustn't go. It's no fun if you're not here. Ask her a sensible question. Go on.

TONY (*to* SHIRLEY: *after a moment*): Why did you want to better yourself, as you put it?

SHIRLEY: Doesn't everybody?

PETER: No.

TONY: What did you expect to get out of it?

PETER: You thought you'd get away from the horrible place where you live.

SHIRLEY: No, I didn't. It's quite nice.

PETER: Surely you see how ugly it is.

SHIRLEY: But it's modern.

PETER: I know. All those little houses with their desolate little gardens. As embarrassing as a new set of false teeth. And with the same absurd pretensions. 'Parkway', 'Grosvenor Lodge', 'Sorrento', 'Berkeley'. They're inhabited by peasants. Why don't they have the honesty of peasants?

SHIRLEY: I don't know what you're talking about.

PETER: But you must see. Look at the shops there. Full of awful stuff. Look at the sweet shops. Dozens of them. Stuffed with sickening muck.

SHIRLEY: Are you a chapel man?

PETER: No. Why?

SHIRLEY: Just wondered. You seem to be against any fun.

TONY *laughs*.

PETER: No, I'm not against having fun. It's just. . . .

SHIRLEY: Look, the fun people have at my end of the town is different from your fun up here, I expect. We're another tribe, see?

PETER: Are you defending it?

SHIRLEY: Why not? My Dad, just taking one, worked hard for all we've got. He was out of work a lot before the war. And when I was a baby he was away in the army for six years. He came back here and worked very hard. Now he's foreman, and we have a bit of money. We've got the house—matter of fact, ours is just *Number 23* Tukehurst Road, nothing fancy—and Mum keeps it very nice. You think we spend our money on lots of silly things. Perhaps we do. We haven't learnt yet, you see. It takes a bit of practice when you've only had it a little while.

PETER: Your father's good to you, is he?

SHIRLEY: Yes, he's always been good. I let him down once.

PETER: How?

SHIRLEY: Never mind. I'm going to make up for it. Anyway, I don't see what all this has got to do with my being your secretary.

PETER: I wanted to know what sort of background you've got. You might have to move in a very different society. Different values. Does that frighten you?

SHIRLEY: No.

PETER: And you might have to travel with me. I mean to go away a lot.

SHIRLEY: Oh, I couldn't do that.

PETER: Why not?

SHIRLEY: I can't leave the town. I didn't understand you wanted that. So there you are, it's no good.

She stands up.

PETER: Wait a minute. You're twenty. Pretty well free to do as you like. Your mother and father can't expect you to stay at home for ever.

SHIRLEY (*pause*): I'm not really free.

PETER: Boy friend?

SHIRLEY: No.

PETER: Then what is it?

SHIRLEY: Something you wouldn't understand.

PETER: Try me.

SHIRLEY: It wouldn't be any good. I'll go.

PETER: No, wait. I think I could arrange for you to work with me just when I'm in the town.

TONY: Let her go.

PETER (*to* SHIRLEY): Would that do?

TONY: Let her go.

> SHIRLEY *has stopped. She looks from* TONY *to* PETER.

SHIRLEY: Yes, that'd do.

PETER: Good. Well, come back here and let's discuss it. The ways and means.

> SHIRLEY *takes a pace or two back into the room, but she does not sit down.*

PETER: What's the mystery?

SHIRLEY: How do you mean?

PETER: Well, you want the job pretty badly, it seems. Some time ago you let your father down, you say. And you can't go away from the town. How do these things add up? Would you like to tell us?

SHIRLEY: Why not? But if you're expecting ever such a tragic story —(*She exaggerates the phrase in a mocking way.*)—you're going to be disappointed. I've got a young baby.

PETER: I see.

SHIRLEY: And I'm not married. (*Pause.*) Never have been. (*Pause.*) Your face.

PETER (*harshly*): What's the matter with my face?

> *Speaking, he turns sharply away from the girl and almost falls. He catches hold of the sofa arm for support.*

PETER: God damn this bloody thing!

> *He straightens up, turns, and looks directly at* SHIRLEY.

PETER (*quietly*): So you've got a baby. And you're on your own. Well, that can't be such an extraordinary thing nowadays. What's it like?

SHIRLEY: It's a she. And they're no different from other kids, you know.

PETER: I didn't mean that. I meant what's it like to be . . .

SHIRLEY: What?

PETER: Never mind. Anyway, that's why you want a job. This job.

SHIRLEY: Yes. I want to be able to feed and clothe her out of my own pocket. Dad's been very good, but he's getting on now and it's not really fair.

PETER: There's something I want to know. Do you feel you've done wrong?

SHIRLEY: Yes.

PETER: You admit it.

SHIRLEY: Of course I do. Why be surprised? It was not only wrong, it was silly.

PETER: Are you going to atone for it?

SHIRLEY: I don't think I quite know what that means. I'm going to make up for it.

PETER: Not the same thing.

SHIRLEY: What I mean is . . . well, look at you. Somewhere you collected that leg of yours. But you haven't let it hold you back. You've gone on and made a success with your book. Good for you, I say.

PETER: This—(*his leg*)—wasn't my fault.

SHIRLEY: Your fault? What are you talking about? Things happen. They just happen. I've learnt that by now. Haven't you. (*To* TONY.) Hasn't he learnt it by now?

TONY: It doesn't look like it.

PETER: I was knocked down by an army truck. It wasn't my fault. I just happened to be in a certain place at a certain time. Surely it can't be said that your—your own predicament was brought about in such a casual way.

SHIRLEY (*she laughs*): You don't know. You just don't know. I *happened* to be at a dance one Saturday night. I never wanted to go . . . but what's all this got to do with my interview?

PETER: Everything. Go on.

SHIRLEY: Well, if you want me to. My girl friend went off and left me. She's good at dancing. I'm not. I was at the café bar . . .

PETER: Eating ice-cream?

SHIRLEY: I expect so. Can't remember. And this soldier came up. He was only a kid.

PETER: How old were you?

SHIRLEY: Seventeen. He came up and stood beside me. He didn't say anything for ever such a long time. But he stared at me. Then he said—he was Welsh—he said— (*She clumsily imitates.*) —'May I have the pleasure of this dance, Miss?' I laughed.

PETER: Why?

SHIRLEY: It was a funny old-fashioned way of picking up.

PETER: And that was it.

SHIRLEY: That was it.

PETER: How long did you know him?

SHIRLEY: Two months. Just while he was up at the camp.

PETER: Did you love him very much?

> *Silence.*

PETER: I said, did you love him very much?

SHIRLEY (*she slowly shakes her head*): No. I was fond of him. He didn't get on with the other fellows at the camp. He was a long way from home. I was sorry for him, I suppose.

PETER: And that was enough?

SHIRLEY: It looks like it, doesn't it? You see, he never talked much. I didn't either, in those days. Then when he was going away he wanted to make love . . . and it was the only way I could show him I was fond of him.

> *A pause. Then* SHIRLEY *says, gently:*

SHIRLEY: That's the way it happens. You wouldn't understand, living here like this. But that's the way it happens.

> TONY *has approached* PETER, *who is looking directly at* SHIRLEY. TONY *touches* PETER *on the arm.*

TONY: Let her go now. Let her go home. (*To* SHIRLEY.) He'll make up his mind and write to you.

> PETER *and* SHIRLEY *watch each other.*

PETER (*to* SHIRLEY): Do you believe in God?

SHIRLEY: Well, Dad's a Labour man. He doesn't, so the question never came up.

PETER: Then let's start at the beginning. Do you know what sin is?

SHIRLEY: I think so. Doing wrong.

PETER: Right. Who do you hurt most when you do wrong?

SHIRLEY (*she considers*): Yourself, I suppose.

PETER: It's an idea. Not generally acceptable, I'd say, but an idea. So you've wronged yourself. In other words, you've been sinful.

SHIRLEY: Look at it like that, yes, I have.

PETER: Do you believe that people who do wrong should be punished?

SHIRLEY: I always got it when I was naughty.

PETER: Have you been punished for this?

SHIRLEY (*almost to herself*): It's not easy. If you want to know. Not easy at all sometimes.

PETER: I can't hear what you say.

SHIRLEY (*aloud*): People. They're funny. The young chaps. Don't go with her. She's got a kid. I know they say that.

PETER: So you are being punished?

SHIRLEY: Well, yes, if it's being left on your own rather a lot.

PETER: Think of the way we should live nowadays.

SHIRLEY: Mind, I've got some good friends.

PETER: You've seen the buses packed to the roof leaving for the country. The holiday camps. The football matches. The dances. The clubs. And you must have heard that voice saying: 'Get together, boys and girls! You don't stand any chance of happiness on your own. No, boys and girls of all ages, it's in big numbers that the gamble's likely to come off. It's not the even chance which makes it today. It's the ten thousand to one chance that does the trick. So get in and win!' And you want to be like that, don't you, Shirley? You want to be in there with the others.

SHIRLEY: I don't want to be different to everybody else, if that's what you mean.

PETER: But you are, and always will be now. Don't go with her. Remember? The young chaps.

SHIRLEY: I'll find somebody.

PETER: No. If you believed in God you could ask forgiveness. But that's no good, is it?

SHIRLEY: Not a bit.

PETER: It's the young chaps' forgiveness you want. And they'll never let you have it.

SHIRLEY: I'll find somebody.

PETER: Never.

SHIRLEY: Some day.

PETER: Look at me. And then say it. We are eruptions on the smooth face of society. It has to be smooth, kept like an old woman's, so as not to alarm. Our cream is soothing for your hands, our paper to your bottom. This will make life easier, velvet-soft; that will make it quieter. Fill your home with the gentle smell of freshly plucked roses. We bring, with our hot drink, the tranquillity of death into life. But there are people like us to ruin this vision. The welfare schemes and help in the home try to soothe us out of existence. More is being done every day. The prisons and mental homes get bigger and safer. There is a place for the bastard and a place for the sinner. Kindness is now an official state. It wears a uniform and badges. But where is ordinary human kindness? The thing which passes between men without thought. The kindness of love.

> SHIRLEY *has been staring at* PETER. *Now, as he goes on, she will look away from him. Soon she will cover her face with her hands and then, when she takes them away, her eyes will be full of tears.*

PETER: For you know perfectly well that no one has given you that sort of kindness. Your father. You say he was good to you, but you only say that because you wish he had been. Really, he's ashamed of you. Remember? Your friends. You haven't got any friends. You can't cart the baby to the palais on Saturday night and so you stay away. Now you pretend you're going to start all over again. You can't. The job, the money, won't alter a thing. You're done for. Like me. Down the High Street we go, you behind your pram and me shuffling and swaying like a drunkard. The wrongdoer and the wronged. Both of us insults to the present perfect way of life.

> *It is now that* SHIRLEY *looks up. She speaks to* TONY.

SHIRLEY: He's right, of course. I do pretend. It seemed the only thing. I'm on my own all right, because of what I did. More on my own than any person should ever be. And he means it'll never be different. He's right. This is it. My lot, as Dad says. For always.

TONY: That's not true.

SHIRLEY (*suddenly very tired*): Well, I don't know. All I do know is that you've got to go on somehow.

TONY: Of course you have.

SHIRLEY: That's why I wanted this job. What about it?

> TONY *glances at* PETER, *giving him a chance to speak.* PETER *turns away.*

TONY: There isn't any job.

SHIRLEY: What?

TONY: There's no job here. You've come to the wrong house. This isn't Mr Dickinson. His name's Peter Sharpe.

SHIRLEY: But you both said . . .

TONY: I know we did. You made a mistake. The house you want is next door. That way.

SHIRLEY: You mean you've been playing some sort of joke?

TONY: Yes.

SHIRLEY (*a cry*): Why?

> *Silence.* PETER *has picked up the walking-stick. He stands leaning forward on it, looking down.*

TONY (*to* SHIRLEY): Come on. If you go now you may still be in time.

SHIRLEY: They said seven o'clock. I've been here ages.

> SHIRLEY *goes to* PETER. *She stands in front of him, trying to look into his face.*

SHIRLEY: Why? Why?

> PETER *looks up at the girl, almost in surprise.*

PETER: No reason. It just happened to be you. You just happened to be here. No reason. No reason at all.

SHIRLEY: Are you dead, or something?

> *She turns away.*

In the hall:

> TONY *and* SHIRLEY *can be seen coming from the room, leaving* PETER *alone.* TONY *brings* SHIRLEY *into the hall and to the front door. She turns to him.*

SHIRLEY: He just had to tell somebody, didn't he? And, as he said, I happened to be here. It wasn't personal, was it? Might have been anybody.

TONY: Come on. You must hurry.

SHIRLEY: Answer the question. It wasn't personal, was it?

TONY: Of course not.

SHIRLEY: You see, I want to think the best of him. Nobody could play a trick like that unless they didn't know what they were doing. I suppose he's got some excuse.

TONY: Yes.

SHIRLEY: Have you?

TONY: What do you mean?

SHIRLEY: Why didn't you say something?

> TONY *shakes his head. He opens the front door. It has begun to rain.* SHIRLEY *goes out on to the step. She turns.*

SHIRLEY: Early on. Why didn't you tell me it was a joke? Because you thought it was funny, I suppose. All right, mister, it's funny to trick me out of a job. I bet you've got one. Now go back and laugh.

> SHIRLEY *turns away and goes down the steps.* TONY *watches her for a moment, and then he shuts the door. As he moves back into the hall* PETER *calls from the room:*

PETER'S VOICE: Well, why didn't you say something?

> TONY *crosses the hall. He does not go back into the drawing-room, but turns into the unlit dining-room.*

In the drawing-room:

> PETER *is watching* TONY *as he goes into the room across the hall.* PETER *calls:*

PETER: Where are you going?

> TONY *does not answer.*

PETER: You could have stopped me, if you'd wanted to. (TONY *has gone from sight:* PETER *shouts.*) Tony!

> In the dining-room:

> TONY *is standing in the bay of the window and pulling the curtain a little aside. Beads of rain are scattered on the darkened window glass, which reflects Tony's face.*

PETER'S VOICE: Tony, come here and amuse me. What are you doing?

> TONY *looks out through the window. As he watches* SHIRLEY *approaches the front door of the next house. All she does will be seen by* TONY *through the distortion of the rain-covered window and in the fall of light from the street lamp.*

PETER'S VOICE: Come here, Tony.

> TONY *watches through the window.* SHIRLEY *runs up the steps of the next house and stands at the front door. She rings the bell.*

> *Music can be heard from the drawing-room: a piano:* PETER *has switched on a radio.*

> TONY *watches* SHIRLEY *as she stands at the door. She is quite near, a matter of ten feet or so off. Light falls on her as the door is opened. She speaks to an unseen person: her words cannot be heard.* SHIRLEY *slowly nods her head as she is answered. Then she turns away into the darkness as the door is shut.*

> TONY *watches her go and then, letting the curtain fall into place, moves away from the window.*

In the drawing-room:
> PETER *is listening to the music.* TONY *comes in from the hall. The music ends: loud and prolonged applause.* TONY *switches off the radio. Silence.*

TONY (*quietly*): What have you proved?

PETER: I wasn't trying to prove anything.

TONY: Why do it then? Can I have some more whisky?

PETER: Help yourself.

TONY: Dickinson turned her away. She didn't get the job.

PETER: She'd never have got it anyway.

> TONY *has poured himself straight whisky, and now he turns to* PETER.

TONY: Explain.

PETER: Analyse, do you mean?

TONY: Oh, balls. Don't use words. Just explain.

PETER: All right. She was standing out there on the steps . . . (*He stops.*)

TONY: And . . .?

PETER: And I saw her . . . go on, laugh . . . I saw her as if she was undressed. . . .

TONY (*flat statement*): I'm not laughing.

PETER: I saw her body shrinking from the cold, shrinking from disappointment, withdrawing from love. . . . Don't look at me like that! . . . and I wanted to hurt her.

TONY: Why?

PETER (*he imitates*): Why? That's what she asked. Why? Why? (*Shortly.*) I thought you'd think it was funny. Something to do. Pass the time. You're always talking about it.

TONY: Are you serious?

PETER: Of course I'm serious.

TONY: You're lying.

PETER: What's the matter with you?

TONY: Why did you want to hurt her?

PETER: Oh, shut up. Forget it.

TONY: Not likely. Come here.

> TONY *moves so that he is close to* PETER. *A pause.* PETER *turns to look at* TONY. PETER *is afraid.*

TONY (*gently*): Sit down.

> PETER *sits on the sofa. In a moment* TONY *will put a cigarette into Peter's mouth, and light it for him. Tony's*

> *manner with* PETER *is patient and not unkind, treating
> him rather as a frightened child. And Peter's confidence to
> TONY is childlike. He might be telling of how he woke to
> see the shadow on the stairs, and how he cried out in the dark
> many years ago.*

TONY: What got into you?

PETER (*staring closely into* TONY'S *face*): Yes, that's what we say, isn't it? What's got *into* you? What *possessed* you to do it? Leave me alone, Tony. Please.

TONY: No.

PETER: If you live as I do it all goes into your head. All the devils. And it's all thought, no feeling. (*He has groped for this word.*) Saints. Nomads. Me. What other people experience . . . all that just goes to the head and becomes a possibility. It sometimes gets pretty crowded up there with maybes. I'm trying to explain. That's what you want, isn't it?

TONY: Yes.

PETER: She was standing there on the step. And I didn't feel anything. Some common tart come to the wrong house. Then I saw her . . . saw her . . . as I said. And I remembered a song. From years ago. I was once in love, believe it or not. Keep me to the point, for God's sake. So there she was. Enquiring. Unknown. And I wanted her to feel something about me. Recognize me, I suppose.

TONY: You wanted to make an enemy.

PETER: Yes. (*Pause.*) Yes! Something positive. It's not often now that people approach me. Either by chance or wish. There she was. I wanted to be remembered by someone. With hatred? Why not? How can I ask for love? And it was meant to be a joke. At first. This'll make Tony laugh. I remember thinking that. But when she told me about the child it wasn't any good. I found I was talking to one of my own kind. I was talking to myself. And it hasn't made you laugh.

TONY: No.

PETER: Why not? I thought we could have it as a secret between us. The day we . . .

TONY: You were wrong.

> TONY *has got up and moved away from* PETER. *It is a
> sudden movement, as if he cannot stand the physical contact
> any longer.*

PETER: And I thought that was the way you saw things. You've never seemed to care about people. You've always seemed so . . . callous. No, I don't mean that. I mean, offhand.

TONY: Just because I call you old boy, old boy . . . just because I wear these silly clothes to make me feel good . . . because of lots of reasons . . . all right, I drink too much and smoke too much. . . . Filth can still make me laugh . . . and it's fun to get a rise out of a girl . . . all right . . . maybe . . . that's the way I look to you. All the same, I'm not your kind of criminal.

PETER: Criminal?

TONY: Yes, sweetheart. What you did tonight was criminal. You make an excuse of the accident to your leg. It's got nothing to do with it. If you were active and got around, if Mummie and Daddie understood you, if you were a success like Brian, it wouldn't make any difference. You'd still want to have somebody concerned in some way with you. Perhaps not in your misery, but in something equally trivial, such as your happiness. Yes, with you up and about and she a bit prettier, alone together, you'd probably have made love to her instead of doing what you did. But either way it's a crime. Engaging another person's emotions to prove that you exist.

PETER: What about us, Tony?

TONY: Oh, I gave up long ago. I'm quite happy to drift on the surface of other peoples' lives. I'm always pleased to see almost anybody. Hullo, old boy. How's it go? You don't say so. Tell me more. Tell me all. I'll lend an ear to any deserving cause.

> *Silence.* PETER *looks up.*
> *In the hall:*
> *A key is being turned in the lock of the front door.*
> *In the drawing-room:*

PETER: You know what you've just said.

TONY: Pretty well.

PETER: That there's no sort of friendship between us. Nothing that you can't have with anybody. You've just said that, haven't you?

TONY: Yes.

> In the hall:
> *The front door is open.* CHARLES *and* LAURA *have come in.*
> *It is now raining hard and a sudden gust of wind swings*

the door as CHARLES *stands on the step shaking the umbrella. After a moment he joins* LAURA *in the hall, shutting the door behind him.* LAURA *is wiping rain from her face with a little handkerchief, and looking into the drawing-room at* PETER *and* TONY.

LAURA (*she calls to them*): So you're still here. Not gone. (*To* CHARLES.) They're still here.

CHARLES: Oh?

CHARLES *and* LAURA *begin to get out of their wet coats.*

In the drawing-room:

PETER *and* TONY *are speaking. Their voices are low, the words hurried.*

PETER: Is there nothing? Nothing at all?

TONY: Self-disgust. That I could stand by and not interfere between you and that girl, just let it go on, because I couldn't get rid of my pity for you. Take that, if you want it.

PETER: Do you hate me?

TONY: I don't love you, Peter.

PETER: Then go. Go away.

LAURA *is coming into the room. She has taken off her coat, but still wears a plastic thing tied over her hat.*

LAURA: You didn't go out, then. You were right. It's pouring with rain. Set in for the night, I shouldn't wonder. The rehearsal went well. But the roof over the stage began to leak, so we had to give up. Daddie just got his bit in. He's going to be very good. He has such authority. We saw a funny thing on the way home. . . .

She stops, staring from PETER *to* TONY.

LAURA: I haven't interrupted you, have I?

TONY: No.

LAURA: I mean, you weren't in the middle of an important conversation, were you?

TONY: No, we were just gossiping.

LAURA: I'm sure that's not true. Daddie and I have always said what a good mind you've got, Tony. I suppose it comes of being in business. It gives you a sensible and practical approach. That's why we like you to see Peter. He was always a bit of a dreamer, even before his accident. It doesn't do to be too sensitive in this world, does it?

TONY: No, it doesn't. I must be going.

CHARLES (*he has come in from the hall*): Oh, stay on for a little. What about a drop of this?

He means the whisky.

TONY: No, thank you, Mr Sharpe.

CHARLES: Peter? (PETER *shakes his head.*) Well, I'm going to. I want to chase that cold out of my head.

As CHARLES *pours the whisky* LAURA *suddenly giggles: a very silly sound, indeed.*

CHARLES: What's the matter with you?

LAURA: I suddenly thought. . . .

CHARLES: What?

LAURA: Of you standing there on the stage just about to speak when —splash!—that water right on your head. And you not moving. Just saying the line as if nothing was happening. (*To* TONY.) Just where he was standing. Such bad luck. They must have that roof seen to.

CHARLES has drained the glass of whisky. Now he stares at his wife.

CHARLES: I understood you thought I was very good in the part.

LAURA: Oh, you are. . . .

CHARLES: Then why make it sound as if I look a fool?

LAURA: I didn't mean to.

TONY (*interrupting: to* CHARLES): These accidents happen. How do you go about acting a character in an amateur play?

CHARLES: Well, you have to get it right, you know. People are very observant. They'll pick out the smallest detail. For example, you have to look right. Clothes, that sort of thing. Take this policeman I'm doing at the moment. I happen to know one of the fellows down at the station. I've had a word with him.

TONY: Really? That's very interesting.

CHARLES: Goes beyond the play. You can see that. I mean, the information's always useful. How the other chap lives. That sort of thing.

TONY: Yes, it must be.

CHARLES: And as for the play, oh, it's very necessary to get it right. Otherwise, you couldn't believe what you were doing. I get right into it, I must say. While it's going on it all seems more . . . real, I suppose, than life itself.

PETER: Show us what you mean, Father.

CHARLES: How?

PETER: Do your bit.

CHARLES: I couldn't do it here. Like this.

PETER: Why not?

CHARLES: Well, I haven't got the atmosphere. Got to have the feel of the thing, you know.

PETER: You mean, there's been no crime here. Is that it?

CHARLES: Yes. And the furniture's different. . . . (*To* TONY.) Are you really interested?

TONY: Of course.

CHARLES: The play takes place in a big country house. I'm not exactly sure where it's supposed to be. Somewhere in England. And these people—there are five of them—have been invited for the weekend by this man. They all think they're going to inherit money. Four of them . . .

LAURA: Who does this belong to?

> LAURA *is holding Shirley's handbag, which she has picked up from the side of the chair.*

CHARLES: Oh, for God's sake, shut up, Laura! You're always butting in! (CHARLES *turns again to* TONY: *speaks to him.*) Four of these people are murdered. Each of them is stabbed to death with a knitting needle. Now one of the characters is an old lady who is always knitting socks. We get a lot of fun out of the fact that it is her needles which keep disappearing. It's all very true to life, though.

TONY: It sounds most exciting.

CHARLES: It is. Then at the end the murderer is discovered by the old lady. She rings me up at the local police station and I come in and make the arrest. Suppose Peter's the man.

PETER: Yes, suppose I'm the man.

CHARLES: Stand there.

> PETER *stands in front of* CHARLES. CHARLES *turns away for a moment, playing the ostrich, pretending not to be there. Then he turns and approaches* PETER.

CHARLES: Henry Heber Percy Armitage, I arrest you for the murder of Sylvia Hardcastle. I must warn you that anything you say may be used in evidence.

PETER: I just want to say this. . . .

CHARLES: No, no. That's the end of the play. He doesn't speak.

PETER: There are extenuating circumstances, Inspector. I was very unhappy when I was a child. I hated my father. It's not an unusual excuse, I know. He was never unkind to me. I wish he had been.

If he could have been so definite I think I could have loved him. But I was nothing to him. The creature he passed on the stairs, the thing underneath his feet which longed to be kicked, but he had no time even for cruelty. Will that be taken into consideration, sir?

> *A bell can be heard from somewhere in the street. It is the kind which ambulances and police cars use. The sound approaches: passes the house: fades: stops.*

> PETER *has heard this. He turns to* LAURA, *holding out his hand for the bag.*

LAURA (*to* CHARLES): There goes another car. Or is it an ambulance?

PETER: What's happening out there?

LAURA: We saw it when we were coming home. I wanted to stop, but Daddie wouldn't let me. It was raining. . . .

PETER: But what did you see?

LAURA: It was by the canal bridge. There were several policemen and some people. Peter, who does this bag belong to?

PETER (*taking the bag from her*): Someone called this evening. They must have left it. What else did you see?

LAURA: Not much. Daddie hurried me past. I saw one of the policemen up to his waist in water. They were flashing torches.

CHARLES: There'd been some sort of accident, obviously. No concern of ours.

> PETER *is looking across at* TONY, *who turns and goes out by the hall to the dining-room.* PETER *watches him.*

LAURA: Was it anybody I know?

PETER (*turning to her*): What do you mean?

LAURA: Who called. And left that.

PETER: No. You don't know her. It was a mistake. Wrong house.

> PETER *opens the bag and looks at what is in it. While he does this he continually glances up at the darkened dining-room, where* TONY *has gone. Then* PETER *snaps the bag shut and goes across to the dining-room.*

> CHARLES *and* LAURA *are left alone.*

CHARLES: What's been going on here? You imagine I don't notice things. I'm no fool.

LAURA: No one suggests that you are. Now sit down. Would you like a hot drink?

CHARLES: Why?

LAURA: For the cold in the head you're going to have.

CHARLES: No. Shut up. Leave me alone. (*Pause.*) That boy . . .

LAURA: Peter? Our boy?

CHARLES: Yes, Peter. Talking about when he was little. How he hated . . . (*He cannot say it.*) He meant me. You know that, don't you?

> CHARLES *looks as if he wants to cry: a sudden moment of despair and no comprehension at all. He stares at* LAURA: *then gives a smile like a whimper.*

CHARLES: He's got a terrible sense of fun, that boy of ours.

> In the dining-room:
>
> PETER *and* TONY *are together at the window. The lights have not been put on.* TONY *is looking out at the street.* PETER *is very close to him.*

PETER: What are you thinking? (*He does not give time for an answer.*) It's impossible. Kill herself? She'd never do such a thing. You mean because of what I did? You're mad. Did she go that way? Towards the bridge? Well, if you think it's happened why don't you go out and see? Ask. Find out. (*Pause:* PETER *follows* TONY's *look.*) You can't see the place from here.

> PETER *turns away from* TONY. *He speaks out of the near darkness of the room. Speaks for himself.*

PETER: You're afraid, aren't you? It may be true. There may be a drowned girl pulled from the river lying out there in the rain. Was she heavy enough to go down? I'd not have thought it. You're scared. You're trying to stop it being true by not finding out. But if it's happened it *is* true. The wretched soaked little thing lies on the stones at the moment. But you believe it won't be true until there's some proof. Nothing less than a body. You're the kind of man who is the despair of the Christian church. (TONY *has turned to look at* PETER: *a moment: suddenly.*) Don't go!

> But TONY *has turned away from the window and is crossing the room.*
>
> *Peter's face is caught by the light: held.*
>
> In the drawing-room:
>
> CHARLES *and* LAURA *turn towards the door as* TONY *comes into the room.*

CHARLES: Now look here, Tony. I've been having a word with my wife. We agree that it's quite natural for you two boys to have . . . Are you going?

> CHARLES *sees that* TONY *has picked up his raincoat as he crossed the hall.*
>
> PETER *has followed* TONY *into the room.*

TONY: Yes. What did you want to say?

CHARLES: My wife and I agree that it's natural for you and Peter to have your differences of opinion. When two people are such close friends of course they sometimes rub each other the wrong way. That's what's happened tonight, isn't it? Now, come on. Be good chaps and make it up. You'll both laugh about this in a week's time, and wonder how it ever could have happened.

LAURA: Yes, it's quite early. There's still time to go out for a drink and a chat. The rain won't worry youngsters like you.

TONY: I'm thirty-six, Mrs Sharpe. And you're wrong. Peter and I haven't quarrelled.

CHARLES: But you haven't said a word to him since we came in. We both noticed it.

TONY: Please let me say goodnight and go.

CHARLES: Peter, I insist that you explain to your mother. . . .

PETER: There's nothing to make up with Tony, Father. We were never friends.

CHARLES: Nonsense.

PETER: It's true. It was an invention of yours. Like most things I possess.

CHARLES: Look, you had your little joke with me earlier on. . . .

PETER: I'm not joking.

> *The doorbell rings. And again, at once.*

CHARLES: Who the hell's that?

> CHARLES *notices a look between* PETER *and* TONY.

CHARLES: Are you expecting someone? (*To* LAURA.) Well, find out out who it is.

> LAURA *goes towards the hall and the front door.*

CHARLES (*to* PETER): Why should I invent anything for you? Haven't I always wanted you to go out and about in the real world and be happy? Tell me what's happened. We've always lived quietly. Come on, boy, this can be settled as everything has been settled before, can't it?

> PETER *speaks to* CHARLES *but watches, with* TONY, *through the open door to the hall.*

PETER: Don't make me answer your questions, Father. We've got to go on living here. Quietly. Together. Perhaps for a long time. By all means try to make the people in your play as true to life as you possibly can. But let us pretend . . . on each other's behalf . . . that . . .

> LAURA *has come back into the room. She stands aside in the doorway to let* SHIRLEY *come in.*

LAURA: This young lady says . . .

PETER (*to* SHIRLEY): You left your bag.

SHIRLEY: Yes.

PETER: Here you are.

> PETER *holds out the bag to* SHIRLEY, *who takes it. She opens the bag and looks inside. She seems satisfied.*

SHIRLEY: Thank you.

> *She is about to turn away and go when* PETER *speaks.*

PETER: Mr Coleman—(*he indicates* TONY)—this is Mr Coleman remember—he was very worried about you.

> TONY *makes a gesture as if he would stop* PETER. *It is ignored.*

PETER (*to* SHIRLEY): My mother told him that they were searching the canal at the bridge, and then he heard the police cars. Mr Coleman thought . . .

SHIRLEY (*to* TONY): Why can't you people take things as they are? Look at you now. Inventing a sad story for me. She ended up in the river. It'd never be like that. Never.

> SHIRLEY *puts her hand on Tony's arm. He does not move.*

SHIRLEY: Still, it was nice of you to be worried. Matter of fact, it was a cat. It had got trapped in a drain. I stayed and watched. It was a stray. They got it out all right. It was starving. They went to a lot of trouble. Got wet. They wouldn't have done it for me. Not likely. Now they've taken it away. They're going to destroy it. Somebody had complained. Its screams were upsetting the neighbourhood. (*She looks at* PETER.) He's right. No doubt about it. The place must be kept quiet so that you and all the other people in this street can die in peace. Goodnight.

> SHIRLEY *goes out of the room. No one tries to detain her. The front door slams shut behind her. Silence.*

LAURA: Who is she? I can't believe that she meant . . .

CHARLES: Be quiet, Laura. I won't have such things discussed in this house. (*A whisper: to* TONY.) You'll stay on and have a little supper?

TONY: No, I must go.

CHARLES: Very well.

LAURA: Shall we see you next Sunday, Tony?

TONY: Well, I was thinking of driving down to the seaside, Mrs Sharpe. I have some people I must see. On business, really . . .

PETER (*he has been watching* TONY *as he struggles*): Leave him alone, Mother.

TONY (*pause*): No, you won't be seeing me next Sunday.

PETER: Goodbye, Tony.

TONY: Goodbye, Peter. (*To* CHARLES *and* LAURA.) Goodnight. No, don't bother. . . .

> This is to LAURA *who has made a movement to go with* TONY *to the door. She stops, and* TONY *goes out of the room.*

CHARLES (*to* LAURA): Let's have something to eat.

LAURA: All right, dear. What would you like?

CHARLES: Oh, I don't know. Whatever there is.

LAURA: It won't be long.

> LAURA *goes out of the room, quietly shutting the door behind her.*
>
> CHARLES *and* PETER *are left alone.* CHARLES *has put on reading glasses, and picked up a newspaper.* PETER *has not moved from where he was standing when* TONY *left.*

CHARLES: Peter . . .

PETER (*turning to* CHARLES): Yes?

CHARLES: What exactly was that girl doing here tonight?

PETER: She came to the wrong place. She wanted the Dickinsons. We played a little joke on her, that's all.

CHARLES: A joke, eh? Haha. Was it a good one?

PETER: Not bad.

CHARLES: You always enjoyed a joke. (*He is shaking out the paper.*) When you were a little boy . . . (*He has folded the paper.*) . . . you couldn't have been more than seven or eight . . . (*He has become absorbed in an item of news.*) . . . I remember very well. . . .

PETER (*after a moment*): What do you remember?

CHARLES (*he looks up*): What? (*He stares at* PETER *as if he had never seen him before.*) What were we talking about?

PETER: We were talking about me, Father.

CHARLES: Well, go on. I'm listening.

CHARLES *leans back in his chair, pushing his glasses up on to his forehead, leaving the newspaper on his knees.*

PETER: You were saying that I always enjoyed a joke. And I was going to say that I'm not sure that I enjoy this one.

CHARLES: Something at the moment?

PETER: Yes, something at the moment.

CHARLES'S *eyes are a little wide with concentration as he stares at* PETER. *He might be dead. His son's voice is calm, a man reflecting on a landscape.*

PETER: I mean living in a desert, like this. At one time I believed that this waste ground must have boundaries. And I thought that if I made my way towards that limit I'd at last meet with people. Well, there's been Tony. And there was Roy and Harry—remember Harry?—and others. But as soon as I took their hand and prepared myself to love them, what did I find? They were not at the beginning of a fertile land, but making for some other, more believable, place than I had in mind. So the most we could do was pass each other, without doing more harm than was necessary.

TONY COLEMAN *is seen. He is in the street, beside his car.*

PETER'S *voice will continue over this and the following visual scenes.*

TONY *is pulling on gloves and turning up his coat collar against the rain. His face, which is closely seen, has relaxed into tiredness and every year of his age. He pulls on his little pimple of a cap, and turns to the car.*

PETER'S VOICE: I've heard of people who live in places where talent and opportunity for a kind of joy in life can flourish. And I really believe they exist. I don't want to make the mistake of thinking that all people in all places are like me. But there are far too many of us. You shouldn't crowd a wilderness. It contradicts its purpose.

There is the sound of the car as TONY *drives away, leaving the street empty.*

PETER *is seen again. He is speaking without bitterness.*

PETER: I lost you and Mother many years ago in the hide and seek of childhood. Did we ever meet again?

LAURA *is seen in the dining-room.*

PETER'S *voice continues over this.*

LAURA *is standing by the sideboard. She has a silver-framed photograph in her hand. There are others in front of her. She stares down at them. She looks for something in the fixed faces.*

PETER'S VOICE: I think I remember—it was a long time ago—when we . . . no, I must have dreamt it. We've never met in this place. You're lost a thousand miles from where I am. Sometimes I think I see distress signals fired into the night. But they die out before they can be interpreted.

> LAURA *puts down the photograph. She turns away.*
> PETER *is seen again.*

PETER: They say you walk in circles in a desert. Past the tennis club, over the bridge, by the new supermarket, and so down the High Street: round the public lavatories and the preserved market cross, up through the old town—fine view of the gasworks—across the meadows, over the bridge, past the tennis club and back here. And sometimes, raising dust like an army, there is a person. Such as that girl. On the march, believing that by putting one foot before another she makes a track for herself to follow.

> SHIRLEY *is seen walking through the town.*
> PETER'S *voice speaks over this.*
> SHIRLEY *goes forward and lights from shops fall on her. She looks ahead. Her movements are definite and hurried. The rain has made her hair ugly to look at.*

PETER'S VOICE: The moment I set eyes on her I knew she was an enemy. She believes in the good land. I don't any more. Not the chance of reaching it, anyway. So I tried to stop her. We fought on shifting ground with no result. Admiring each others' wounds we agreed to call it off. Nothing is even mortal in this place.

> SHIRLEY *has gone from sight down the street.*
> PETER'S *last words are spoken over:*
> *The town square: swept with rain. The station: a train is leaving.*

PETER'S VOICE: But it has been some sort of encounter. It's made a landmark, something to catch the eye, like litter on the hills. Something to occupy my mind as I go—forward?—in this labyrinth without walls. Something to remember. Something. . . .

> *A by-pass road, lit by sodium lamps and deserted, goes straight into the distance.*

CURTAIN

THE DEVILS

INTRODUCTORY NOTE

WHEN Peter Hall approached him in 1960 for a large-scale costume play, Whiting offered to adapt either Aldous Huxley's *The Devils of Loudun* or Frederick Rolfe's *Hadrian VII*. *The Devils* was produced at the Aldwych in February 1961 with Richard Johnson as Grandier, Dorothy Tutin as Soeur Jeanne, Diana Rigg as Phillipe, Patrick Wymark as De Laubardement and Max Adrian as Barré. Peter Wood directed in a set by Sean Kenny.

The production suffered from Whiting's normal bad luck. On the first night Patrick Allen (d'Armagnac) had to duck to avoid having his hat knocked off by an arch which was being flown in and Richard Johnson (Grandier) was ill with influenza. He played with a temperature of 102 but his performance suffered and his understudy David Sumner took over on the second night.

It got a better press than any previous Whiting play.

The Times:

. . . a play which is rich in ironic implication and has a fascination of its own. It wastes itself in the end in scenes of torture which are merely painful to witness.

W. A. Darlington in the *Daily Telegraph*:

. . . three long acts of intermittent power and tremendous atmosphere.

Philip Hope-Wallace in the *Guardian*:

A flawed masterpiece . . . this piece of history, for all Mr Whiting's skill and elevation of thought, refuses to bend into a dramatic shape.

Robert Muller in the *Daily Mail*:

Much was expected; more was fulfilled . . . a play of depth, force, terror and beauty. . . . The effect is of a Jacobean dramatist writing a contemporary tragedy.

J. C. Trewin in the *Birmingham Post*:

> It is still hard to know why it was brought to the Aldwych stage.

T. C. Worsley in the *Financial Times*:

> I don't remember in twenty years of reviewing plays ever before having been tempted to use the word masterpiece about a new English play . . . I shall not resist the temptation. . . . Not one word or scene is wasted.

Milton Shulman in the *Evening Standard*:

> Whiting has neither the intellectual power of Shaw nor the political fervour of Miller.

Alan Brien in the *Sunday Telegraph*:

> There are speeches where sense and poetry are brilliantly interwoven. But it has not been dramatized.

Kenneth Tynan in the *Observer*:

> Tiring of the tortures and tiring of hating the torturers, I found myself with little left to feel, save perhaps a vague suspicion, finally mounting to certainty, that a squalid footnote to the history of superstition had been dignified beyond its deserts by an extremely gifted dramatist.

H. A. L. Craig in the *New Statesman*:

> There are speeches in this play that for power haven't been written by an Englishman in the English theatre since Webster. . . . Mr Whiting makes the best of our playwrights since the war seem mere byways in the drama. *The Devils* is our only highroad.

The play was kept in the Royal Shakespeare Company's 1962 repertoire and in February 1962 Hans Lietzau directed it at Berlin's Schillertheater.

In New York it wasn't premièred until November 1965 when Michael Cacoyannis directed it at the Broadway Theatre with Jason Robards and Anne Bancroft.

Walter Kerr wrote in the *New York Herald Tribune*:

> *The Devils* is a play of massive height and width and no depth at all. . . . Possibly the irony—the almost too simple irony—of the overall plan forces this thinness upon us. . . . Mr Robards is clearly bent on some

sort of penitential self-destruction. But we are not told why. More than that, we are not made to feel why.

But Howard Taubman gave it a rave in the *New York Times*:

A stunning play, one of the finest of our age, has come to town. *The Devils* . . . has an Elizabethan sweep and richness of dramatic texture.

But luck as usual was working against Whiting. There was a transport strike in New York and Anne Bancroft had a fall which injured her back. Though bookings had been made as far ahead as June, the play was taken off after about six weeks.

PERSONS

MANNOURY, *a surgeon*
ADAM, *a chemist*
LOUIS TRINCANT, *the Public Prosecutor*
PHILLIPE TRINCANT
JEAN D'ARMAGNAC, *the Governor of Loudun*
GUILLAUME DE CERISAY, *the Chief Magistrate*
A SEWERMAN
URBAIN GRANDIER, *the Vicar of St Peter's Church*
NINON, *a widow*
DE LA ROCHEPOZAY, *the Bishop of Poitiers*
FATHER RANGIER
FATHER BARRÉ
SISTER JEANNE OF THE ANGELS, *the prioress of St Ursula's Convent*
SISTER CLAIRE
SISTER LOUISE
DE LAUBARDEMONT, *the King's Special Commissioner to Loudun*
FATHER MIGNON
SISTER GABRIELLE
PRINCE HENRI DE CONDÉ
RICHELIEU
LOUIS XIII, *King of France*
BONTEMPS, *a gaoler*
FATHER AMBROSE
A CLERK
Townspeople, People from the Country, Capuchins, Carmelites, Jesuits and Soldiers

The action of this play takes place in and near the town of Loudun, and briefly at Paris, between the years 1623 and 1634

ACT ONE

The streets of Loudun. Day.
A corpse hangs from the municipal gallows. Nearby, a sewerman works in a
shallow drain.
People are coming from Saint Peter's Church. ADAM, *a chemist, and*
MANNOURY, *a surgeon, among others.*

MANNOURY: Shall we go together?

ADAM: By all means.

MANNOURY: Don't catch my sleeve. He spoke as if he were
God.

ADAM: Grandier?

MANNOURY: Grandier.

ADAM: Very rousing to the spirit.

MANNOURY: You think so? Hm.

ADAM: So small a town is lucky to have such a caretaker of souls.
Did I say that as if I meant it?

MANNOURY: No. There are things, my dear Adam.

ADAM: Things, Mannoury?

MANNOURY: Don't gape. Things said and things done.

ADAM: By the priest? Yes, I've heard.

MANNOURY: Then see.

> NINON, *a young widow, has come from the church. She goes away along*
> *the street.*

ADAM: With my own eyes.

MANNOURY: I've attended her. Medically.

ADAM: Have you?

MANNOURY: It's not widowhood gives that contentment. That
walk.

ADAM: It takes a visit.

MANNOURY: It does.

> *They have come beneath the gallows.*

ADAM: Hoo, he dangles.

141

MANNOURY: What idiot is this?

ADAM: They put him up last night.

MANNOURY: Compelling sight. What resides, Adam?

ADAM: I don't understand you.

MANNOURY: What's left, man? After that.

ADAM: Ah, you've something in your head.

MANNOURY: Has he? That's the point. Come to dinner.

> ADAM *and* MANNOURY *go.*
>
> LOUIS TRINCANT *and his daughter,* PHILLIPE, *have come from th*
> *church.*

TRINCANT: Fold your hands, child. You walk like a peasant.

PHILLIPE: Who's to see?

TRINCANT: The world. Let it set eyes on a lady.

> *They have come near the gallows.*

PHILLIPE: Was he young or old?

TRINCANT: Don't look.

PHILLIPE: You want me to be filled with nice and useful experience
Father, so tell me something: does death unmask the face in
heaven?

TRINCANT: A question for a priest.

PHILLIPE: I'm sorry. Let's talk of how my legs move in the dance
And of marriage. And love. Not death. For death smells bad. And
there is scent upon a pillow.

TRINCANT: Chatter. Come along. Mind the step.

> TRINCANT *and* PHILLIPE *go.*
>
> JEAN D'ARMAGNAC, *Governor of the town, and* GUILLAUME DI
> CERISAY, *the Chief Magistrate, have come from the church into th*
> *street.*

D'ARMAGNAC: Grandier seems to have got it into his head that the
forces of good are a kind of political party, needing a leader.

DE CERISAY: His mind's been running on such things.

D'ARMAGNAC: Politics? All the same, the terms seem strange
coming from a pulpit.

DE CERISAY: So does wit.

D'ARMAGNAC: Yes. I disgraced myself this morning. I laughed
aloud. Is that more becoming to the Governor of the town than
yawning his way through the sermon, as I used to do before
Grandier came here?

DE CERISAY: Have you sent the carriage on?

D'ARMAGNAC: Yes, I thought we'd walk. Tell me—

DE CERISAY: Yes?

D'ARMAGNAC: This is a small town. Can it contain a Father Grandier? That proud man. Shall we go this way?

D'ARMAGNAC and DE CERISAY go.

The crowd has gone. The church doorway is empty.

FATHER URBAIN GRANDIER, *Vicar of Saint Peter's Church, appears. He comes into the street. A bucket of filth dredged up by the sewerman splashes his gown.*

SEWERMAN: Sorry.

GRANDIER: It doesn't matter.

SEWERMAN: It's wrong, though. Shit on the holy purple.

GRANDIER: My son—

SEWERMAN: Father?

GRANDIER: Your words suit your condition.

SEWERMAN: How would you have it?

GRANDIER: Otherwise.

SEWERMAN: But I'm a man, sir. A dirty, sinful man. And my job is in the drains of the city. Why expect clean words from me? Let me oblige you, all the same. I regret, sir, splashing your gown with the excrement of the poor. Better?

GRANDIER (*he laughs*): It'll do.

SEWERMAN: Lovely day. Hot.

GRANDIER: Yes. How can you bear to work down there?

SEWERMAN: Well, I used to keep my mind on higher things.

GRANDIER: I'm very pleased to hear it. What were they?

SEWERMAN: My wife and my dinner.

GRANDIER: I see. But now—

SEWERMAN: There's not the need. I've grown used to the sink. Nobody can live forty-three years and not have it happen. If you were a man, sir, and not a priest, perhaps I could make you understand.

GRANDIER: Try, even so.

SEWERMAN: Well, every man is his own drain. He carries his main sewer with him. Gutters run about him to carry off the dirt—

GRANDIER: They also carry the blood of life.

SEWERMAN: Mere plumbing. Elementary sanitation. Don't interrupt. And what makes a man happy? To eat, and set the drains awash. To sit in the sun and ferment the rubbish. To go home, and find comfort in his wife's conduit. Then why should I feel ashamed or out of place down here?

GRANDIER: Put in that way I can see no reason at all. It must be almost a pleasure.

SEWERMAN: It's clear, sir, that your precious juices will never flow here. As this misguided creature has dripped through his toes all night.

GRANDIER: Don't mock the thing!

SEWERMAN: Sorry.

GRANDIER: He was a man. A young man. Eighteen years old. They brought him to kneel at the church door on his way here. He told me his sins.

SEWERMAN: What were they?

GRANDIER: Being alive.

SEWERMAN: Comprehensive.

GRANDIER: Heinous, it seemed. Manhood led him into the power of the senses. With them he worshipped in total adoration a young girl. But he learnt too quickly. He learnt that only gold can decorate the naked body. And so he stole.

SEWERMAN: And so he hanged.

GRANDIER: He confessed something to me alone. It was not for God to hear. It was a man speaking to a man. He said that when he adorned the girl the metal looked colourless, valueless, against her golden skin. That was repentance. When will they take him down?

SEWERMAN: Tomorrow. When it's dark.

GRANDIER: See that it's done with some kind of decency.

GRANDIER *goes*.

DE CERISAY: D'ARMAGNAC: TRINCANT.

D'ARMAGNAC: Provincial life, my dear Trincant.

TRINCANT: You feel it has a bad effect on the art of poetry?

D'ARMAGNAC: Ask De Cerisay.

DE CERISAY: Well, you and I, Trincant, as Public Prosecutor and Magistrate, are brought close to the ground by our work. I've always understood poetry to be an elevated art.

TRINCANT: I assure you that during composition I think the right thoughts. My mind, if I may put it this way, is filled with nobility.

DE CERISAY: Why don't you show this latest bunch of Latin epigrams to Grandier?

TRINCANT: The priest?

DE CERISAY: As a priest his secular senses are well developed. Make a selection. Submit them. The man is a scholar.

TRINCANT: Very well. I don't seek praise, but I'll do as you say. Yes.

TRINCANT goes.

D'ARMAGNAC: Poor Trincant. He loves the Muses but, alas, they don't seem to love him. I hope your suggestion about Grandier was not malicious.

DE CERISAY: Not at all, sir. As with any author, the greater Trincant's audience the less burden of doubt on his closer friends.

D'ARMAGNAC: Grandier came to see me this morning. I was having breakfast in the garden. He didn't know that I could observe him as he walked towards me. Vulnerable: smiling. He visibly breathed the air. He stopped to watch the peacocks. He fondled a rose as if it were the secret part of a woman. He laughed with the gardener's child. Then he composed himself, and it was another man who sat down beside me and talked for an hour. Where will this other man climb on his ladder of doubt and laughter?

DE CERISAY: Probably to the highest offices of the church.

D'ARMAGNAC: And the man I saw in the garden?

Silence.

GRANDIER *with* NINON. *A disordered bed: biretta on the bedpost.*

NINON: Tell me.

GRANDIER: Now what do you need to be told? Words are playthings in our situation. Expect music from them, but not sense.

NINON: Don't laugh at me. I never understand. I'm not a clever woman.

GRANDIER: You're too humble, Ninon. It's a female vice. It will never do. Ask your question.

NINON: Why do you come to me?

GRANDIER: That would be a wise question if we were in your drawing-room. As it is—

NINON: There are pretty young girls in the town.

GRANDIER: They didn't need consolation for the untimely death of their husband, the rich wine merchant. That was the reason for my first visit, remember. How many Tuesdays ago was it? I asked you to believe that God loved you, and had you in His eternal care. That the bursting of your husband's heart at the dinner table, when his blood ran with his wholesale wine, was an act of love. That all things, however incomprehensible, are an act of love. But you couldn't bring yourself to believe any of this. Your soul is as tiny as your mind, Ninon, and you had to fall back on a most human gesture: you wept. Tears must be wiped away. How can that be done without a caress?

NINON: I saw you that day just as a man. What's the matter?

GRANDIER: I wish words like that could still hurt me.

He is putting scent on his handkerchief.

NINON: I've never seen you as anything but a man. Do you want to be more?

GRANDIER: Of course. Or less.

NINON: But how can you be a man of God without being a man?

GRANDIER: My dear child, you ask questions out of your time, and far beyond your experience. Your mouth . . .

A bell is sounding.

NINON: You possess me.

GRANDIER: Go to sleep now. You've been a good little animal today. Let the thought of it comfort you. Be happy.

GRANDIER *goes.*

ADAM *and* MANNOURY: *a table between them.*

MANNOURY: This human head fills me with anticipation, my dear Adam.

ADAM: It's a common enough object.

MANNOURY: Every man wears one on his shoulders, certainly. But when a head comes into my hands disassociated from the grosser parts of the body I always feel an elevation of spirit. Think, this is the residence of reason.

ADAM: Indeed! Ah, yes. Very true.

MANNOURY: Isn't it possible that one day in the most commonplace dissection I might find—

ADAM: What Mannoury? Don't hesitate to tell me.

MANNOURY: I might stumble upon the very meaning of reason. Isn't it possible that the divinity of man, enclosed in an infinitesimal bag, might rest upon the point of my knife? I have dreamed of the moment. I have seen myself. I lift the particle, taken from the cerebellum and, Adam, I know!

ADAM: What do you know, Mannoury?

MANNOURY: Come, my dear friend, I am speaking in the most comprehensive sense. I know—everything. All—is revealed.

ADAM: God bless my soul!

MANNOURY: Let's take this thing to your house. We'll spend the evening on it.

They begin to go down into the street.

MANNOURY: Everyone is speaking of your treatment of the Duke's love disease.

ADAM: Yes, I think we're getting on top of it. Too soon to be certain.

MANNOURY: Your metallic compound. Does it affect the potency?

ADAM: Disastrously. But as I jokingly told the Duke, Science must concern itself with primary causes. It cannot turn its head to observe destructive side issues.

MANNOURY: And never will, we must hope.

ADAM: Is Madam Who Shall Be Nameless delivered?

MANNOURY: Prematurely. The foetus was interesting. It had a tiny cap drawn over its head.

ADAM: Hardly surprising with all this talk about the coachman.

They are now in the street. GRANDIER *is approaching them.*

MANNOURY: Look who's coming.

ADAM: Studied indifference, if you please.

GRANDIER: Good evening, Mister Surgeon. And Mister Chemist.

MANNOURY: Good evening, sir.

ADAM: Sir.

GRANDIER: It's been a fine day.

MANNOURY: Yes.

ADAM: It has.

GRANDIER: But now—rain, do you think?

ADAM: The sky is clear.

MANNOURY: It is.

GRANDIER: But it may cloud before night.

ADAM: Indeed.

MANNOURY: Indeed, it may.

GRANDIER: Darken, you know. What have you got in that bucket?

MANNOURY: A man's head.

GRANDIER: A friend?

MANNOURY: A criminal.

ADAM: The body was taken down from the gallows last night.

GRANDIER (*after silence*): I hope they didn't overcharge you, in the interest of Science.

MANNOURY: Ninepence.

GRANDIER: Reasonable. A bargain. Let me see. Poor pickle.

ADAM: Yes. Mannoury and I have been discussing the human predicament with this relic as centrepiece.

GRANDIER: I'm sure you said some very interesting things.

ADAM: Well, Mannoury did observe that the seat of reason is situated here.

GRANDIER: How true! But you'll have said that, Adam.

ADAM: I did.

GRANDIER: And we mustn't forget looking down on this pudding that man's fiddledeevinity is what you may say only to the greater purpose of his hohumha.

ADAM: I beg your pardon.

GRANDIER: I quite agree. But I mustn't stay exchanging profundities with you, however much you may tempt me. So goodbye, Mister Surgeon and Mister Chemist.

GRANDIER *goes. The bell is sounding.*

MANNOURY: You fell into his trap, Adam. Never engage Mister Clever.

ADAM: He smelled of the widow woman. Filth.

MANNOURY: Of course. He's just come from her.

ADAM: After tickling himself in the confessional with the sins of young girls this morning—

MANNOURY: He consummates himself in the widow's bed this afternoon—

ADAM: And then comes and yawns in our faces.

MANNOURY: Tonight—

ADAM: Tonight he'll spend in some great house. D'Armagnac's, De Cerisay's. Fed, comforted and flattered by the laughter of women.

MANNOURY: What a—I'm so sorry. What were you going to say?

ADAM: I was going to say, What a life!

MANNOURY: So was I.

ADAM: We're never asked to such places.

MANNOURY: I've thought of it often.

ADAM: How do you console yourself?

MANNOURY: By remembering that I'm an honest man doing an honest job.

ADAM: Is that enough?

MANNOURY: What do you mean?

ADAM: Pick up the head and come with me.

They go along the street and into a house.

GRANDIER *enters the church. He kneels at the altar: prays.*

GRANDIER: O my dear Father, it is the wish of Your humble child to come to Your Grace. I speak in the weariness of thirty-five years. Years heavy with pride and ambition, love of women and love of self. Years scandalously marred by adornment and luxury, time taken up with being that nothing, a man.

I prostrate myself before You now in ravaged humility of spirit. I ask You to look upon me with love. I beg that You will answer my prayer. Show me a way. Or let a way be made.

Silence.

O God, O my God, my God! Release me. Free me. These needs! Have mercy. Free me. Four o'clock of a Tuesday afternoon. Free me.

He rises: cries out.

Rex tremendae majestatis, qui salvandos salvas gratis, salva me, salva me, fons pietatis!

DE LA ROCHEPOZAY, *Bishop of Poitiers: Capuchins and Carmelites.*

DE LA ROCHEPOZAY: I have been alone for many days now. You will want to know if I have found some kind of grace. Perhaps, for I am filled with weariness and disgust at the folly and wickedness of mankind. Is this the beneficence of God, you ask? It may well be. Let me tell you the circumstances of the revelation.

Shut in my room for seven days, fasting and at prayer, I came to see myself as the humble instrument of God's will. It was a state of such happiness, such bliss and such abasement that I wished never to return to you. I longed for this husk to wither away, leaving only the purity of spirit. But my sense of duty as your bishop forced me to leave this paradise. I came back to the world.

A priest of Loudun, called Grandier, wished to see me. He is my child, as you all are, my darling, and I would wish to love him. But his handkerchief was scented.

If this man had struck me in the face it would have humiliated me less. The assault on my senses was so obscene that I was in a state of terror. Scent, for a man to whom the taste of water was like fire, and the sound of the birds in the garden like the screams of the damned.

I am very tired. Take these rings from my fingers.

Perhaps on your way here from your parish a child smiled at you, or you were attracted by a flower, or the smell of new grass by the road. Did you think of these things with anything but pleasure? One of you may have lost your way and been directed by a stranger. Did you think of it as anything but kindness?

Let me say this to you. There is no innocence, none! Suspect goodness in men, and reject kindness.

For all vanities are an assertion of self, and the assertion of self in Man is the ascendancy of the Devil.

When that handkerchief was flourished in my face this morning I saw it as if in a vision. It became a mighty banner flung across the world, stinking, enveloping, overwhelming our beloved Church in shamelessness and lust. We are in peril!

Take me away. Take me away.

DE LA ROCHEPOZAY *is led away.* FATHER BARRÉ *and* FATHER RANGIER *are left alone.*

RANGIER: How are things in your part of the world?

BARRÉ: I'm kept very busy.

RANGIER: Is he among you?

BARRÉ: Incessantly.

RANGIER: Can we name him?

BARRÉ: If you want to. Satan.

RANGIER: How is the struggle?

BARRÉ: I shan't give up.

RANGIER: You look tired.

BARRÉ: It goes on day and night.

RANGIER: Your spirit is shining.

BARRÉ: Unbroken, at any rate. But there's never a moment's peace at Chinon now. Only the other day I was conducting a marriage. Everything was going very well. I had before me a young couple, ignorant, I thought, but pure. It never entered my head that they were anything else. I'd reached the blessing, and was about to send them out to the world as man and wife, when there was a disturbance at the west door. A cow had come into the church, and was trying to force its way through the congregation. I knew at once, of course.

RANGIER: That it was he?

BARRÉ: Say it, Rangier, say it. (*He shouts.*) It was Satan!

RANGIER: You're never taken in.

BARRÉ: Before I could act he had passed from the cow to the bride's mother, who fell to the ground in a kind of convulsion. There was the most dreadful confusion, of course, but I began exorcism at once. There's a couple that won't forget their wedding day in a hurry.

RANGIER: How did it end?

BARRÉ: The spirit screamed from the church like a great wind. A kind of black slime was found smeared on the girl's forehead. She said she'd fallen, but of course I know better. That's not all. Two days later the husband came to me and said he'd found himself quite unable to perform his necessary duty. The usual kind of spell, you know. I've now started investigations into the whole family.

RANGIER: This sort of thing must bring a lot of people to Chinon.

BARRÉ: Thousands.

RANGIER: There's great popular interest in evil nowadays.

BARRÉ: It's certainly helped to offset the sadly declining attendance at my shrine. The image of Notre-Dame de Recouvrance.

RANGIER: Well, you know how that's come about.

BARRÉ: Certainly. They all flock to Loudun now. This Grandier person, who's upset the bishop, is responsible for that. He touts for his place disgracefully.

RANGIER: There are fashions in miracle-working images, just as there are in women's hats.

BARRÉ: That's true. But there's a satisfying constancy in evil. I must go.

RANGIER: Anything interesting?

BARRÉ: I have to call at a farm. They say that something is speaking through the umbilicus of a child. The child herself is now in conversation with it, and I'm told the two voices have evolved a quite astonishing creed of profanation.

BARRÉ *and* RANGIER *go separate ways.*

GRANDIER *alone. He has a sheaf of poems in his hand.* TRINCANT *comes to him.*

TRINCANT: So good of you to call, Father Grandier.

GRANDIER: Not at all. I've brought back your poetry.

TRINCANT: So I see. D'Armagnac holds that any insufficiency must be put down to life in the provinces.

GRANDIER: You write them when you get back from the office.

TRINCANT: Every day.

GRANDIER: Amid the cooking smells.

TRINCANT: They drift up.

GRANDIER: And the clatter of family life.

TRINCANT: It intrudes.

GRANDIER: And so naturally you achieve—these.

TRINCANT: Put me out of my misery. I want an honest opinion.

GRANDIER: You're an important man in this town, Trincant. Men in public positions can't expect honesty.

TRINCANT: Speak to me as a poet, not as Public Prosecutor.

GRANDIER: Very well. Your poetry—

PHILLIPE TRINCANT *has come in.*

TRINCANT: What is it?

PHILLIPE: I want my sewing, Father.

TRINCANT: Please take it. (*To* GRANDIER.) This is my elder daughter, Phillipe. What were you saying?

GRANDIER: I was about to say that your creations—these—have great merit. They seem to be moral observations of a most uncommon kind.

TRINCANT: Really?

GRANDIER (*to* PHILLIPE): Don't you think so? I'm speaking of your father's poetry.

TRINCANT: She's very ignorant about such things. Young girls, you know, dear me. Dancing, music and laughter. Finer things can go hang.

GRANDIER: She should be instructed.

TRINCANT: It's so difficult to find anyone suitable in this town. Unless—

GRANDIER (*to* PHILLIPE): Do you speak any Latin?

PHILLIPE: A little.

GRANDIER: That's not enough.

TRINCANT: Unless—

GRANDIER: It's an exact language. Makes it possible to say just what you mean. That's rare nowadays. Don't you agree?

PHILLIPE: Yes, it is.

TRINCANT: Unless you, Father Grandier, would undertake the instruction.

GRANDIER: Of your daughter?

TRINCANT: Yes.

GRANDIER: I'm a busy man.

TRINCANT: Just one day a week. A few hours in the appreciation of finer things. It could be done by conversation. Perhaps the reading of suitable Latin verse.

GRANDIER: Very well.

TRINCANT: Shall we say Tuesday?

GRANDIER: No. Not Tuesday. The next day.

ADAM *and* MANNOURY: *they sit in the pharmacy, beneath a stuffed crocodile and hanging bladders. Light is reflected through bottles which hold malformed creatures.*

ADAM (*he is reading from a small book*): At half-past five on Tuesday he left the widow's house.

MANNOURY: The man is a machine. Interesting, though. Can sexual response be conditioned by the clock?

ADAM: At half-past seven he was observed in public conversation with D'Armagnac. The subject is in doubt, although Grandier was seen to snigger twice. He dined alone, later than usual, at nine o'clock. A light burned in his room until after midnight.

MANNOURY: I suppose it's possible. I say to a woman: At four-thirty on Tuesday I shall arrive to pleasure you. I do so on the dot for some weeks. It no longer becomes necessary to say that I shall do so. Anticipation speaks for me. Tuesday: half-past four. Usual physiological manifestations. Subject for treatise. Must think.

ADAM (*he turns a page*): Discovered at dawn prostrate before altar. Great languor through the morning. A meal at a quarter past two. Sweetbreads in cream, followed by a rank cheese. Wine. Three o'clock: entered Trincant's house for instruction of Trincant's daughter, Phillipe.

MANNOURY: Adam, you're a wit.

ADAM: Am I, now?

MANNOURY: Your inflexion on the word 'instruction' was masterly.

ADAM: Thank you.

MANNOURY: But forgive me, my dear friend, if I ask you something. How do we go on? Your observations of Grandier's movements are a marvel. But these are the habits of any man. We shall never catch him on such evidence.

ADAM: You must give me time, Mannoury. We shall never expose him on his habits, certainly. But lust is leading him by the nose. And lust must have a partner. The widow, Ninon? Phillipe Trincant? Another? Who knows? But there will be a time. Patience.

SISTER JEANNE DES ANGES *alone: kneeling.*

JEANNE: I dedicate myself humbly to Your service. You have made me, both in stature and in spirit, a little woman. And I have a small imagination, too. That is why, in Your infinite wisdom, You have given me this visible burden on my back to remind me day by day of what I must carry. O my dear Lord, I find it difficult to turn in my bed, and so in the small and desperate hours I am reminded of Your burden, the Cross, on the long road.

You have brought meaning to my life by my appointment to this Ursuline house. I will try to guide the Sisters of this place. I will do my duty as I see it. (*Silence.*) Lord . . . Lord, I have had great difficulty with prayer ever since I was a little girl. I have longed for another and greater voice within me to praise you. By Your grace I have come young to this office. Have mercy on Your child. Let her aspire. Meanwhile, the floors shall be swept, the beds neatly made, and the pots kept clean.

(*Silence.*) Mercy. (*Silence.*) I will find a way. Yes, I will find a way to You. I shall come. You will enfold me in Your sacred arms. The blood will flow between us, uniting us. My innocence is Yours.

(*Silence: precisely.*) Please God, take away my hump so that I can lie on my back without lolling my head. (*Silence.*) There is a way to be found. May the light of Your eternal love . . . (*whispers.*)

Amen

SISTER JEANNE *rises: goes.*

GRANDIER *and* PHILLIPE: *she is reading.*

PHILLIPE: Foeda est in coitu et brevis voluptas, et taedet
       Veneris statis peractae.
GRANDIER: Translate as you go. Line by line.
PHILLIPE: Pleasure in love is . . .
GRANDIER: Lust.
PHILLIPE: Pleasure in lust is nasty and short, And sickness . . .
GRANDIER: Weariness.
PHILLIPE: And weariness follows on desire.
GRANDIER: Go on.
PHILLIPE: non ergo ut pecudes libidinosae caeci protinus irruamus
       illuc (nam languescit amor peritque flamma); (*pause.*)
       We're not like animals to rush at it,
       Love dies there, and the flame goes out.
GRANDIER: Prosaic, but fair. Give me the book. (*He translates.*)
       But in everlasting leisure,
       Like this, like this, lie still
       And kiss time away.
       No weariness and no shame,
       Now, then and shall be all pleasure.
       No end to it,
       But an eternal beginning.
  My child, why are you crying?
PHILLIPE: I haven't been well.
GRANDIER: Do you find our little lessons too much for you?

PHILLIPE: No, no, I love—I enjoy them very much.

GRANDIER: Well, we've only had six. I thought they might go on
say to the end of the year.

PHILLIPE: Of course. As long as you like.

GRANDIER: As long as *you* like, Phillipe. They're for your benefit.

PHILLIPE: I want very much to understand. All things.

GRANDIER: All things?

PHILLIPE: There are forces inside me as a woman which must be
understood if they are to be resisted.

GRANDIER: What forces, Phillipe?

PHILLIPE: Inclinations—

GRANDIER: Go on.

PHILLIPE: Inclinations towards sin.

   Silence.

D'ARMAGNAC *stands at a high point on the fortifications of the town.*
A Council of State. Distant figures: LOUIS XIII, *King of France, and*
RICHELIEU.

RICHELIEU: It is a simple matter to understand, sir. You have that
paper upside down. The self-government of the small provincial
towns of France must be brought to an end. The first step is to
pull down all kinds of fortification.

   GRANDIER *has approached* D'ARMAGNAC *from below.*

D'ARMAGNAC: So it's the turn of this city.

GRANDIER: Is everything to come down?

D'ARMAGNAC: That's what they want. It's a trick, of course.
Richelieu sits with the King in Paris. He whispers in his ear.

RICHELIEU: France must be free within herself is she is to deter-
mine her own destiny.

D'ARMAGNAC: Ignorant and crafty provincials like us cannot see
beyond the city walls. So we have this order from the Cardinal to
tear them down. Will it broaden our view?

RICHELIEU: Such men as your friend D'Armagnac, sir, see with
little vision. Their loyalty is to their town, not to France.

GRANDIER: Have they given any reason for this order?

D'ARMAGNAC: When a man's intent on power, as Richelieu is, he
can justify his actions with absurdities.

RICHELIEU: Such fortifications provide opportunities for an uprising by the Protestants.

D'ARMAGNAC: Look. An old city. Those walls keep out more than the draught. Those towers are more than ornament. And from that fortress I have tried to administer my small sovereignty with reasonable wisdom. For I love the place.

GRANDIER: You must refuse to destroy it. Will other provincial governors stand against the order?

D'ARMAGNAC: It's very doubtful.

GRANDIER: Shall we?

D'ARMAGNAC: We?

GRANDIER: Let me help you in this matter, sir.

D'ARMAGNAC: Do you mean it? There is a churchman beside the King in Paris. As another, beside me here, do you also want to use this matter for your own ends?

GRANDIER: Conflict attracts me, sir. Resistance compels me.

D'ARMAGNAC: They can destroy you.

GRANDIER: I am weak, it's true. But equal power cannot be conflict. It is negation. Peace. So let me help you with all the passion of my failure.

D'ARMAGNAC: Don't smile. They can destroy you.

DE LAUBARDEMONT, *the King's Commissioner, has come to stand below* RICHELIEU *and the* KING. RICHELIEU *speaks to him.*

RICHELIEU: D'Armagnac, the Governor of Loudun, has refused to obey the order. Go to the town. You've served me before. Wait. There is a man. His name is Grandier. He is a priest. Yes, there is a man called Grandier. Remember that.

DE LAUBARDEMONT *goes.*

An unseen woman's voice:

> Lux aeterna luceat eis, Domine, cum sanctis tuis in aeternum, quia pius est.
> Requiem aeternam dona eis, Domine, et lux perpetua luceat eis.

SISTER JEANNE DES ANGES: SISTER CLAIRE OF ST JOHN: SISTER LOUISE OF JESUS: SISTER GABRIELLE OF THE INCARNATION: *they enter.*

JEANNE: We have suffered a great loss, Sisters. Canon Moussaut was a good old man.

CLAIRE: It is God's will.

LOUISE: God's will.

JEANNE: So we have been taught. All the same, his death leaves us with a problem. We lack a director. The old man served this place well for many years, it's true, but the life of sinful children must go on. Penitents, we must have a confessor.

LOUISE: Have you chosen, Mother?

JEANNE: God will choose.

CLAIRE: We will pray.

JEANNE: Do so. There is a—(*fit of coughing*) Don't touch my back! (*stillness: exhaustion.*) There is a man. His name is Grandier. He is young. I have never seen him, but God has often put him in my thoughts lately. I mean to . . . (*Silence.*)

CLAIRE: What's the matter?

JEANNE: Claire?

CLAIRE: Why stare at me like that? Have I done something wrong?

JEANNE (*seeing the girl*): No, no. I mean to write to this good man and invite him to be our new director. Grandier. Grandier. It is guidance, you understand. He has been put in my thoughts. Grandier.

CLAIRE: It is God's will.

LOUISE: God's will.

JEANNE (*sudden harsh laughter*): I am tired to death. (*Silence: calmly.*) It is a very excellent and practical solution. He can advise us on the method of education for the children put in our care. He will oversee our spiritual needs. (*Laughter again.*) He can sort out these damned problems of theological progression which muddle me day after day. Yes, it will be a good appointment. Leave me alone.

The Sisters go: JEANNE *calls back* CLAIRE.

JEANNE: Claire!

CLAIRE: Yes?

JEANNE: They say I have beautiful eyes. Is it true?

CLAIRE: Yes, Mother.

JEANNE: Too beautiful to close even in sleep, it seems. Go with the others.

JEANNE *alone.*

JEANNE: A summer morning. Children playing. Boy and girl. Paper boats sail the pond. Sun shone so hot upon the head that day. Children crouched, staring at each other across the sheet of water. Was it love? Flick. A toad upon a slab. Croak. Boy, head to one side, smiling, gentle voice whispering over the water: Look. Speak to your brother, Jeanne. There. Green brother. Hophop. Speak to him, Jeanne. (*Laughter: silence.*) God, forgive my laughter. But you haven't given me much defence, have You?

JEANNE *goes to a window and opens it. She stares down through the grille upon:*

A street. There is a market stall. People of the town are coming and going, buying and selling. Children. A cart passes. A song is heard.
GRANDIER *comes through the crowd. He is in full canonicals, magnificent, golden, in the dying light of day. His tread is quick, confident and gay.*
JEANNE *cries out.*
The sound is not heard by the crowd, but GRANDIER *stops. He looks around him, into the faces of the crowd, wondering which man or woman could have been moved to such a cry of agony in the middle of such careless activity.*
GRANDIER *goes on by way of ascending steps.*
JEANNE *is writing. Rapid, angular hand, ornamented.*

The street. ADAM *and* MANNOURY *are among the crowd. They come forward.*
MANNOURY: The first thing to do is to draw up some kind of document.
ADAM: An accusation against Grandier.
MANNOURY: Exactly. We know about his debauchery.
ADAM: Profanity.
MANNOURY: And impiety.
ADAM: Is it enough?
MANNOURY: It'll have to do.
ADAM: For the time being.
MANNOURY: We'll present the paper to the Bishop.
ADAM: It must be properly done.

MANNOURY: Of course. Framed in correct language, decent to handle—

ADAM: Something's just occurred to me.

MANNOURY: Oh?

ADAM: What a lot of criticism we middle classes come in for just because we like things nice. I'm sorry. Go on. What will the document say?

MANNOURY: Say? (*Pause.*) We shall have to decide.

ADAM: It's not important.

MANNOURY: No. Just the means.

ADAM: We must keep the end in sight.

MANNOURY: Always.

> *They go.*

A confessional: GRANDIER *and* PHILLIPE. *They speak in whisper. throughout.*

GRANDIER: When was your last confession, child?

PHILLIPE: A week ago, Father.

GRANDIER: What have you to tell me?

PHILLIPE: Father, I have sinned. I have suffered from pride.

GRANDIER: We must always be on guard.

PHILLIPE: I finished some needlework yesterday, and I was pleased with myself.

GRANDIER: God allows us satisfaction in the work we do.

PHILLIPE: I have been in error through anger.

GRANDIER: Tell me.

PHILLIPE: My sister teased me. I wished her—elsewhere.

GRANDIER: You're absolved. Anything else? (*Silence.*) Come now others are waiting.

PHILLIPE: I've had unclean thoughts.

GRANDIER: Of what nature?

PHILLIPE: About a man.

GRANDIER: My child—

PHILLIPE: In the early hours of the morning . . . my bedroom is suffocatingly hot . . . I've asked them to take away the velvet curtains . . . my thoughts fester . . . and yet they are so tender . . my body . . . Father . . . my body . . . I wish to be touched.

GRANDIER: Have you tried to suppress these thoughts?

PHILLIPE: Yes.

GRANDIER: Are they an indulgence?

PHILLIPE: No. I have prayed.

GRANDIER: Do you wish to be saved from this? (*Silence.*) Answer, child.

PHILLIPE: No! I want him to take—no, possess—no, destroy me. I love you. Him. I love him!

GRANDIER *comes out from the box: compassion. After a moment he draws aside the curtain and* PHILLIPE *is seen. They stand facing each other.*

DE LA ROCHEPOZAY. ADAM *and* MANNOURY *humbly before him.*

DE LA ROCHEPOZAY: I have considered this document you have presented against the priest, Grandier. He is known to us as an impious and dangerous man. A few months ago we ourselves suffered insult and humiliation by his presence. But this is neither here nor there. What is your complaint?

MANNOURY: We feel, my lord bishop, that Grandier should be forbidden to exercise the sacerdotal function.

DE LA ROCHEPOZAY: What is your profession?

MANNOURY: I'm a surgeon.

DE LA ROCHEPOZAE: Would it amuse you if I came and instructed you in your business?

MANNOURY: I'm always prepared to take advice.

DE LA ROCHEPOZAY: Don't talk like a fool. This grubby and ill-composed document tells us nothing we did not know about the man. Vague and yet somewhat hysterical accusations concerning lonely widows and amorous virgins are all that I can find here. I'm not prepared to conduct the affairs of this diocese on the level of a police court.

ADAM: He has powerful friends.

DE LA ROCHEPOZAY: Stop whispering. What did you say?

ADAM: Grandier is protected by his friends.

DE LA ROCHEPOZAY: What are their names?

MANNOURY (*to* ADAM: *a nudge*): Go on.

ADAM: D'Armagnac. De Cerisay. Others.

DE LA ROCHEPOZAY: I'll accept your reasonable intentions in coming here. Although, God knows, if there's anyone I distrust it's the good citizen going about his civic duty. His motive is usually hate or money. But I will not accept your opinions, your advice, nor, for a moment longer, your presence.

ADAM *and* MANNOURY *go.*

DE LA ROCHEPOZAY (*to his attendant*): It is vital that the Church should be protected from the democratic principle that every man must have his say. Those two probably spoke the truth, but they must not be allowed to think that they influence our judgement in any way.

JEANNE *alone: a book of devotions. Night.* CLAIRE *comes to her.*

CLAIRE: This was just delivered at the gate.

JEANNE *takes a letter from* CLAIRE, *breaks it open, and reads.*

JEANNE: He has refused.

CLAIRE: Father Grandier?

JEANNE (*she reads aloud*): My dear Sister: It is with great regret that I must refuse your invitation to become Director of your House. The pressing duties I have in the town would not allow me the time to devote my energies to the advantage of your Sisterhood. I very much appreciate all you say of my qualities and . . .

JEANNE *tears the letter across and presses it to her body.*

JEANNE: Thank you, Sister.

CLAIRE *goes.*

JEANNE *alone.*

JEANNE: What is this divine mystery? Let me see. Let me see. (*Laughter.*) I was about to address myself to God in this matter. Habit. Habit. It would never do. No. It must be to Man.

She whispers the name: Grandier.

You wake up. Dawn has broken over others before you. Look at the little grey window. Then turn. She lies beside you. The attitude is of prayer or the womb. Her mouth tastes of wine and the sea. Her skin is smooth and silky, rank with sweat. The native odours of her body have exhausted in the night the scents of day.

PHILLIPE, *naked, is seen making love with* GRANDIER. *They will continue to be seen in the touching formal attitudes of passion throughout* JEANNE'S *words.*

JEANNE: Look down at her. What do you feel? Sadness? It must be sadness. You are a man. Ah, now she stretches her arms above her head. Are you not moved? This is not the sophistry of a whore, whatever you may pretend. She shifts her legs, entwines them, lays a finger on your lips and her mouth upon her finger. She whispers. Those words were taught. She only repeats the lesson. Such filth is love to her, and the speaking of it is an act of faith. (*Sudden laughter.*) What was that you did? Stretching out to clutch the falling bed-clothes. Was it to cover your nakedness? Is there modesty here?

(*Silence: in wonder.*) How strange. Can you laugh, too? That's something I didn't know. Pain, oblivion, unreason, mania. These I thought would be in your bed. But laughter . . .

How young you both look. Quiet again.

The girl is heavy in your arms. She yawned, and you have taken up the shudder of her body. You tremble, in spite of yourself. Look, the sun is breaking up the mists in the fields. You're going to be engulfed by day. Take what you can. Let both take what they can. Now.

Now.

(*She weeps.*) This frenzy, this ripping apart, this meat on a butcher's slab. Where are you? Love? Love? What are you? Now. Now. Now.

JEANNE *falls on her knees, convulsed.* GRANDIER *and* PHILLIPE *can no longer be seen.*

JEANNE (*suffocated, young voice*): O my God, is that it? Is that it? *Darkness.*

D'ARMAGNAC: DE CERISAY: DE LAUBARDEMONT.

DE LAUBARDEMONT: It's not a question of compromise. I'm here as His Majesty's Special Commissioner, but I have no power to negotiate. I'm sorry, D'Armagnac.

D'ARMAGNAC: You know, Laubardemont, grown men in this country are getting a little tired of the father figures which keep arising, so we are told, for our own good. France may very well be looked on as a woman, and submissive, but she's not a baby.

DE LAUBARDEMONT: I'm inclined to agree with you. But I'm not here for argument. I simply brought a message.

D'ARMAGNAC: An order. Pull down the fortifications.

DE LAUBARDEMONT: That was the message. What answer may I take back?

D'ARMAGNAC: That I refuse.

DE LAUBARDEMONT: I have a curious feeling.

D'ARMAGNAC: Fear?

DE LAUBARDEMONT: No, no. Just that you've been influenced in this decision. And that there is pressure behind your obduracy.

D'ARMAGNAC: The decision is entirely mine. As governor of the town.

GRANDIER *approaches.*

D'ARMAGNAC: Do you know Father Grandier?

DE LAUBARDEMONT: I've heard of him.

D'ARMAGNAC: Well, this is he.

DE LAUBARDEMONT (*turning*): Ah, Father. Can't you bring your influence to bear on the Governor in this matter of the demolition. As a man of peace I'm sure you want it brought about.

GRANDIER: As a man of peace, I do. As a man of principle, I'd prefer the city walls to remain standing.

DE LAUBARDEMONT: I see. Well, I seem to be alone in this. If you change your mind, and I earnestly hope you will, I shall be in Loudun for a few days.

DE LAUBARDEMONT *goes.*

D'ARMAGNAC: Look at him, Grandier.

GRANDIER: A funny little man.

D'ARMAGNAC: My dear fellow, we are all romantic. We see our lives being changed by a winged messenger on a black horse. But more often than not it turns out to be a shabby little man, who stumbles across our path.

A cloister. JEANNE *and* FATHER MIGNON, *a foolish old man, walking together.*

JEANNE: We are all of us so happy, Father Mignon, that you've been able to accept. We shall look forward to having you as our director for many years to come.

MIGNON: You're very kind, my child. You have a direct simplicity which an old man like myself finds very touching.

JEANNE: There are many problems in a place like this. I shall need your advice and guidance.

MIGNON: Always at your disposal.

JEANNE: For example, nearly all the Sisters here are young women. I think you'll agree that youth is more exposed to temptation than age.

MIGNON: That's so. I remember when I was a young man—

JEANNE: I have myself—

MIGNON: What's that?

JEANNE: I was about to say that I have myself recently suffered from visions of a diabolical nature.

MIGNON: In living close to God one becomes a natural prey to the Devil. I shouldn't worry about them too much.

JEANNE: I can speak about this in the daytime. But at night—

MIGNON: It is a well-known fact, my dear, that the spirit is at its weakest in the small hours.

JEANNE: Yes. I managed to resist the vision. Several hours of prayer and I was myself again. But the visitation—

MIGNON: Visitation?

JEANNE: The dead Canon Moussaut, your predecessor, came to me in the night. He stood at the foot of my bed.

MIGNON: But this was a visit of love, my child. Moussaut was a good man. You were fond of him. Did he speak to you?

JEANNE: Yes.

MIGNON: What did he say?

JEANNE: Filth.

MIGNON: What's that?

JEANNE: He spoke filth. Dirt. Jeering, contemptuous, hurtful obscenity.

MIGNON: My beloved Sister—

JEANNE: He was not in his own person.

MIGNON: What do you mean?

JEANNE: He came to me as another. A different man.

MIGNON: Did you recognize this man?

JEANNE: Yes.

MIGNON: Who was it?

JEANNE: Grandier. Father Grandier.
Silence.
MIGNON: My dear, do you understand the seriousness of what you're saying?
JEANNE (*calmly*): Yes. Help me, Father.

GRANDIER: *in the pulpit.*
GRANDIER: . . . For some lewd fellows go about the town and speak against me. I know them. And you will know them when I say that Surgery and Chemistry go hand in hand, vermination against the wall. They have borne false witness. They spy. They sneak. They snigger. And the first sinful man was called Adam, and he begot murder. Why do they pursue me? I am not sick!

If they be here, in this holy place, let them stand before me and declare their hatred, and give the reason for it. I am not afraid to speak openly of what they attempt to discover secretly. If they be in this church let them stand before me. (*Silence.*) No, they are in some hole in the ground, scratching, so that more venom may come to the surface, and infect us all; distilling bile in retorts; revealing lust, envy and blight with the turn of a scalpel.

During this DE LAUBARDEMONT, *with two attendants, has approached, listened and moved on.*

O my dear children, I should not speak to you so from this place. And I should not speak to you in bitterness as your pastor.

Do they provoke me to anger? saith the Lord: do they not provoke themselves to the confusion of their own faces?

The pharmacy: ADAM *and* MANNOURY.
ADAM: It's after ten o'clock. Would you believe it?
MANNOURY: Well, we have had a nice talk.
ADAM: Have we got anywhere?
MANNOURY: Somebody at the door.
ADAM: Can't be.
MANNOURY: Is.

ADAM *opens the door.* DE LAUBARDEMONT *stands there.*

ADAM: No business. Shut.

DE LAUBARDEMONT: My name is Jean de Martin, Baron de Laubardemont. I am His Majesty's Special Commissioner to Loudun.

ADAM: Can I help you?

DE LAUBARDEMONT: I hope so.

DE LAUBARDEMONT *comes into the shop.*

DE LAUBARDEMONT: I am visiting the town for a kind of investigation.

MANNOURY (*carefully*): We are both honest men.

DE LAUBARDEMONT: I know. That's why I'm here. I've always found in cases like this that there are perhaps two incorruptible men in the town. Usually close friends, professional men, middle class, backbone of the nation. Deep civic interest. Patriotic. Lost sons in a war. Happily married. Managing to make ends meet in spite of taxation. Austere lives, but what they have they like to be nice. Gentlemen, am I right?

ADAM: Quite correct.

DE LAUBARDEMONT: Good. I want you to tell me all you know about a man called Grandier. Father Grandier, of Saint Peter's Church.

ADAM: My dear Mannoury, at last!

GRANDIER *and* PHILLIPE: *a secluded place.*

PHILLIPE: I must go home now.

GRANDIER: Yes.

PHILLIPE: I don't like walking through the streets at night. Dogs bark. Listen, they're at it now.

GRANDIER: I wish I could come with you. I would like—oh, words, words!

PHILLIPE: What is it?

GRANDIER: Come here. Gently. I want to tell you—

PHILLIPE: Yes?

GRANDIER: You know the love-making—

PHILLIPE: Yes.

GRANDIER: I want to tell you, Phillipe. Among the clothes dropped on the floor, the soiled linen, the instruction, the apparatus, the surgery—among all this there is a kind of passion of the heart.

PHILLIPE: I know. It is love. Human love.

Silence.

GRANDIER: You understand it that way?

PHILLIPE: I think so.

GRANDIER: Do I love you?

PHILLIPE: I believe so.

GRANDIER: Then what comfort can I give you?

Silence.

PHILLIPE: I am a simple person. I see the world and myself as I have been taught. I am deeply sinful, but my love of God has not deserted me. It is said by Man that those in our state should stand before God. I believe this to be right. And I would not be afraid to declare myself to Him with you beside me, even in our transgression, for I believe Him to be good, wise and always merciful.

Silence.

GRANDIER: You shame me.

The pharmacy. DE LAUBARDEMONT: MANNOURY: ADAM. *They have been joined by* FATHER MIGNON.

MIGNON: I couldn't get any more out of the prioress. I can prove nothing. She may be just an hysterical woman.

ADAM: Does it matter?

MIGNON: I'd very much like you, as a surgeon, Mannoury, and you, Adam, as a chemist, to be there.

DE LAUBARDEMONT: May I attend as a disinterested party?

MIGNON: Certainly. If this is a genuine case, the more the—(*he stops.*)

DE LAUBARDEMONT: Were you going to say merrier?

MIGNON: I've sent a message to Father Barré, at Chinon. He's our great local expert in these matters.

MANNOURY: I shall be only too happy to give you any medical advice, Father.

ADAM: And I'll comment on any chemical or biological manifestations.

MIGNON: She already complains of a spasmodic but acute swelling of the belly.

ADAM: Fascinating!

MANNOURY: Not unusual. Sense of false pregnancy. Known it before. Nothing to do with the Devil. Wind?

DE LAUBARDEMONT: Conjecture is useless. It'll soon be morning.

Dawn. JEANNE *at prayer beside her simple bed.*

JEANNE: Please God, make me a good girl. Take care of my dear father and mother and look after my dog, Captain, who loved me and didn't understand why I had to leave him behind all that time ago. Lord . . . Lord, I would like to make formal prayers to You, but I can only do that out of a book in the chapel. (*Silence.*) Love me. (*Silence.*) Love me. Amen.

JEANNE *gets up and goes from the room to a great open space where stand:*

DE LAUBARDEMONT: MANNOURY: ADAM: MIGNON: RANGIER *and* BARRÉ. JEANNE *approaches them.*

BARRÉ: Let me deal with this. Good morning, Sister. Are you well?

JEANNE: I'm very well, thank you, Father.

BARRÉ: Excellent. Will you kneel down?

JEANNE *does so.* BARRÉ *goes to her.*

BARRÉ (*sudden shout*): Are you there! Are you there! (*Silence: to the others.*) They never answer at once. Afraid of committing themselves. (*To* JEANNE.) Come now, declare yourself! In the name of Our Lord Jesus Christ—

Suddenly JEANNE *throws back her crooked head and peals of masculine laughter pour from her open, distorted mouth.*

BARRÉ (*with satisfaction: to the others*): Always does the trick.

JEANNE (*deep man's voice*): Here we are, and here we stay.

BARRÉ: One question.

JEANNE: Pooh!

BARRÉ: Don't be impudent. One question. How did you gain entry to this poor women?

JEANNE (*deep voice*): Good offices of a friend.

BARRÉ: His name?

JEANNE: Asmodeus.

BARRÉ: That's your name. What is the name of your friend?

JEANNE *is swaying on her knees. She gives inarticulate cries which gradually form themselves into the word:*
JEANNE: Grandier! Grandier! Grandier!
Deep, sullen laughter.

CURTAIN

ACT TWO

Saint Peter's Church. Night.
GRANDIER *is at the altar.* PHILLIPE *kneels below him.*
GRANDIER *holds up a salver. Speaks:*

GRANDIER: Benedic, ✠ Domine, hunc annulum, quem nos in tuo
nomine benedicimus, ✠ ut quae eum gestaverit, fidelitatem inte-
gram suo sponso tenens, in pace et voluntate tua permaneat, atque
in mutua caritate semper vivat Per Christum Dominum nostrum.
PHILLIPE: Amen.
    GRANDIER *sprinkles the ring with holy water, and then, taking the
ring from the salver, comes down to kneel beside* PHILLIPE.
GRANDIER: With this ring I thee wed: this gold and silver I thee
give; with my body I thee worship; and with all my worldly goods
I thee endow.
    GRANDIER *places the ring on the thumb of Phillipe's hand, saying:*
GRANDIER: In the name of the Father: (*then on the second finger, saying*)
And of the Son: (*then on the third finger, saying*) And of the Holy
Ghost: (*lastly on the fourth finger, saying*) Amen.
    And there he leaves the ring.
    GRANDIER *mounts the altar steps.*
GRANDIER: Confirma hoc, Deus, quod operatus es in nobis.
PHILLIPE: A templo sancto tuo, quod est in Jerusalem.
GRANDIER: Kyrie eleison.
PHILLIPE: Christe eleison.
GRANDIER: Kyrie eleison.
    They speak together:
Pater noster—
—*and their voices whisper into silence.*

A street.
    THE SEWERMAN *is sitting at ease. He holds a cage with a bird in it.*
    GRANDIER *and* PHILLIPE *come from the church.*
171

PHILLIPE: We should step out into the sunlight. Bells should tell the world about us. It shouldn't be night. And as quiet as this. Dear God, my husband, kiss me.

They kiss. THE SEWERMAN *speaks:*

SEWERMAN: So it's done. I saw you go into the church.

GRANDIER: It's done. And well done. Does the bird sing?

SEWERMAN: Not its purpose. Tongueless.

GRANDIER: Do you carry it for love?

SEWERMAN: An idea which would only occur to a good man. Or one careless with hope. No, I carry the thing so that it may die, and I live. He's my saviour. Who's yours?

GRANDIER: You—

SEWERMAN: Blaspheme?

GRANDIER: Yes.

SEWERMAN: Sorry. You know the pits at the edge of the town? Where even your beloved here sends in my buckets. Well, there are days when the place gives off poison. So I always approach it with this creature on a pole before me. His many predecessors have died in the miasma. When this happens I know it's no place for me. So I let the drains run foul for a day or two, and I spend my time catching another victim to shut up here. You'll understand what I mean.

Silence.

GRANDIER: I have put my trust in this child. She is not a victim.

SEWERMAN: Just as you say.

GRANDIER: Come now, even at this hopeless hour you must admit more passes between human beings than the actions which provide you and the laundry with a job.

SEWERMAN: I'm not arguing.

GRANDIER: There is a way of salvation through each other.

SEWERMAN: Are you trying to convince me?

GRANDIER: I'd like to.

SEWERMAN: What about yourself? Has the little ceremony in there done the trick?

GRANDIER: It has given me hope.

SEWERMAN: Hope of what?

GRANDIER: Hope of coming to God by way of a fellow being. Hope that the path, which taken alone, in awful solitude, is a way of despair, can be enlightened by the love of a woman. I have come to believe that by this simple act of committal, which I have done with my heart, it may be possible to reach God by way of happiness.

SEWERMAN: What was that last word?

GRANDIER: Happiness.

SEWERMAN: I don't know what it means. You must have made it up for the occasion. It's getting light.

PHILLIPE: I must go.

SEWERMAN: Yes. They mustn't find the bed empty. On the other hand, they mustn't find it too full.

PHILLIPE (*to* GRANDIER): Speak to me.

SEWERMAN: Say it.

GRANDIER: I love you, Phillipe.

PHILLIPE *goes.*

SEWERMAN: Speaking of love, some very odd things are going on up at the convent.

GRANDIER: So I'm told.

SEWERMAN: It seems your name is being bandied about by the crazy ladies.

GRANDIER: We must pity them.

SEWERMAN: Will they pity you, that's the point?

GRANDIER: What do you mean? They're deluded.

SEWERMAN: What were you, a few minutes ago, with that girl?

GRANDIER: I was in my right mind, and I knew what I was doing. You may mock me, my son, if you wish. What seems to you a meaningless act, the marriage of an unmarriageable priest, has meaning for me. The lonely and the proud sometimes need to avail themselves of simple means. I, too, have made fun of the innocent before now. Your debasement has given you an unholy elevation. From your superior position be kind, be wise. Pity me. Pity me.

SEWERMAN: All right. Let's hope the good women of Saint Ursula's will do the same.

Daylight.

JEANNE, *on her knees. Facing her,* BARRÉ, RANGIER *and* MIGNON.

BARRÉ: Exorcise te, immundissime spiritus, omnis incursio adversarii, omne phantasma, omnis legio, in nomine Domini nostri Jesus Christi, eradicare et effugare ab hoc plasmate Dei.

RANGIER *and* MIGNON *come forward.* RANGIER *splashes holy water:* MIGNON *lays on the stole.* ASMODEUS, *in a deep voice, speaks through* JEANNE.

ASMODEUS: You gentlemen are wasting your time. You're soaking the lady, but you're not touching me.

BARRÉ (*to* MIGNON): Give me the relic. (MIGNON *hands* BARRÉ *a small box. It is applied to* JEANNE'S *back.*) Adjure te, serpens antique, per judicem vivorum et mortuorum. . . .

ASMODEUS: Excuse me.

BARRÉ: . . . per factorum tuum, per factorum mundi. . . .

ASMODEUS: I'm sorry to interrupt you.

BARRÉ: Well, what is it?

ASMODEUS: I don't understand a word you're saying. I'm a heathen devil. Latin—I suppose it is Latin—is a foreign language to me.

BARRÉ: It is customary to carry out exorcism in Latin.

ASMODEUS: Hidebound, that's what you are. Can't we continue our earlier conversation, which interested me so much, about the sexual activities of priests?

BARRÉ: Certainly not!

ASMODEUS: Is it true that men of your parish . . . (*insane giggles*) . . . is it true that they . . . Bend low. Let me whisper.

JEANNE: O dear God, release this thing from me.

ASMODEUS: Be quiet, woman. You're interrupting a theological discussion.

JEANNE: Father, help me.

BARRÉ: My dear child, I'm doing all I can.

BARRÉ *takes* RANGIER *and* MIGNON *aside: speaks to* RANGIER.

BARRÉ: The wretch thinks I'm defeated.

ASMODEUS: You are.

BARRÉ: He seems at the moment to be lodged in the lower bowel. Are Adam and Mannoury here?

RANGIER: They're waiting. In there.

BARRÉ: Ask them to get ready, will you. Consecrate the water, while you're about it.

RANGIER *goes out through the small, low door.* BARRÉ *turns to* JEANNE.

BARRÉ: My beloved Sister, it must be extreme measures.

JEANNE: What do you mean, Father?

BARRÉ: The fiend must be forced from you.

JEANNE: Is there any way, but exorcism?

BARRÉ: Haha! They say the Devil takes residence only in the innocent. It's true in this case, it seems. Yes, child, there is another way. (*He shouts.*) Do you hear me, Asmodeus?

ASMODEUS (*is it* JEANNE'S *voice?*): Mercy. Mercy.

BARRÉ (*a scream*): Nonsense!

Silence.

RANGIER *comes out from the inner room.*

BARRÉ: My dear boy, you look quite pale. The use of such methods in our job distresses you. Wait till you've been at it as long as I have. Anyway, the Church must keep up with the times. (*To* JEANNE.) Come, my dear Sister. Through that little door. There lies your salvation. She looks like a child, doesn't she? Touching. Um. Go along, now. Pretty, pretty. A few steps. (JEANNE *moves forward towards the small door.*) Let the power of good propel you. Not much further. There!

JEANNE *is standing in the doorway staring into the small, dark room —and then at once she is struggling in* BARRÉ'S *arms, a howling animal.*

BARRÉ (*powerful: confident*): Help me, Rangier!

RANGIER *comes to* BARRÉ, *and together they hold the woman.*

JEANNE: No, no! I didn't mean it!

BARRÉ: Too late, Asmodeus. Do you expect mercy now, after your blasphemy and filth against Our Lord?

JEANNE: Father! Father Barré, it is I speaking to you now, Sister Jane of the Angels—

BARRÉ: Ah, Asmodeus, you spoke with many voices.

JEANNE: But it's I, Father. Beloved Mother of this dear convent, protector of little children—

BARRÉ: Silence, beast! Let's get her in there, Rangier. Are you ready, Adam?

ADAM (*from within*): Quite ready.

BARRÉ *and* RANGIER *carry the struggling woman into the room. The door slams shut.* MIGNON, *left alone, gets down on his knees and begins to pray.*

There is a scream from JEANNE *inside the room: it dissolves into sobs and laughter.* MIGNON *prays louder. His empty, excited little voice ascends to nothingness.*

D'ARMAGNAC, DE CERISAY *and* GRANDIER *move into the foreground.*

DE CERISAY: The devil, it seems, departed from the woman at two o'clock precisely.

D'ARMAGNAC: What about the others?

DE CERISAY: The Fathers are working on them now.

D'ARMAGNAC: Same method?

DE CERISAY: No. It seems that after the Prioress more normal methods of exorcism are proving successful. A little holy water—applied externally—a few prayers, and the devils go.

D'ARMAGNAC: Then we can hope for some peace.

DE CERISAY: I don't know.

D'ARMAGNAC: Can't you do something if it starts again? As Magistrate. I'd say such goings-on constitute a civil disorder.

DE CERISAY: I saw Barré and Rangier the other day and questioned the legality of their methods. Next time the convent door was shut in my face. I put myself in a difficult position if I use force against priests. They've asked me to be present at an interrogation of Sister Jane. I'm on my way there now.

D'ARMAGNAC (*to* GRANDIER): You know your name is constantly being mentioned in this affair.

GRANDIER: Yes, sir.

D'ARMAGNAC: Wouldn't it be a good thing to take steps to clear yourself?

DE CERISAY: Have you offended this woman in some way?

GRANDIER: I don't know how that's possible. I've never seen her.

DE CERISAY: Then why has she chosen you as the devilish perpetrator?

GRANDIER: You look frightened, De Cerisay. Forgive me.

D'ARMAGNAC: You're the one who should be frightened, Father. There was a case some years ago—I forget the man's name—

GRANDIER: I don't, poor devil. There have been many cases, sir.

D'ARMAGNAC: You're in danger.

GRANDIER: Of death? But surely not by a farce such as the convent's putting on. Come, sir, death must be more magnificent, more significant for a man of my kind.

D'ARMAGNAC: How did these other men end?

GRANDIER: At the stake. But they were ridiculous and obscure Proper matter for sacrifice, that's all.

DE CERISAY: D'Armagnac and I will give you any help we can, Father.

GRANDIER: Can't I talk either of you out of this? When I came here this morning I heard the stories on the streets. I laughed. I thought you'd be doing the same. Is the possession genuine?

DE CERISAY: Not from the evidence I have. As I say, I shall see the woman today. I'll let you know what happens. But you haven't answered my question. Why should it be you?

GRANDIER: Secluded women. They give themselves to God, but something remains which cries out to be given to Man. With the truly pure in heart it can be given in the form of charity, but for the weaker members it is not so easy. It's sad. Very sad, indeed, when you think about it. Imagine being awakened in the night by a quite innocent dream. A dream of your childhood, or of a friend not seen for many years, or even the vision of a good meal. Now, this is a sin. And so you must take up your little whip and scourge your body. We call that discipline. But pain is sensuality, and in its vortex spin images of horror and lust. My beloved Sister in Jesus seems to have fixed her mind on me. There is no reason, De Cerisay. A dropped handkerchief, a scribbled note, a piece of gossip. Any of these things found in the desert of mind and body caused by continual prayer can bring hope. And with hope comes love. And, as we all know, with love comes hate. So I possess this woman. God help her in her terror and unhappiness. God help her. (*To* D'ARMAGNAC.) Now, sir, the business I called on. I've the new plans for your garden summer house. Will you come and see them? I've revised and modified the frivolity of the design. As you wished.

GRANDIER *and* D'ARMAGNAC *go.* DE CERISAY *stares after them for a moment, and then moves on to enter—*

A high-ceilinged room, furnished with two small beds. One is occupied by JEANNE. BARRÉ, RANGIER *and* MIGNON *are present. Also* ADAM *and* MANNOURY. A CLERK *sits writing.*

BARRÉ: Dear Sister in Christ, I must question you further.

JEANNE: Yes, Father.

BARRÉ: Do you remember the first time your thoughts were turned to these evil things?

JEANNE: Very well.

BARRÉ: Tell us.

JEANNE: I was walking in the garden. I stopped. Lying at my fee was a stick of hawthorn. I was sinfully possessed by anger, for that very morning I'd had cause to admonish two of the Sisters for neglecting their duties in the garden. I picked up the unsightly thing in rage. It must have been thorned, for blood ran from my body. Seeing the blood, I was filled with tenderness.

RANGIER: But this revelation may have come from a very different source.

BARRÉ: All the same—(*to the clerk*.) Are you getting this down?

JEANNE: There was another time.

BARRÉ: Tell us.

JEANNE: A day or two later. It was a beautiful morning. I'd had a night of dreamless sleep. On the threshold of my room lay a bunch of roses. I picked them up and tucked them into my belt. Suddenly, I was seized by a violent trembling in my right arm. And a great knowledge of love. This persisted throughout my orisons. I was unable to put my mind to anything. It was entirely filled with the representation of a man which had been deeply and inwardly impressed upon me.

BARRÉ: Do you know who sent those flowers?

JEANNE (*long silence: quietly*): Grandier. Grandier.

BARRÉ: What is his rank?

JEANNE: Priest.

BARRÉ: Of what church?

JEANNE: Saint Peter's.

> BARRÉ *turns to stare in silence at* DE CERISAY.

DE CERISAY (*quietly*): This is nothing.

> BARRÉ *turns back to* JEANNE.

BARRÉ: We are unconvinced, my dear Sister. And if our conviction remains untouched I do not have to remind you that you face eternal damnation.

> JEANNE *suddenly throws herself across the bed: she utters grunts like a small pig: she grinds her teeth: she disorders the bed. The men draw back from her.* JEANNE *sits upright, staring at them.*

BARRÉ (*with great urgency*): Speak! Speak!

JEANNE: It . . . was . . . night. Day's done!

BARRÉ: Yes?

JEANNE: I had tied back my hair, and scrubbed my face. to Back childhood, eh? Poor Jane. Grown woman. Made for—for. . . .

BARRÉ: Go on.

JEANNE: He came to me.

BARRÉ: Name him!

JEANNE (*at once*): Grandier! Grandier! The beautiful, golden lion entered my room, smiling.

BARRÉ: Was he alone?

JEANNE: No. Six of his creatures were with him.

BARRÉ: Then?

JEANNE: He took me gently in his arms and carried me to the chapel. His creatures each took one of my beloved sisters.

BARRÉ: What took place?

JEANNE (*smiling*): Oh, my dear Father, think of our little chapel, so simple, so unadorned. That night it was a place of luxury and scented heat. Let me tell you. It was full of laughter and music. There were velvets, silks, metals, and the wood wasn't scrubbed, no, not at all. Yes, and there was food. High animal flesh, and wine, heavy, like the fruit from the East. I'd read about it all. How we stuffed ourselves.

DE CERISAY: This is an innocent vision of hell.

BARRÉ: Ssh! Go on.

JEANNE: I forgot. We were beautifully dressed. I wore my clothes as if they were part of my body. Later, when I was naked, I fell among the thorns. Yes, there were thorns strewn on the floor. I fell among them. Come here.

She beckons to BARRÉ, *who leans towards her. She whispers and then laughs.*

BARRÉ (*bleakly*): She says that she and her sisters were compelled to form themselves into an obscene altar, and were worshipped.

JEANNE: Again.

Again she whispers: laughs.

BARRÉ: She says demons tended Grandier, and her beloved sisters incited her. You'll understand what I mean, gentlemen.

JEANNE *again draws* BARRÉ *to her. She whispers frantically, and gradually her words become audible.*

JEANNE: . . . and so we vanquished God from his house. He fled in horror at the senses fixed in men by another hand. Free of Him, we celebrated His departure again and again. (*She lies back.*) To one who has known what I have known, God is dead. I have found peace.

Silence. MIGNON *has fallen on his knees and is praying.* BARRÉ *takes* DE CERISAY *by the arm. As they speak they will move far from* JEANNE *and the others.*

BARRÉ: This was an innocent woman.

DE CERISAY: That was no devil. She spoke with her own voice. The voice of an unhappy woman, that's all.

BARRÉ: But the degraded imagination and filthy language she used in other depositions. These cannot spring unaided from a cloistered woman. She is a pupil.

DE CERISAY: Of Grandier?

BARRÉ: Yes.

DE CERISAY: But the man swears he's never been in the place.

BARRÉ: Not in his own person.

DE CERISAY: There must be some way of proving what she says. Will you let my people into the house? They will conduct an investigation on a police level.

BARRÉ: Proof? Three of the Sisters have made statements saying that they have undergone copulation with demons and been deflowered. Mannoury has examined them, and it's true that none of them is intact.

DE CERISAY: My dear Father, I don't want to offend your susceptibilities, but we all know about the sentimental attachments which go on between the young women in these places.

BARRÉ: You don't wish to be convinced.

DE CERISAY: I do. Very much. One way or another.

DE CERISAY *goes.* BARRÉ *turns.* MANNOURY *and* ADAM *are approaching.*

ADAM: Well, there, now.

MANNOURY: Fascinating.

ADAM: Unusual.

MANNOURY: Must say. Hell can't be as dull as some people make out. Haha! What?

ADAM: Such things.

MANNOURY: You know, I think a privately printed testament of this case might have quite a sale. Shall we write it up?

ADAM: Let's.

They have approached BARRÉ.

BARRÉ: Have you examined her?

MANNOURY: Yes. I'll let you have my report later.

BARRÉ: Can you give me anything to go on, meantime?

MANNOURY: As a professional man—

ADAM: He speaks for me.

MANNOURY: I don't like to commit myself.

BARRÉ: Even so—

MANNOURY: Well, let's put it this way. There's been hanky-panky.

BARRÉ: Don't mince words. There's been fornication!

MANNOURY: Rather!

BARRÉ: Lust! She's been had!

ADAM: I'll say.

BARRÉ: Thank you, gentlemen. That's all I need. Look.

> *They are silent.* GRANDIER *is walking in the distance.* BARRÉ,
> MANNOURY *and* ADAM *go.*

> GRANDIER *approaches.* PHILLIPE *comes quickly to him.*

PHILLIPE: They said you were at the Governor's house.

GRANDIER: I've just come from there. What's the matter?

PHILLIPE: I want to know. Was I restless last night? I had to leave
you before it was light. I went as quietly as I could. Did I disturb
you? It's important that I should know.

GRANDIER: I can't remember. Why is it important?

PHILLIPE: You can't remember.

> *She gives a sudden, startling, harsh laugh.*

GRANDIER: Walk to the church with me.

PHILLIPE: No.

GRANDIER: Very well.

PHILLIPE: There's no need to go into the confessional to say what
I have to tell you. I'm pregnant.

> *Silence.*

GRANDIER: So it ends.

PHILLIPE: I'm frightened.

GRANDIER: Of course. How can I own the child?

PHILLIPE: I'm very frightened.

GRANDIER: And there was such bravery in love, wasn't there,
Phillipe? All through the summer nights. How unafraid we were
each time we huddled down together. We laughed as we roused
the animal. Remember? Now it has devoured us.

PHILLIPE: Help me.

GRANDIER: And we were to have been each other's salvation. Did
I really believe it was possible?

PHILLIPE: I love you.

GRANDIER: Yes, I did believe it. I remember leaving you one day—you had been unusually adroit—

PHILLIPE: O God!

GRANDIER: I was filled with that indecent confidence which comes after perfect coupling. And as I went I thought—yes, solemnly I thought—the body can transcend its purpose. It can become a thing of such purity that it can be worshipped to the limits of imagination. Anything is allowed. All is right. And such perfection makes for an understanding of the hideous state of existence.

PHILLIPE: Touch me.

GRANDIER: But what is it now? An egg. A thing of weariness, loathing and sickness. So it ends.

PHILLIPE: Where is love?

GRANDIER: Where, indeed? Go to your father. Tell him the truth. Let him find some good man. They exist.

PHILLIPE: Help me.

GRANDIER: How can I help you? Take my hand. There. Like touching the dead, isn't it? Goodbye, Phillipe.

    GRANDIER *goes.*

The pharmacy. ADAM, MANNOURY *and* FATHER MIGNON.

There is a harsh cry from FATHER BARRÉ *as he appears at the top of the stairway. He moves like a drunken man. The others scatter in alarm.*

BARRÉ: I was denied entrance to the convent tonight. By armed guards.

MIGNON: My God, my God, what's wrong?

BARRÉ: The Archbishop has issued an ordinance against further exorcism or investigation.

MIGNON: Never!

BARRÉ: It was done at the request of De Cerisay and D'Armagnac. What's more, the Archbishop's personal physician—that rationalist fool!—got hold of the women without my knowledge. He examined them, and gave it as his opinion that there was no genuine possession.

MIGNON: What shall we do? Oh, what shall we do?

    BARRÉ *comes down into the room.*

BARRÉ: De Cerisay sees it as an act of justice. He doesn't understand that such things play straight into the hands of the devil. Allow reasonable doubt for a man's sin, and the devil snaps it up. (*He shouts wearily.*) There can be no reasonable doubt in sin. All or nothing!

MIGNON: Of course. Of course. Justice has nothing to do with salvation. Sit down. Sit down.

BARRÉ: My life's work is threatened by a corrupt archbishop, a liberal doctor and an ignorant lawyer. Ah, gentlemen, there'll be happiness in hell tonight.

Silence.

MANNOURY: Are we done for, then?

ADAM: Seems so.

MANNOURY: All up.

ADAM: Dear me.

MANNOURY: Pity.

MIGNON: Let us pray.

ADAM: I beg your pardon?

MIGNON: Let us pray.

ADAM: What for?

MIGNON: Well, let me think—

ADAM: Right you are.

MIGNON: I know!

ADAM: Yes?

MIGNON: Let us pray that the Archbishop has a diabolic vision. . . .

BARRÉ (*to* MANNOURY): I shall go back to my parish.

MIGNON (*to* ADAM): . . . of a particularly horrible nature. . . .

BARRÉ (*to* MANNOURY): There's work for me there.

MIGNON (*to* ADAM): He's an old man, too. Perhaps we can frighten him to death.

BARRÉ: Be quiet, Mignon. You rave.

MIGNON: Don't leave us.

BARRÉ: I must.

MIGNON: You're naturally a little depressed by this setback. But we'll find a way.

BARRÉ: No. The Archbishop's ordinance has made evil impossible in this place. For the moment. But the ordinance doesn't apply in my parish, and you can be sure that Satan is trumpeting there. I must answer the call.

MIGNON: We shall miss you very much.

BARRÉ: My dear friend, a whisper from hell and I shall be back.

D'ARMAGNAC *and* DE CERISAY *at a table.* GRANDIER *formally approaches them.*

GRANDIER: I believe I must thank you, De Cerisay, for having this persecution stopped. Very well. I do so now.

DE CERISAY: I acted for you, Father, but not entirely on your behalf. The circus up at the convent was beginning to attract a lot of unwelcome attention to the town. It's my job to keep some sort of order in the place.

D'ARMAGNAC: You don't make it easy for your friends, Grandier. Trincant has told me about his daughter. You have your whores. Why did you have to do this?

GRANDIER: It seemed a way.

D'ARMAGNAC: A way to what?

GRANDIER: All worldly things have a single purpose for a man of my kind. Politics, power, the senses, riches, pride and authority. I choose them with the same care that you, sir, select a weapon. But my intention is different. I need to turn them against myself.

D'ARMAGNAC: To bring about your end?

GRANDIER: Yes. I have a great need to be united with God. Living has drained the need for life from me. My exercise of the senses has flagged to total exhaustion. I am a dead man, compelled to live.

D'ARMAGNAC: You disgust me. This is a sickness.

GRANDIER: No, sir. It is the meaning and purpose.

D'ARMAGNAC: I'm not one for sophisticated argument, but tell me something. I can see that the obvious short-cut, self-destruction, is not possible. But isn't creating the circumstances for your death, which is what you seem to be doing, equally sinful?

GRANDIER: Leave me some hope.

D'ARMAGNAC: The hope that God will smile upon your efforts to create an enemy so malignant as to bring you down, and so send you—up?

GRANDIER: Yes.

D'ARMAGNAC: I've a letter here from Paris. It should make you happy. By supporting me in this matter of the fortifications you have made an excellent enemy. Richelieu. So far the King is standing with me against the Cardinal. But should the King fail or falter this city will come down, and you will probably have your wish, for you are deeply implicated. All the same, I shall continue to protect you from what I think to be a most dreadful course, and a most blasphemous philosophy.

GRANDIER: It is what I seek, sir. Don't hold it from me. Think what it must be like. I reach the end of a long day. I am warm, fed and satisfied. I go home. On the way I stare at a stranger across the street, perhaps a child. I greet a friend. I lie looking down on the face of a sleeping woman. I see these with wonder and hope, and ask myself: Is this, perhaps, the means to my end? And I am denied.

GRANDIER *suddenly hides his face in his hands.*

GRANDIER: O my God, my God! All things fail me.

D'ARMAGNAC: Afraid, Grandier?

GRANDIER: Yes. Yes. Yes. Forsaken.

The convent garden. JEANNE *and* CLAIRE *are sitting on a bench.* LOUISE *and* GABRIELLE *are on the ground at their feet. Two lay sisters stand nearby. Great stillness.*

LOUISE: What shall we do, Mother?

JEANNE: Do?

LOUISE: People are taking their children away from us.

JEANNE: Who can blame them?

CLAIRE: There's no one to help. We have to do all the housework ourselves. It's very tiring.

JEANNE (*sudden laughter*): Why don't you ask the devils to lend a hand?

CLAIRE: Mother!

GABRIELLE: I've taken in a little washing and sewing. I hope you don't mind, Mother.

JEANNE: Sensible girl. When hell fails to provide one can fall back on hard work, eh?

GABRIELLE: I know you've never liked us to do menial tasks.

JEANNE: I said it diminished women in our vocation. (*She laughs.*) Did I say that?

GABRIELLE: Yes.

Silence.

LOUISE: Mother—

JEANNE: Yes, child?

LOUISE: Why has the Archbishop forbidden Father Barré to come and see us any more?

JEANNE: Because the Archbishop has been told that we are foolish and deluded women.

LOUISE: Mother—

JEANNE: Yes?

LOUISE: Have we sinned?

JEANNE: By what we've done?

LOUISE: Yes. Have we mocked God?

JEANNE: It was not the intention.

But to make a mockery of Man. That's a different matter!

For what a splendid creature he makes to be fooled. He might have been created for no other purpose. With his head in the air, besotted with his own achievement, he asks to be tripped. Deep in the invention of mumbo-jumbo to justify his existence, he is deaf to laughter. With no eyes for anything but himself, he's blind to the gesture of ridicule made in front of his face.

So, drunk, deaf and blind, he goes on. The perfect subject for the practical joke. And that, my sisters, is where the children of misfortune—like me—play a part. We do not mock our beloved Father in Heaven. Our laughter is kept for His wretched and sinful children who get above their station, and come to believe they have some other purpose in this world than to die.

After the delusions of power come the delusions of love. When men cannot destroy they start to believe they can be saved by creeping into a fellow human being. And so perpetuating themselves. Love me, they say over and over again, love me. Cherish me. Defend me. Save me. They say it to their wives, their whores, their children, and some to the whole human race. Never to God. These are probably the most ridiculous of all, and most worthy of derision. For they do not understand the glory of mortality, the purpose of man: loneliness and death.

Let us go in.

On the fortifications. Night.

D'ARMAGNAC *and* DE CERISAY *enter from different ways. They are wrapped against the rain, and they shout above the wind.*

DE CERISAY: D'Armagnac, are you there?

D'ARMAGNAC: The horseman fell at the gate. They found these papers, scattered.

DE CERISAY: What are they?

D'ARMAGNAC: The king has gone back on his word. Richelieu has won. The town fortifications are to come down. It is to be a little place. I shall have no more power than a tradesman.

GRANDIER *has appeared far below them.*

D'ARMAGNAC: Is that the priest?

DE CERISAY: Yes. (*He shouts.*) Grandier!

D'ARMAGNAC: He will suffer. (*He shouts.*) Grandier!

GRANDIER: What's the matter?

D'ARMAGNAC: The Cardinal has moved against us.

DE CERISAY: The King has lost his nerve.

D'ARMAGNAC: All this is to come down.

DE CERISAY: You are mentioned—

D'ARMAGNAC: We shan't stand here much longer.

DE CERISAY: —named for your resistance.

D'ARMAGNAC: You are in danger.

GRANDIER: Thank God.

D'ARMAGNAC: What do you say? I can't hear you. Are you mad? Is he mad? Let's go down.

D'ARMAGNAC *and* DE CERISAY *go.* GRANDIER *kneels. The wind and rain sweep about him.*

GRANDIER: Heavenly Father, You have restored strength to my enemies, and hope to Your sinful child. I give myself into the hands of the world secure in the faith of Your mysterious ways. You have made the way possible. I understand, and I accept. But You work beyond a curtain of majesty. I am afraid to raise my eyes, and see. Reveal Yourself. Reveal Yourself.

His voice is lost.

Stillness.

DE LAUBARDEMONT *and* MIGNON.

DE LAUBARDEMONT: We shall have to act quickly.

MIGNON: Yes. Yes.

DE LAUBARDEMONT: I must start for Paris tonight.

MIGNON: So soon?

DE LAUBARDEMONT: Can it be done in the time?

MIGNON: We must try.

DE LAUBARDEMONT: Sort out your thoughts on the subject.

MIGNON: I've been reading it up. There was the appalling Gauffridy case. In Marseilles, twenty years ago. The priest bewitched and debauched several Ursulines—

DE LAUBARDEMONT: We don't need precedents. We need results. Here and now. Call them in.

MIGNON *leads* JEANNE *forward. They are followed by* CLAIRE, LOUISE, GABRIELLE *and the two lay sisters.* DE LAUBARDEMONT *stands apart.*

MIGNON: My beloved sisters in Christ, I am only a foolish old man who hasn't much time left on this earth to do God's will—

DE LAUBARDEMONT: Well then, get on with it.

MIGNON: My children, do you trust me?

JEANNE: Of course, Father.

MIGNON: As your spiritual instructor, do you trust me?

JEANNE: Always.

MIGNON: Very well. I am deeply disturbed by this sudden cessation of diabolical manifestations in you. Dreadful stories are being put about in the town and farther afield. They say you were not truly possessed by demons, but that you were playing parts, making a mockery both of your sublime state, and your superiors in the Church.

JEANNE: That is what we were told by the Archbishop's doctor. He talked about hysteria. The cry from the womb.

MIGNON: But as a good woman it was up to you to prove him wrong. Oh, assure me that it was true. You were possessed.

JEANNE: It was true. We were possessed by hell.

MIGNON: And the instigator, the foul magician—

JEANNE: Grandier! Grandier!

THE SISTERS: Grandier! Grandier!

MIGNON: But now I fear for you in another way. The evidence is all against you. The silence of the devils condemns you.

Silence.

MIGNON: You see, they do not speak. There is no proof of your virtue. Ah, my sisters, this stillness presages your eternal damnation. I fear for you. I dread. Forsaken by God and forsaken by the Devil you stand in the most desolate limbo for ever. I beg you, consider your position.

JEANNE: Father, we are afraid.

MIGNON: And well you may be, my child.

JEANNE: Don't leave us!

MIGNON: What else can I do? I will pray for you.

MIGNON *turns away towards* DE LAUBARDEMONT.

LEVIATHAN (*speaking through* JEANNE): May I put in a word?

MIGNON: God be praised! What is your name?

LEVIATHAN: Leviathan.

MIGNON: Where are you lodged, unholy thing?

LEVIATHAN: In the lady's forehead.

BEHERIT (*speaking through* JEANNE): I am in the woman's stomach. My name is Beherit.

ISACAARON (*speaking through* JEANNE): Isacaaron speaking. From under the last rib on the left.

ELYMI (*speaking through* CLAIRE): I am here. (*Another voice.*) And I.

EAZAZ (*speaking through* LOUISE): And I. (*Another voice.*) And I am here.

Clamour of diabolical voices. Derisive laughter: grunts, squeals, howls.

DE LAUBARDEMONT *moves to* MIGNON.

DE LAUBARDEMONT: Well done. Barré must be got back from Chinon. He must begin exorcism at once. In public. A representative of the Court will attend. See to it.

DE LAUBARDEMONT *goes.* MIGNON *runs forward, shouting:*

MIGNON: Open the gates! Open the gates!

A crowd floods into the palace. Men and women of the town. THE SEWERMAN. ADAM *and* MANNOURY. TRINCANT. *A dwarf. A creature. A trumpeter. Laughing women. Dogs. Children climb to points of vantage and look down.*

Below: the Sisters laboriously perform their antics. JEANNE *is on her hands and knees, snuffling the ground.* CLAIRE *has the skirts of her habit over her head, exposing herself in a dull promenade.* LOUISE *and* GABRIELLE *are locked in an embrace, making a beast. And from all of them come the hoarse, masculine cries of diabolic voices: inarticulate, whining, commanding, a dissonance of obscenity.*

The townspeople are very amused. They point out especially delectable gestures to each other. Some urge the Sisters to greater excesses. A lay sister, agile as a tumbler, is applauded. A party has settled down to eat and drink and watch.

Thunder of bells from Saint Peter's spire.

BARRÉ *enters in glory. He carries a gold, jewelled crucifix, which twists and glitters in his nervous hands.* RANGIER *comes from another way. Three Carmelites from another.* MIGNON *approaches them. All meet.*

BARRÉ: I have been sent for.

MIGNON: Yes. Yes.

BARRÉ: The triumph of good!

MIGNON: It is. Yes.

BARRÉ: De Cerisay—

MIGNON: Bah!

BARRÉ: D'Armagnac—

MIGNON: Filth!

BARRÉ: Are they here?

MIGNON: No.

RANGIER: Dare not show their faces.

BARRÉ: The triumph of good! I am in love with the words. I must say them again. It is the triumph of good!

A lay sister is scrabbling at BARRÉ'S *feet.*

BARRÉ: Peace, Sister.

BARRÉ *lays on the crucifix. It has no effect, so he savagely kicks the woman aside.*

RANGIER: The King's man is here.

BARRÉ: Who have they sent?

RANGIER: Prince Henri de Condé.

BARRÉ: One of the blood!

RANGIER: No less.

BARRÉ: Excellent. (*He shouts.*) Constables!

Archers enter, and press back the crowd. Near silence. The archers range themselves against the crowd, isolating the Sisters.

LEVIATHAN (*speaking through* JEANNE *in a loud voice*): Where is the enemy?

BARRÉ (*in great exaltation*): I am here.

LEVIATHAN: Who are you?

BARRÉ: I am only a humble man. But I speak for the Lord Jesus Christ.

A terrible scream from LEVIATHAN. *Babel of voices from the other devils. Delight of the crowd.*

BARRÉ: Mignon: water, a missal, the stoles, the ciborium, the saint's fingernail, the piece of the true cross. Let me have them all.

MIGNON: God's armoury! It's here.

The Carmelites have brought forward and are arranging the relics.

BARRÉ: I must prepare myself.

BARRÉ *falls on his knees: prays. The crowd is silent.*

HENRI DE CONDÉ *enters. This exquisite and handsome sodomite is supported by painted boys. He regards* BARRÉ *for a moment: speaks.*

DE CONDÉ: I don't wish, my dear Father, to disturb your devotions, and I would never suggest that a member of the royal family took precedence over God . . . all the same. . . .

BARRÉ (*he has got to his feet*): I'm at your service, sir.

DE CONDÉ: Thank you. These are the raving women, I take it.

BARRÉ: All of them are possessed by one or more devils.

DE CONDÉ: And the instigator is a man of your own people?

BARRÉ: A priest, yes.

DE CONDÉ: You don't seem amused.

BARRÉ: Amused?

DE CONDÉ: Never mind.

BARRÉ: If you'll take your place, sir, I'll proceed.

DE CONDÉ: Very well.

DE CONDÉ *goes to a prepared part nearby, and sits overlooking the scene. The boys play around him like butterflies.*

The Sisters are now in an untidy heap, exhausted, mere rubbish on the ground. BARRÉ *is robing and preparing himself with the help of* MIGNON *and* RANGIER.

DE CONDÉ *draws one of the boys to him.*

DE CONDÉ: These are women, darling. Look well. Vomit, if you wish. Man is born of them. Gross things. Nasty. Breeding ground. Eggs hatch out in hot dung. Don't wrinkle your little nose, pet. Take this scent. Some men love them. The priest, Grandier, for example. He's picked the gobbets from the stew. He's—(DE CONDÉ *whispers in the boy's ear. The child's eyes widen.* DE CONDÉ *laughs.*)

BARRÉ *has come forward.*

BARRÉ: With your permission, sir, I'll begin.

DE CONDÉ: Please do so.

BARRÉ: But first I have a declaration to make. This, sir—(*He holds up the ciborium.*)—contains the holy eucharist.

BARRÉ *places the ciborium on his head and kneels.*

BARRÉ: Heavenly Father, I pray that I may be confounded and that the maledictions of Dathan and Abiram may fall upon me, if I have sinned or been at fault in any way in this affair.

DE CONDÉ: A very commendable gesture. Bravo!

BARRÉ *rises, and goes towards* JEANNE.

BARRÉ: Leviathan! Leviathan!

LEVIATHAN (*speaking through* JEANNE: *sleepy*): Go away.

BARRÉ: Rouse yourself.

LEVIATHAN (*speaking through* JEANNE): You bore me.

BARRÉ: In the name of Our Lord Jesus Christ—

LEVIATHAN (*speaking through* JEANNE): Don't keep bringing that impostor's name into the conversation.

BARRÉ: It disturbs you, eh?

LEVIATHAN (*speaking through* JEANNE): I don't tolerate fools gladly All that talk about love. It has a softening effect on the character. And what's more, the fellow wasn't a gentleman.

DE CONDÉ: Reverend Father—

BARRÉ: Yes, sir?

DE CONDÉ: I notice that you don't speak to these creatures in Latin, as is usual. Why is that?

BARRÉ: They're not conversant with the language. You'll understand, sir, that there are uneducated as well as educated devils.

DE CONDÉ: Quite.

LEVIATHAN (*speaking through* JEANNE): I haven't travelled much.
    Deep laughter, taken up by the other devils.

BARRÉ: Listen, Filth—

LEVIATHAN (*speaking through* JEANNE): You're always so personal.

BARRÉ: I'm going to speak a name to you. Grandier!

LEVIATHAN (*speaking through* JEANNE): Oh, that's a sweet noise. Do it again.

BARRÉ: Grandier!

LEVIATHAN (*speaking through* JEANNE): Yes, I like that.

BARRÉ: You know him?

LEVIATHAN (*speaking through* JEANNE): We serve him. Don't we?

ZABULON (*speaking through* CLAIRE): Yes.

ISACAARON (*speaking through* JEANNE): We do. We do.

BEHERIT (*speaking through* JEANNE): Grandier! Grandier!

EAZAZ (*speaking through* LOUISE): Oh, my love, my darling, hold me, take—take—aah!—

ZABULON (*speaking through* CLAIRE): Grandier! Grandier!

BEHERIT (*speaking through* JEANNE): Grandier! Grandier!

EAZAZ (*speaking through* LOUISE): Grandier! Grandier!

LEVIATHAN (*speaking through* JEANNE): Grandier! Grandier!
    Pandemonium.

BARRÉ: Let one speak for all!

RANGIER *and* MIGNON *move in among the Sisters scattering holy water. The screams and shouts gradually die away.*

DE CONDÉ: Father, may I question these things?

BARRÉ: By all means, sir.

RANGIER, MIGNON *and the Carmelites hustle the wretched Sisters forward until they are ranged in front of* DE CONDÉ, *who stares down at them.*

DE CONDÉ (*addressing the Sisters*): Gentlemen. You have given us your views on the character and worth of our blessed Saviour. (*Hissing from the devils.*) Which of you will answer me on a matter of merely national importance?

BEHERIT (*speaking through* JEANNE): I'll try.

DE CONDÉ: You will? Good. What's your name?

BEHERIT (*speaking through* JEANNE): Beherit.

DE CONDÉ: Well, Beherit, tell me this. What's your opinion of His Majesty, the King of France, and his adviser, the great Cardinal? *Silence.*

DE CONDÉ: Come now, as a political devil you must have some views. Or do you find yourself in the quandary of most Oppositions? Having to speak with more than one voice.

BEHERIT (*speaking through* JEANNE: *muttering*): Don't understand.

DE CONDÉ: You understand very well. If you, Beherit, praise the King and his minister you condone, and imply that their policy is hellish. If you, Sister Jane, dispraise them, you run the risk of treason against powerful men. I sympathize with your difficulty. Father Barré—

BARRÉ *comes forward, as* DE CONDÉ *takes a small box from one of the boys.*

DE CONDÉ: I have here a relic of the most holy worth. It has been lent to me by a great cathedral of the north. I feel the bits and pieces which you've assembled from local sources may not be powerful enough to dispel these impudent demons. So why not try this?

BARRÉ: What is in the box, sir?

DE CONDÉ: A phial of the blood of our Lord Jesus Christ.

BARRÉ *reverently takes the box in his hands: kisses it.*

DE CONDÉ: Tell me, Father, what effect would the close proximity of this relic have on devils such as these?

BARRÉ: It would put them to flight.

DE CONDÉ: At once?

BARRÉ: Immediately. I couldn't guarantee, of course, that when the relic was removed they wouldn't return.

DE CONDÉ: Of course not. That would be asking too much. Would you like to try?

BARRÉ goes towards JEANNE.

BARRÉ: In the name of our Heavenly Father, I conjure thee, most frightful beings, by this most sacred substance, to depart!

BARRÉ applies the box to Jeanne's forehead. At once, in a number of horrible screams, the devils leave her body by way of her distorted mouth. Silence. Then JEANNE *rises to her full height. She speaks calmly, with the voice of a young girl, in her own person.*

JEANNE: I am free. I am free.

She goes to DE CONDÉ, *kneels, and kisses his hands.*

DE CONDÉ: I'm very pleased to have been of some service, madam.

BARRÉ (*triumphantly*): You see!

DE CONDÉ takes the box from BARRÉ, *opens it, and holds it upside down: it is empty.*

DE CONDÉ: You see, Father?

BARRÉ (*after a moment*): Ah, sir, what sort of trick have you played on us?

DE CONDÉ: Reverend Sir, what sort of trick are you playing on *us*?

Silence between the two men, DE CONDÉ *smiling: hushed crowd: terrified women.*

The moment is broken by MIGNON. *He starts to run in tiny circles, holding his little head in his hands.*

LEVIATHAN (*speaking through* MIGNON): Fooled again!

BEHERIT (*speaking through* MIGNON): Make way!

MIGNON cries out, as BEHERIT *forces an entry.*

RANGIER suddenly begins to neigh like a horse, and high stepping in fine style, proceeds to exhibit. The Sisters begin to grunt and groan in sympathy, one of them offering herself obscenely to RANGIER, *who mounts. Only* JEANNE *stands alone and still. A boy by* DE CONDÉ *begins to laugh in a ringing, hysterical way. There is a disturbance in the crowd. Two women have become possessed.*

BARRÉ stares about him in horror. Then, wielding the crucifix like a club, he plunges among the devils, laying about him.

BARRÉ: We are besieged! Clear the place at once!

The Carmelites hurry away the Sisters, and the dancing MIGNON *and* RANGIER. *The guards disperse the crowd.* BARRÉ *is passing among the people, laying the cross on possessed and unpossessed alike, and shouting:*

BARRÉ: . . . per factorem mundi, per eum qui habet potestatem mittendi te in gehennam, ut ab hoc famulo Dei, qui ad sinum Ecclesiae recurrit, cum metu et exercitu furoris tui festinus discedas.

    RANGIER, MIGNON *and the Sisters go into the distance, followed by* BARRÉ. *The crowd go yawning home.*

    The boy standing beside DE CONDÉ *still laughs himself to tears.*

DE CONDÉ (*smiling*): Be quiet, child.

    DE CONDÉ *stares across at* JEANNE, *who stands alone, some way off.*

DE CONDÉ: Mother, I am often accused of libertinage. Very well. Being born so high I have to stoop lower than other men. Soiled, dabbling myself, I know what I am doing and what I must give. I'd say you'll have your wish about this man Grandier, seeing the way the world goes. But do you know what you must give? (*Casually.*) Your immortal soul to damnation in an infinite desert of eternal bestiality.

    DE CONDÉ *and the boys go.*

    CLAIRE *and* LOUISE *enter apart from* JEANNE. *Gay voices.*

CLAIRE: I was never any good at prayer.

LOUISE: Neither was I.

CLAIRE: We could have spent our lives on our knees.

LOUISE: And no one would have heard of us.

CLAIRE: They're selling my picture in the town.

LOUISE: We're famous all over France.

CLAIRE: Are you still worried about being damned?

LOUISE: Not any more.

CLAIRE: Not since your beautiful legs have been so admired.

LOUISE: Sweetheart, what do you think of in chapel now?

CLAIRE: This and that. New ways.

LOUISE: To amuse?

CLAIRE: Yes. (*A bell.*) Come on.

    Laughing, they go. JEANNE *stands silent for a moment. Then:*

LEVIATHAN (*speaking through* JEANNE): Clear your mind of cant, you absurd little monster.

JEANNE: I'm afraid.

LEVIATHAN (*speaking through* JEANNE): Nonsense. We'll support you in anything you do.

JEANNE: I wish to be pure.

LEVIATHAN (*speaking through* JEANNE): There is no such thing.

JEANNE: O God: God, yes, there is.
> *Women's voices are raised from the nearby chapel.*

LEVIATHAN (*speaking through* JEANNE): No, there isn't. Now think, my dear. Remember the night-time visions. He and—(*obscene giggles*)—oh, that thing—and you, agape—no, no, my darling, not purity, not even dignity. What are you thinking of? Not only all impure, but all absurd. Remember?
> JEANNE *starts to laugh:* LEVIATHAN *joins her.*
> *Darkness.*

A Council of State. Night.
> LOUIS XIII, RICHELIEU, FATHER JOSEPH *and* LA VRILLIERE, *Secretary of State.*
> DE CONDÉ *is apart.*
> DE LAUBARDEMONT *comes forward and speaks to the Council. A clerk stands beside him, handing over relevant papers from time to time.*

DE LAUBARDEMONT: Your Majesty. Your Eminence. You have asked me to report on the case of possession at Loudun. The man's name is Urbain Grandier.

DE CONDÉ: He is innocent.
> *Both men speak to the Council.*

DE LAUBARDEMONT: I have been advised by priests of the district and by reputable medical men that the possession is genuine.

DE CONDÉ: I have also been there. The man is innocent.

DE LAUBARDEMONT: Grandier's house has been searched. Various manuscripts have been found. There was a pamphlet written some years ago and directed against Your Eminence. Other papers confirmed Grandier's support of D'Armagnac in his defiant attitude about the fortifications of the town, which has distressed you so much, Your Majesty. There were letters and notebooks of a more personal kind. A treatise on Sacerdotal Celibacy was found. The man seems to have been in love when this was written. It is reported that a mock marriage took place with a daughter of the Public Prosecutor. There were letters from other women, one of which appears to suggest that he has committed the veneric act in church.

DE CONDÉ: For the love of Jesus Christ, if you wish to destroy the man, then destroy him. I'm not here to plead for his life. But your methods are shameful. He deserves better. Any man does. Kill him with power, but don't pilfer his house, and hold evidence of this sort against him. What man could face arraignment on the idiocy of youth, old love letters, and the pathetic objects stuffed in drawers or at the bottom of cupboards, kept for the fear that one day he would need to be reminded that he was once loved? No. Destroy a man for his opposition, his strength or his majesty. But not for this!

Silence.

DE LAUBARDEMONT (*to the Council*): I should now give you any evidence in the man's favour. . . . (*He is interrupted by a sign from* RICHELIEU.)

RICHELIEU: The Devil must never be believed, even when he tells the truth.

DE LAUBARDEMONT: I shall act on your instructions at once.

DE LAUBARDEMONT *comes forward. Guards gather about him. They move off.*

A brilliant morning.

GRANDIER *comes to* THE SEWERMAN, *carrying flowers.*

SEWERMAN: Why, whatever's this?

GRANDIER: I must have picked them somewhere. I can't remember. You have them.

SEWERMAN: Thank you. They smell sweet. Very suitable.

GRANDIER: Can I sit with you?

SEWERMAN: Of course. I've no sins this morning, though. Sorry.

GRANDIER: Let me look at you.

SEWERMAN: Do you like what you see?

GRANDIER: Very much.

SEWERMAN: What's happened? You're drunk with mystery.

GRANDIER: I've been out of the town. An old man was dying. I sat with him for two nights and a day. I was seeing death for the hundredth time. It was an obscene struggle. It always is. Once again a senile, foolish and sinful old man had left it rather late to come to terms. He held my hand so tightly that I could not move.

His grimy face stared up at me in blank surprise at what was happening to him. So I sat there in the rancid smell of the kitchen, while in the darkness the family argued in whispers, between weeping, about how much money there would be under the bed.

He was dirty and old and not very bright. And I loved him so much. I envied him so much, for he was standing on the threshold of everlasting life. I wanted him to turn his face to God, and not peer back through the smoky light, and stare longingly at this mere preliminary. I said to him: Be glad, be glad. But he did not understand.

His spirit weakened at dawn. It could not mount another day. There were cries of alarm from the family. I took out the necessary properties which I travel in this bag. The vulgar little sins were confessed, absolved, and the man could die. He did so. Brutally, holding on to the last. I spoke my usual words to the family, with my priest's face. My duty was done.

But I could not forget my love for the man.

I came out of the house. I thought I'd walk back, air myself after the death cell. I was very tired. I could hear Saint Peter's bell.

The road was dusty. I remembered the day I came here. I was wearing new shoes. They were white with dust. Do you know, I flicked them over with my stole before being received by the bishop. I was vain and foolish, then. Ambitious, too.

I walked on. They were working in the fields and called to me. I remembered how I loved to work with my hands when I was a boy. But my father said it was unsuitable for one of my birth.

I could see my church in the distance. I was very proud, in a humble way. I thought of my love for the beauty of this not very beautiful place. And I remembered night in the building, with the gold, lit by candlelight, against the darkness.

I thought of you. I remembered you as a friend.

I rested. The country was stretched out. Do you know where the rivers join? I once made love there.

Children came past me. Yes, of course, that's where I got the flowers. I didn't pick them. They were given to me.

I watched the children go. Yes, I was very tired. I could see far beyond the point my eyes could see. Castles, cities, mountains, oceans, plains, forests—and—

And then—oh, my son, my son—and then—I want to tell you—

SEWERMAN: Do so. Be calm.

GRANDIER: My son, I—Am I mad?

SEWERMAN: No. Quite sane. Tell me. What did you do?

GRANDIER: I created God!

Silence.

GRANDIER: I created Him from the light and the air, from the dust of the road, from the sweat of my hands, from gold, from filth, from the memory of women's faces, from great rivers, from children, from the works of man, from the past, the present, the future and the unknown. I caused Him to be from fear and despair. I gathered in everything from this mighty act, all I have known, seen and experienced. My sin, my presumption, my vanity, my love, my hate, my lust. And last I gave myself and so made God. And He was magnificent. For He is all these things.

I was utterly in His presence. I knelt by the road. I took out the bread and the wine. Panem vinum in salutis consecramus hostiam. And in this understanding He gave Himself humbly and faithfully to me, as I had given myself to Him.

Silence.

SEWERMAN: You've found peace.

GRANDIER: More. I've found meaning.

SEWERMAN: That makes me happy.

GRANDIER: And, my son, I have found reason.

SEWERMAN: And that is sanity.

GRANDIER: I must go now. I must go to worship Him in His house, adore Him in His shrine. I must go to church.

GRANDIER *moves forward and enters the church.*

Soldiers lounge against the altar. DE LAUBARDEMONT *comes forward.*

DE LAUBARDEMONT: You are forbidden this place.

GRANDIER: Forbidden?

DE LAUBARDEMONT: You are an impious and libertine priest. You must not enter.

GRANDIER: It is my church! My beloved church!

DE LAUBARDEMONT: No longer. You're under arrest. Charges will be read. Come with me. Bring him.

GRANDIER, *between soldiers, is brought from the church into the sunlight,* DE LAUBARDEMONT *leading the way. They pass through the street.*

ADAM, MANNOURY *ad* TRINCANT *lean from an upper window, jeering.*

PHILLIPE TRINCANT, *with a silent old man beside her, watches.*

RANGIER *and* MIGNON *move in the church with a censer, intoning, exorcising.*

BARRÉ *is on his knees in the street as* GRANDIER *passes.*

THE SEWERMAN *watches. A crowd of townspeople gather round him, noisy and enquiring.*

And as GRANDIER *moves on the street and the church are filled with the clamour and laughter of devils, issuing from every mouth.*

Laughter. Laughter.

CURTAIN

ACT THREE

Night.
A cell. Another room above. GRANDIER *alone.*
Distant shouts and laughter from an unseen crowd.
BONTEMPS, *a gaoler, comes to* GRANDIER.

BONTEMPS: Have you slept?

GRANDIER: No. No, the noise. The crowd. Have they slept?

BONTEMPS: Thirty thousand people have come into the town. Where do you expect them to find beds?

GRANDIER: Why should they want to sleep, anyway? Did I, as a child, the night before the treat?

BONTEMPS: They're certainly looking forward to it.

GRANDIER: What? Say it.

BONTEMPS: The execution.

GRANDIER: I haven't been tried yet.

BONTEMPS: All right. Have it your own way. The trial, then.

GRANDIER: Are you a merciful man?

BONTEMPS: Look, this is your system. Just be thankful that you can get men to do the job. Don't ask that they should be humane as well. I came to tell you that you're to be called early. So try and get some sleep.

GRANDIER: Thank you.

BONTEMPS: Is there anything you want? There's not much I can offer.

GRANDIER: Nothing. Nothing.

JEANNE *and* FATHER MIGNON.

JEANNE: Don't go!

MIGNON: It's three o'clock in the morning. I'm an old man. Need sleep.

JEANNE: I don't want to be left alone with him.

MIGNON: With your persecutor? Grandier?

JEANNE: Yes.

MIGNON: He's under close guard.

JEANNE: No. He's here. Within me. Like a child. He never revealed to me what sort of man he was. I knew him to be beautiful. Many said he was clever, and many said he was wicked. But for all his violence to my soul and body he never came to me in anything but love. No, let me speak. He's within me, I say. I'm possessed. But he is still, lying beneath my heart, living through my breath and my blood. And he makes me afraid. Afraid that I may have fallen into the gravest error in this matter.

MIGNON: What do you mean?

JEANNE: Have I been mistaken? Did Satan take on the person of my love, my darling, so as to delude me?

MIGNON: Never. The man is his agent.

JEANNE: I have such a little body. It is a small battleground in which to decide this terrible struggle between good and evil, between love and hate. Was I wrong to allow it?

MIGNON: No, no. Don't you understand? These very thoughts are put in your mind by the forces of dread. It's wrong to believe that Hell always fights with the clamour of arms. It is now, in the small hours, that Satan sends his secret agents, whispering, with their messages of doubt.

JEANNE: I don't know. I don't know. You all speak with so many voices. And I am very tired. (*She cries out.*) Father! Father!

GRANDIER *alone in his cell.*

GRANDIER: There will be pain. It will kill God. My fear is driving Him out already.

Yes. Yes. We are flies upon the wall. Buzzing in the heat. That's so. That's so. No, no. We're monsters made up in a day. Clay in a baby's hands. Horrible, we should be bottled and hung in the pharmacy. Curiosities, for amusement only.

So. Nothing.

Shall I withstand the pain? Mother, mother, remember my fear!

Oh, nothing. This morning on the road. What was that? It was a little delusion of meaning. A trick of the sun, some fatigue of the body, and a man starts to believe that he's immortal. Look at me now. Wringing my hands, trying to convince myself that this flesh and bone is meaningful.

Sad, sad, though, very sad. To make a man see in the morning what the glory might be, and by night to snatch it from him.

Most Heavenly Father, though I struggle in Your arms like a fretful child—

This need to create a meaning. What arrogance it is! Expendable, that's what we are. Nothing proceeding to nothing.

Let me look into this void. Let me look into myself. Is there one thing, past or present, which makes for a purpose? (*Silence.*) Nothing. Nothing.

Who's there?

FATHER AMBROSE, *an old man, has come in.*

AMBROSE: My name is Ambrose.

GRANDIER: I know you, Father.

AMBROSE: I was told of your trouble, my son. The night can be very long.

GRANDIER: Yes. Stay with me.

AMBROSE: I thought I might read to you. Or, if you'd like it better, we can pray together.

GRANDIER: No. Help me.

AMBROSE: Let me try.

GRANDIER: They are destroying my faith. By fear and loneliness now. Later, by pain.

AMBROSE: Go to God, my son.

GRANDIER: Nothing going to nothing.

AMBROSE: God is here, and Christ is now.

GRANDIER: Yes. That is my faith. But how can I defend it?

AMBROSE: By remembering the will of God.

GRANDIER: Yes. Yes.

AMBROSE: By remembering that nothing must be asked of him, and nothing refused.

GRANDIER: Yes. But this is all in the books. I've read them, and understood them. And it is not enough. Not enough. Not now.

AMBROSE: God is here, and Christ is here.

GRANDIER: You're an old man. Have you gathered no more than this fustian in all your years? I'm sorry. You came in pure charity. The only one who has done so. I'm sorry.

AMBROSE *opens a book.*

AMBROSE: Suffering must be willed, affliction must be willed, humiliation must be willed, and in the act of willing—

GRANDIER: They'll be understood. I know. I know.

AMBROSE: Then you know everything.

GRANDIER: I know nothing. Speak to me as a man, Father. Talk about simple things.

AMBROSE: I came to help you, my son.

GRANDIER: You can help me. By speaking as a man. So shut your books. Forget other men's words. Speak to me.

AMBROSE: Ah, you believe there is some secret in simplicity. I am a simple man, it's true. I've never had any great doubt. Plain and shy, I have been less tempted than others, of course. The devil likes more magnificence than I've ever been able to offer. A peasant boy who clung to the love of God because he was too awkward to ask for the love of man. I'm not a good example, my son. That's why I brought the books.

GRANDIER: You think too little of yourself. What must we give God?

AMBROSE: Ourselves.

GRANDIER: But I am unworthy.

AMBROSE: Have you greatly sinned?

GRANDIER: Greatly.

AMBROSE: Even young girls come to me nowadays and confess things I don't know about. So it's hardly likely that I'll understand the sins of a young man of the world such as you. But let me try.

GRANDIER: There have been women and lust: power and ambition: worldliness and mockery.

AMBROSE: Remember. God is here. You speak before Him. Christ is now. You suffer with Him.

GRANDIER: I dread the pain to come. The humiliation.

AMBROSE: Did you dread the ecstasy of love?

GRANDIER: No.

AMBROSE: Or its humiliation?

GRANDIER: I gloried in it. I have lived by the senses.

AMBROSE: Then die by them.

GRANDIER: What did you say?

AMBROSE: Offer God pain, convulsion and disgust.

GRANDIER: Yes. Give Him myself.

AMBROSE: Let Him reveal Himself in the only way you can understand.

GRANDIER: Yes! Yes!

AMBROSE: It is all any of us can do. We live a little while, and in that little while we sin. We go to Him as we can. All is forgiven.

GRANDIER: Yes. I am His child. It is true. Let Him take me as I am. So there is meaning. There is meaning, after all. I am a sinful man and I can be accepted. It is not nothing going to nothing. It is sin going to forgiveness. It is a human creature going to love.

　　BONTEMPS *has come in.*

BONTEMPS: He's got to leave. If you want a priest they say you can ask for Father Barré or Father Rangier.

GRANDIER: They say?

BONTEMPS: Out there.

GRANDIER: De Laubardemont?

BONTEMPS: That's right.

AMBROSE: Must I go? Does he say I must go?

GRANDIER: Yes, Father. You are dangerous in your innocence. But they are too late.

AMBROSE: I don't understand.

GRANDIER: It is better that way. Let me kiss you.

　　BONTEMPS *and* FATHER AMBROSE *go.*

　　GRANDIER *alone.*

GRANDIER: What? Tears? When was the last time this happened? What are they for? They must be for what is lost, not for what has been found.

　　For God is here.

Sudden daylight. Laughter.

　　CLAIRE, GABRIELLE *and* LOUISE *come into the open air.*

GABRIELLE: The town's like a fairground.

CLAIRE: They were singing not far from my window all night.

GABRIELLE: There are acrobats. I wish we could see them. I loved acrobats.

CLAIRE: Haven't we entertained each other enough in that way?

　　They laugh.

LOUISE: We don't seem to amuse other people any more. None of the Fathers or the great Parisians have been near us for days.

　　JEANNE *has come up to them, unobserved.*

JEANNE: You must understand, Louise, that the darlings of the
  public have their day, which ends, like any other.
LOUISE: Is it all over, Mother?
JEANNE: Soon. He's appearing before his judges this morning to
  make his last statement.
LOUISE: I didn't mean Father Grandier. I meant us. What shall
  we—
JEANNE: Then they'll speak the sentence. And at last there will be
  the Question.
LOUISE: But what will become of us, Mother?
JEANNE: We shall live. You've a lifetime before you, pretty Louise.
  Think of that.

    A cell: MANNOURY *alone.*
    ADAM *is let in.*
ADAM: Hullo.
MANNOURY: Hullo.
ADAM: Were you sent for?
MANNOURY: Yes.
ADAM: So was I. By De Laubardemont?
MANNOURY: That's it.
ADAM: I've brought my things. Have you?
MANNOURY: Yes.
ADAM: What I thought would be necessary.
MANNOURY: Difficult to say, isn't it?
ADAM: Have you done this before?
MANNOURY: No.
ADAM: Neither have I. Hm. Cold in here.
MANNOURY: Yes.
ADAM: Cold out.
MANNOURY: 'Tis.
ADAM: For a summer day.
MANNOURY: August. Yes.
    DE LAUBARDEMONT *comes in.*
DE LAUBARDEMONT: Good morning, gentlemen. Glad to find you
  here. He's being brought back from the court. Should be on his
  way now.

MANNOURY: What exactly do you want us to do?

DE LAUBARDEMONT: Prepare the man. A decision has been reached. Unanimously. He is condemned.

ADAM: Well, well.

MANNOURY: Not surprising.

ADAM: There it is.

DE LAUBARDEMONT: I want you to be as quick as you can. There was an extraordinary amount of sympathy for the creature when he made his statement. There were even some unhealthy tears. So I want him ready and back there to hear the sentence as soon as possible.

MANNOURY: We'll do our best.

DE LAUBARDEMONT: Adam, would you be good enough to go and see the gaoler? He's getting all the necessary stuff together. Bring it in when he's done.

ADAM: All right.

ADAM *goes.*

DE LAUBARDEMONT: The man made something of an impression. Father Barré explained that it was the devil's doing. He said the calm was the brazen insolence of hell, and the dignity nothing but unrepentant pride. Still, the man made quite an impression.

GRANDIER *is brought in by a captain of the guard.* GRANDIER *is dressed in full canonicals, looking his finest.*

GRANDIER: Good morning, Mister Surgeon.

MANNOURY: And good morning to you.

GRANDIER: De Laubardemont I've already seen.

DE LAUBARDEMONT: You must return to the court at once.

GRANDIER: Very well.

DE LAUBARDEMONT: For the sentence.

GRANDIER: I understand.

DE LAUBARDEMONT: So now I must ask you to undress.

GRANDIER: Undress?

DE LAUBARDEMONT: You can't go like that.

GRANDIER: I suppose not.

GRANDIER *takes off his biretta, and then begins to remove his cape.* ADAM *comes in with* BONTEMPS. ADAM *carries a tray, on which there is a bowl of water, some oil and a razor.*

GRANDIER: Good morning, Mister Chemist. What have you got there?

ADAM (*stammering*): It's a razor.

GRANDIER (*after a moment: to* DE LAUBARDEMONT): Must it be this way?

DE LAUBARDEMONT: Yes. Order of the court.

MANNOURY *has taken the razor: tests it on his thumb.*

GRANDIER: Well, Mister Surgeon, all your study and training have brought you only to this. Those late nights spent discussing the existence of existence have brought you only here. To be a barber.

DE LAUBARDEMONT: Get on with it.

GRANDIER: Just a moment.

GRANDIER *touches his black curls, and then fingers his moustaches.*

GRANDIER: Have you a glass?

DE LAUBARDEMONT: No, no. Of course not.

BONTEMPS: There's this.

BONTEMPS *takes an empty metal cup from the tray. He polishes the base of the cup on his sleeve and gives it to* GRANDIER.

GRANDIER *stands looking long and deeply at his reflection.*

A public place.

A large crowd. Town and country people. Yawning, at ease, calling to each other. Apart: an enclosure holding some well-dressed women of the bourgeoisie. Chatter from them. There is a clerk within a mountain of books.

Sudden silence. All heads turn towards us.

THE CLERK *rises. He reads:*

CLERK: Urbain Grandier, you have been found guilty of commerce with the devil. And that you used this unholy alliance to possess, seduce and debauch certain Sisters of the holy order of Saint Ursula (they are fully named in this document). You have also been found guilty of obscenity, blasphemy and sacrilege.

It is ordered that you proceed and kneel at the doors of Saint Peter's and Saint Ursula's and there, with a rope round your neck and a two-pound taper in your hand, ask pardon of God, the King and Justice. Next, it is ordered that you be taken to the Place Sainte-Croix, tied to a stake and burned alive: after which your ashes will be scattered to the four winds.

It has been decided that a commemorative plaque shall be set up in the Ursulines' chapel. The cost of this, yet to be ascertained, will be chargeable to your confiscated estate.

Lastly, before sentence is carried out, you will be subjected to the Question, both ordinary and extraordinary.

Pronounced at Loudun, 18 August 1634, and executed the same day.

GRANDIER *slowly comes into sight. His hands are tied behind his back. He is dressed in a nightgown and slippers, but with a skull cap and biretta on his head.* DE LAUBARDEMONT, MANNOURY *and* ADAM *accompany him. Also* BARRÉ, RANGIER *and* MIGNON, *who are scattering holy water with consecrated whisks and intoning formulas of exorcism.*

DE LAUBARDEMONT *steps forward. He snatches the hat and cap from Grandier's head, and flings them to the ground.* GRANDIER *is revealed. He is completely shaven. Gone are the magnificent curls, the moustaches, even the eyebrows. He stands, a bald fool.*

There is a sudden, hysterical giggle from the women in the enclosure. Silence.

GRANDIER *speaks to us.*

GRANDIER: My lords, I call God the Father, God the Son and God the Holy Ghost, together with the Virgin, to witness that I have never been a sorcerer. The only magic I have practised is that of the Holy Scripture. I am innocent.

Silence. Then murmurs from the women: a silly laugh.

I am innocent, and I am afraid. I fear for my salvation. I am prepared to go and meet God, but the horrible torment you have ordered for me on the way may drive my wretched soul to despair. Despair, my lords. It is the gravest of sins. It is the short way to eternal damnation. Surely in your wisdom you do not mean to kill a soul. So may I ask you, in your mercy, to mitigate, if only a little, my punishment.

GRANDIER *looks from face to face: silence.*

Very well. When I was a child I was told about the martyrs. I loved the men and women who died for the honour of Jesus Christ. In a time of loneliness I have often wished to be of their company. Now, foolish and obscure priest that I am, I cannot presume to place myself among these great and holy men. But may I say that I have the hope in my heart that as this day ends Almighty God, my beloved Father in Heaven, will glance aside and let my suffering atone for my vain and disordered life. Amen.

Silence. Then somewhere in the crowd a man's voice clearly echoes Grandier's amen. Then another. Silence again. Only the sound of a woman bitterly weeping.

DE LAUBARDEMONT *to the captain of the guard:*

DE LAUBARDEMONT: Get them all out of here!

At once the guards begin to clear the place. The public go away along corridors and down steps, complaining, some protesting.

GRANDIER *is left with* DE LAUBARDEMONT, THE CLERK, BARRÉ, RANGIER *and* MIGNON. *He has not moved, as he stands facing his judges.*

DE CERISAY *and* D'ARMAGNAC *can be seen. They are apart, overlooking the scene.*

DE LAUBARDEMONT *faces* GRANDIER: *speaks to him.*

DE LAUBARDEMONT: Confess your guilt. Tell us the names of your accomplices. Then perhaps my lords, the judges, will consider your appeal.

GRANDIER: I cannot name accomplices I've never had, nor confess to crimes I've not done.

DE LAUBARDEMONT: This attitude will do you no good. You will suffer for it.

GRANDIER: I know that. And I am proud.

DE LAUBARDEMONT: Proud, sir? That word does not become your situation. Now look here, my dear fellow—untie his hands—this document is a simple confession. Here is a pen. Just put your name to this paper and we can forget the next stage of the proceedings.

GRANDIER: You must excuse me. No.

DE LAUBARDEMONT: I just want your signature. Here. That's all.

GRANDIER: My conscience forbids me to put my name to something which is untrue.

DE LAUBARDEMONT: You'll save us all a lot of trouble if you'll sign. The document being true, of course. (*He shouts.*) True! You've been found guilty.

GRANDIER: I'm sorry.

DE LAUBARDEMONT: I fear for you, Grandier. I fear for you very much. I have seen men before you take this brave standing in the shadow of the Question. It was unwise, Grandier. Think again.

GRANDIER: No.

DE LAUBARDEMONT: You will go into the darkness before your death. Let me talk to you for a moment about pain. It is very difficult for us standing here, both healthy men, to imagine the shattering effect of agony. The sun's warm on your face at the moment, isn't it? And you can curl your toes if you want in your slippers. You are alive, and you know it. But when you are stretched out in that little room, with the pain screaming through you like a voice, let me tell you what you will think. First: how can man do this to man? Then: how can God allow it? Then: there can be no God. Then: there is no God. The voice of pain will grow stronger, and your resolution weaker. Despair, Grandier. You used the word yourself. You called it the gravest sin. Don't reject God at this moment. Reconcile yourself. For you have bitterly offended Him. Confess.

GRANDIER: No.

D'ARMAGNAC: Are those tears on De Laubardemont's face?

DE CERISAY: I'm afraid so.

D'ARMAGNAC: Does he believe what he's saying?

DE CERISAY: Yes. Touching, isn't it?

DE LAUBARDEMONT (*to* GRANDIER): Very well. I ask you once more. Once more! Will you sign?

    GRANDIER *shakes his head.*

DE LAUBARDEMONT: Take him away.

    The guard surrounds GRANDIER.

GRANDIER: I would like to ask something.

DE LAUBARDEMONT: What?

GRANDIER: May I have Father Ambrose with me?

DE LAUBARDEMONT: No.

GRANDIER: He's a harmless old man. He won't impede you.

DE LAUBARDEMONT: He's no longer in the town. He's been sent away. If you want spiritual consolation address yourself to one of these gentlemen.

    GRANDIER *stares at* BARRÉ, RANGIER *and* MIGNON *for a moment before turning away between the guards and going.* DE LAUBARDEMONT *and* THE CLERK *follow.*

MIGNON: I found the Commissioner's last appeal very moving.

RANGIER: Very.

BARRÉ: I suppose you understand that Grandier's refusal to sign was the final proof of guilt.

MIGNON: Yes. Yes, I suppose so.

BARRÉ: Lucifer has sealed his mouth: hardened his heart against repentance.

MIGNON: Of course. That's the reason.

BARRÉ: Shall we go?

    BARRÉ, RANGIER *and* MIGNON *go.*

D'ARMAGNAC: Come to my house with me, De Cerisay.

DE CERISAY: All right, sir.

D'ARMAGNAC: I don't want you to talk to me.

DE CERISAY: Very well.

D'ARMAGNAC: We'll just sit together. And think over the day. Two
—I hope—reasonable men. We'll sit and—we'll drink. Yes, that's
it, we'll get drunk. Drunk enough to see visions. Come on.

    D'ARMAGNAC *and* DE CERISAY *go.*

A garden. JEANNE *enters. She is bare-headed, and dressed only in a
simple white under-garment. Her little, deformed person looks childlike.
She has a rope round her neck, and carries a candle in her hand. She stands
quite still.*

    CLAIRE, GABRIELLE *and* LOUISE *gather some little way from*
JEANNE, *frightened, watching her. Then* CLAIRE *comes forward to her.*

CLAIRE: Come in, dear Mother.

JEANNE: No, child.

CLAIRE: But the sun is very hot after the rain. It will do you no
good.

JEANNE: Find me a place—it needn't be so high—where I can tie
this rope. I have been looking.

CLAIRE: No, Mother. It is the most terrible sin.

JEANEN: Sin?

CLAIRE: Yes.

    CLAIRE *unknots the rope and takes it away.* LOUISE *comes forward
with a cloak, which she puts about* JEANNE.

LOUISE: Don't frighten us, Mother.

JEANNE: I have been woken night after night by the sound of
weeping. I've gone about trying to find out who it is. I have a
heart like anyone else. It can be broken by such a sound.

LOUISE: It's no one here.

JEANNE: I'd never have thought it was possible for anyone to suffer
such despair, such desolation.

LOUISE: But it's no one.

JEANNE: No one?

CLAIRE: It is the devil. He can snivel to order. Yes, Mother, think. Father Grandier would have you go to hell with him. So he gets the devil to cry at night and break your heart, makes you put a rope round your neck, and hang yourself. Don't be deceived.

JEANNE: Is there no way? And is that Claire speaking? Claire, who used to talk to me of the innocence of Christ? What's the time?

LOUISE: Just past noon.

JEANNE: Let me sit here. I promise not to harm myself. Leave me.

CLAIRE, LOUISE *and* GABRIELLE *go, leaving* JEANNE *alone. The silence is broken by a hideous sound of hammering. A scream.*

The upper room. GRANDIER *is stretched on the floor, bound. His legs, from the knees to the feet, are enclosed in a kind of box. Movable boards within the box, driven inward by huge wedges, crush his legs.* BONTEMPS *is hammering the wedges home.*

MANNOURY, ADAM *and* MIGNON *are crouched in the lower room.*

BARRÉ, *who is sitting by Grandier's head, leans forward.*

BARRÉ: Will you confess?

Slowly, GRANDIER *shakes his head.* BARRÉ *glances at* DE LAUBARDEMONT, *who stands against the wall.*

DE LAUBARDEMONT (*to* BONTEMPS): Another.

BONTEMPS *picks up another wedge, but it is at once snatched out of his hand by* RANGIER.

RANGIER: Just a moment! (*He sprinkles the wedge with holy water, and makes signs over it.*) Very necessary. The devil has the power, you see, to make the pain less than it should be.

BONTEMPS: Finished?

RANGIER: Yes.

He gives the wedge to BONTEMPS, *who inserts it.*

BARRÉ: Hit! Hit!

BONTEMPS *strikes with the mallet. A scream.*

In the lower room.

MANNOURY: What's the cubic capacity of a man's breath?

ADAM: Don't know.

MANNOURY: Just wondered.

ADAM: It doesn't occur to you when you start something, that—Hm.

MANNOURY: What did you say?

ADAM: Nothing. Just thinking aloud.

A blow with the mallet. BARRÉ *leans forward.*

BARRÉ: Confess.

GRANDIER: I'm only too ready to confess my real sins. I have been a man, I have loved women. I have been proud. I have longed for power.

BARRÉ: That's not what we want. You've been a magician. You've had commerce with devils.

GRANDIER: No. No.

BARRÉ: Another. Oh, give it to me!

BARRÉ *snatches the wedge and the mallet from* BONTEMPS *and, with the wedge unexorcised, drives it home with two mighty blows.*

GRANDIER'S *scream echoes in the garden where* JEANNE *sits alone.*

JEANNE: Is it only in the very depths that one finds God? Look at me. First I wanted to come to Him in innocence. It was not enough. Then there was the lying and play-acting. The guilt, the humiliation. It was not enough. There were the antics done for the dirty eyes of priests. The squalor. It was not enough. Down, down further.

The sound of hammering. GRANDIER'S *voice:*

GRANDIER: God. God. God. Don't abandon me. Don't let this pain make me forget You.

JEANNE: Down. Down. Into idiot oblivion. No thought. No feeling. Nothing. Is God here?

The upper room. DE LAUBARDEMONT *comes forward.*

DE LAUBARDEMONT: Take him out. It's no good.

BARRÉ, RANGIER *and* BONTEMPS *lift* GRANDIER *from the box and seat him on a stool.* BONTEMPS *covers* GRANDIER'S *shattered legs with a rug.* GRANDIER *stares down at himself.*

GRANDIER: Attendite et videte si est dolor sicut dolor meus.

JEANNE *gets up.*

JEANNE: Where are You? Where are You?

JEANNE *goes from the garden.*

BARRÉ *and* RANGIER *have come down into the lower room.*

ADAM: Any good?

BARRÉ: No.

MANNOURY: No confession?

BARRÉ: No.

ADAM: I say!

BARRÉ: Perfectly good reason.

MANNOURY: What?

BARRÉ: He called on God to give him strength. His god is the devil and did so. Made him insensible to pain. We'll get nowhere like this.

ADAM: Insensible to pain? What were all those screams?

BARRÉ: A mockery.

BARRÉ, MIGNON *and* RANGIER *go down into the street.*

The upper room.

GRANDIER: Take no notice of these tears. They're only weakness.

DE LAUBARDEMONT: Remorse?

GRANDIER: No.

DE LAUBARDEMONT: Confess.

GRANDIER: No. There are two things a man should never be asked to do in front of other men. Perform with a woman, and suffer pain. You people know how to bring hell on earth for someone like me. Make it all public.

DE LAUBARDEMONT: That is vanity, Father.

GRANDIER: Is it? I don't think so. A man is a private thing. He belongs to himself. Those two most intimate experiences, love and pain, have nothing to do with the mob. How can they concern it? For the mob can feel neither.

DE LAUBARDEMONT: The mob is made up of Christian souls. Six thousand of them are waiting for you in the market place. Tell me, do you love the Church?

GRANDIER: With all my heart.

DE LAUBARDEMONT: Do you want to see it grow more powerful, more benevolent, until it embraces every human soul on this earth?

GRANDIER: That would be my wish.

DE LAUBARDEMONT: Then help us to achieve this great purpose. Go to the market place a penitent man. Confess, and by confessing, proclaim to these thousands that you have returned to the Church's arms. By going to the stake unrepentant you do God a disservice. You give hope to the sceptics and unbelievers. You make them glad. Such an act can mine the very foundations of the Church.

Think. You are no longer important. Are you any longer important?

GRANDIER: No.

DE LAUBARDEMONT: Then make a last supreme gesture for the Catholic faith.

Silence. DE LAUBARDEMONT *eagerly leans forward. Then* GRANDIER *looks up. His face is drawn in an agonized smile.*

GRANDIER: This is sophistry, Laubardemont, and you're too intelligent not to know it. Pay me the same compliment.

DE LAUBARDEMONT: You can laugh? Now?

GRANDIER: Yes. Because I know more about it than you.

DE LAUBARDEMONT: When I tell you, Grandier—

GRANDIER: Don't persist. I can destroy you. At least in argument. Keep your illusions, Mister Commissioner. You'll need them all to deal with the men who will come after me.

DE LAUBARDEMONT: Confess.

GRANDIER: No.

DE LAUBARDEMONT: Confess.

GRANDIER: No.

DE LAUBARDEMONT: Sign.

GRANDIER: No.

DE LAUBARDEMONT *goes to the door. He calls down the stairs.*

DE LAUBARDEMONT: Let me have the guard here!

A street.

A crowd is staring into the distance. The people are quiet, shifting, uneasy, withheld. BARRÉ, RANGIER *and* MIGNON *come towards them.* RANGIER *and* MIGNON *are scattering holy water and intoning exorcisms.* BARRÉ *moves along the crowd, taking men and women by the arm, speaking to them individually.*

BARRÉ: My dear children, you are about to witness the passage of a wicked and unrepentant man to hell. I beg of you—you, sir—take the sight to your heart. Let it be a lesson that will stay with you—my good woman—all your life. Watch this infamous magician who has trafficked with devils and ask yourself—my child—is this what a man comes to when he scorns God?

A drum. GRANDIER *comes into sight. He is seated on a chair which*

*has been lashed to a kind of litter, and is carried by four soldiers. He wears
a shirt impregnated with sulphur, a vivid yellow, and there is a rope round
his neck. His broken legs dangle. He is a ridiculous, hairless, shattered doll.*
THE CLERK *walks beside him.* DE LAUBARDEMONT *and soldiers
follow.*

Saint Ursula's Convent.
The procession comes to the convent door and stops. THE CLERK *puts
a two-pound taper into Grandier's hand.*

DE LAUBARDEMONT: You must get down here.

GRANDIER: What is this place?

DE LAUBARDEMONT: It is the Convent of Saint Ursula. A place
you have defiled.

A soldier lifts GRANDIER *from the litter like a child, and puts him
on the ground.*

DE LAUBARDEMONT: Do what must be done.

GRANDIER: In this strange and unknown place I ask pardon of
God, the King and Justice. I beg that I may—(*He falls forward on
his face: cries out.*) Deus meus, miserere mei Deus!

The convent door opens and from the dark entrance come JEANNE,
GABRIELLE, CLAIRE *and* LOUISE.

DE LAUBARDEMONT: Ask pardon of this Prioress, and these good
Sisters.

GRANDIER: Who are these women?

DE LAUBARDEMONT: They are the people you have wronged. Ask
their forgiveness.

GRANDIER: I have done no such thing. I can only ask that God will
forgive them.

Utter silence as GRANDIER *and* JEANNE *stare at each other.*

JEANNE: They always spoke of your beauty. Now I see it with my
own eyes and I know it to be true.

GRANDIER: Look at this thing which I am, and learn the meaning
of love.

The drum. GRANDIER *is lifted back on to the litter. The procession
moves on into the distance.*

A great bell. Voices:

Dies irae, dies illa, solvet saeclum in favilla, teste David cum
Sybilla.

Quantus tremor est futurus, quando judex est venturus, cuncta stricte discussurus!

JEANNE, *alone, comes forward. Darkness.*

The streets of Loudun. Night.

The town seems to be on fire. Distant buildings are silhouetted against a harsh red sky. A church door gapes like a sulphurous mouth. Armed men with banners cross a bridge. A man is climbing a ladder, waving into the distance in hopeless distress.

The crowd (which watched GRANDIER *into the distance) has broken up and is rushing, hysterical, screaming, laughing, through the streets.*

JEANNE *wanders on alone.*

MANNOURY *and* ADAM.

MANNOURY: Very odd, you know.

ADAM: What?

MANNOURY: That business of human fat being rendered down by heat to the consistency of candle wax and then igniting with a flame of such exquisite colour.

ADAM: Rum business, altogether.

MANNOURY: Interesting, though. I'd say, Adam, if there's any aesthetic appeal in your work as a chemist it lies in that direction. Wouldn't you?

ADAM: Maybe.

They go.

BARRÉ, MIGNON *and* RANGIER.

BARRÉ: He's in hell. Be sure of it.

MIGNON: Tonight he roasts.

BARRÉ: Unrepentant, frightful man!

RANGIER: You know, I saw his women sitting there, watching. One was in tears, it's true. But she was watching. Never turned away.

BARRÉ: Devils. All devils. What's the matter with you?

MIGNON: I don't feel very well.

BARRÉ (*hitting him on the back*): Smoke got down you, I expect.

MIGNON: I think I'll go to bed now, if you don't mind.

BARRÉ: We're all going to get to our beds, Mignon. How long we shall be allowed to lie there depends on friend Satan. We vanquished him and brought peace to his place today. But you can be sure that even now he is creeping back. Ah, my dear friends, men of our kind will never lack employment.

They go.

PHILLIPE TRINCANT. *She is monstrously pregnant, and lumbers forward leading the old man by the hand.*

PHILLIPE: Come along home, dear husband. You must try to walk a little quicker. What? (*The old man whispers to her.*) Watching all this today has made you quite excited. (*He whispers again.*) Yes, you shall do whatever you like. And I'll do all I can for you. Wipe your mouth. We've many happy years ahead together. What? Yes, of course there's a way. I'll turn and turn about for you. Jesus, I will. I'll show you tricks. So come home, darling.

PHILLIPE *and the old man go.*

D'ARMAGNAC *and* DE CERISAY. *They are drunk.*

D'ARMAGNAC: We shouldn't be doing this, De Cerisay. We are the rational, forward-looking men of our age. We should be taking a stand.

DE CERISAY: Quite right.

D'ARMAGNAC: About something or other. I'm not quite sure what. Why is the air full of insects tonight? What was I saying?

DE CERISAY: We should take a stand.

D'ARMAGNAC: And assert ourselves.

DE CERISAY: What about?

D'ARMAGNAC: What we believe.

DE CERISAY: And what do we believe?

D'ARMAGNAC: Ask me tomorrow. Am I mad? Were they fornicating in the street up there? And what did that old woman have in the basket? Human remains? Why was that animal leading a man on a rope. What is the strange, sweet smell that hangs over the place? And that musician crucified upon the harp. What does it all mean, De Cerisay? As rational men we should be able to explain it.

DE CERISAY: I can't.

D'ARMAGNAC: Neither can I. So take me home.

They go.

JEANNE'S *wandering through the streets has brought her to* THE SEWERMAN.

SEWERMAN: When it was done they shovelled him to the north, the south, the east and the west.

JEANNE: Do you know who I am?

SEWERMAN: Yes, madam, I know.

   Some of the crowd are passing. They are fighting among themselves for
   some objects which are passed from hand to hand.

JEANNE: What are they doing?

SEWERMAN: It's bits of the body they're after.

JEANNE: As relics?

SEWERMAN: Don't try to comfort yourself. No, they want them as
   charms. There's a difference, you know. (*He snatches a charred bone*
   from one of the men.) They don't want to adore this. They want it to
   cure their constipation or their headache, to have it bring back
   their virility or their wife. They want it for love or hate. (*He holds*
   out the bone.) Do you want it for anything?

   JEANNE *shakes her head. The crowd has gone.* THE SEWERMAN *goes.*
   JEANNE *alone. She cries out in her own voice:*

JEANNE: Grandier! Grandier!
   Silence.

                           CURTAIN

NOMAN

INTRODUCTORY NOTE

IN THE *Encore* interview, John Whiting was asked about the six years between *The Gates of Summer* and *The Devils*:

And then—for six years—you wrote primarily for films?

WHITING: Yes. But I did begin two plays. I wrote half of one. It was hopeless, it wouldn't work at all. I put it away, and I started another one, of which again I wrote half. A very fascinating subject. Couldn't ever work, never worked, boring beyond words, so I put that away. It was only recently that I realized that the first play I started is perfectly all right. I've just changed the place and I've changed the basic idea. It was simply that I was writing the wrong play, that's all.

The play he half finished was *Noman,* which two years previously he'd started planning as a novel. And the play has a great deal in common with his unpublished novel *Not a Foot of Land*.[1] In this, Timothy Crashaw and his accomplices, three men and a girl, plan to destroy the shrine of 'the holy Master', who is venerated by the whole of society. Like so much else in the novel, the motives for the destruction are never explained, though Timothy seems to want to make a gesture against life. In one episode, he recalls the fear he felt after a childhood fall. 'I looked up at the sky and was overcome with unreasoning terror. . . . All acts of violence were inexplicable to me. . . . Revenge, premeditated revenge of the bloodiest kind was the answer!' One character calls Timothy's attitude 'falling in love with death'. There is also a reference in the novel to old Paul, a celebrated pamphleteer who was hanged for his writings. Perhaps *Not a Foot of Land* even more than *Saint's Day* deserves to be described as an anthology on which Whiting drew for the rest of his life.

Noman was to have been in two acts. There are some notes dated 18 August 1958 and there is a complete draft of Act One in manuscript dated 21 August 1958 and there is a manuscript redraft of about two-thirds of it dated 20 October 1958. What follows is the notes, the second draft as far as it goes, and the end of the first draft. The continuity is only an approximate one for Whiting was changing a great deal as he rewrote. There is also some repetition. The incident

[1] Here I am particularly indebted to the work of Dr Scott Robinson.

of taking the plaster hands out of the glass case is absent-mindedly used twice in the redraft. And in the first draft he ends the act with it. It therefore figures three times in this duplex version of the first half of the play.

When he started rewriting the play in 1961 under the title *The Nomads,* he changed very much more than the place and the basic idea. It's quite unrecognizable as the same play, just as *A Walk in the Desert* is unrecognizable as the same play as *Conditions of Agreement,* though this is how Whiting thought of it.

Apart from their intrinsic interest, these fragments are invaluable for the light they throw on Whiting's change of style between *The Gates of Summer* and *The Devils.* But obviously they should not be read in the same way as his finished work and he should not be judged by them. *Noman,* had he thought it worth continuing in 1958, might have been changed drastically in the process of redrafting. As it is, the pressure often gets very slack. It's a brilliant basic idea to make Lang survive the 'murder' and act as the curator of the museum devoted to his own memory. But Whiting hadn't yet found a way of making this idea work theatrically. By keeping the audience ignorant of the deception Lang is practising, Whiting was building up to a magnificent revelation at the end of Act Two, but this meant wasting the irony of the situation throughout most of the play, and there isn't nearly enough action to sustain the discussion. Whether he could have eliminated these faults by reworking the material and whether he would have persevered in 1958 had his earlier plays been more successful are two unanswerable questions. Whether he would have gone on with *The Nomads* in 1963 if he had lived is another.

He made four abortive attempts at it. The first is dated 23 September 1961; the last is dated January 1963. He died in June.

NOTES—18th August 1958

PLACE

Set town (by plan).

A museum on a street.

Front door: stairs to: two main rooms of relics (define these): 3 or 4 stairs to: small living room (confusion) bed. stove: ladder to: attic: rubbish: small window looking over town: other rooms, other windows:

House above the Taurian Steps (40 of them?) The place of assassination (a plaque?): The steps go down to the town. A lamp-post.

Town church clocks.
Draw all this from actual place.
(Perhaps composite.)

TWO ACTS.

TIME:

Between late evening (nightfall) summer and morning of the following day.

Actual year?

PEOPLE

Visitors to the museum:
schoolchildren: schoolmaster (woman?) back to bus: a man with camera: old woman:
People in the street:
workers: general activity: lamplighter.

Man—woman (a child) on steps through night. Tramps on the move.

Reality—to these, the common people, is what comes within the immediate experience.

225

The Caretaker.
The Leader: Meyer—Mayer.
1st Man.
2nd Man.
3rd Man
Girl.

LANG. Brendel.
(Let us look at these people.)
NAMES.
Mayer. Meyer.
Ganze.
Helm.
Walter.
Elisabeth.
Lucie.
Jakob. Jake.
Peter.

1st Man. too old for this sort of thing. 45–50?—trying to be young —pathetic—contempt from others —and from Caretaker. Background? (Walter?)

Stresses within the group.

Group's title: Union for?

2nd Man. 22: young working man: cool foul-mouth: (Peter?) brothers.

3rd Man. 24. Intellectual: with girl. (Jakob. Jake)

Group action—revolutionary action —opposed to that of the individual.

Meyer keeps to himself the need to kill the Caretaker in last resort. *All resolves itself to two men.*

Girl:

Why bring her? Women's place. Balls!

Meyer: [no doubt here].
The Caretaker [NAME?] Lang.

The Power of Revolt.

SCHEME

In two parts:
Part I ending with destruction of museum.
Part II ending with murder on the steps. (By Walter?)

1. Open with schoolchildren on steps.
Schoolmaster.
Old woman in house.
Man (with camera) and wife [tourists] in house.
Brendel.

Tell story of Lang through these people.

(Arrival of Meyer, Elisabeth, Peter, Walter and Jakob through this action. They come separately— Jake and Elisabeth together—and go into house.)

2. Closing of museum, Brendel and handbell.
Distraction by children. (To cover concealment of the 5.)

3. Visitors go: dying movement in the street: cyclist: lamplighter.
Brendel to his room: pot on stove: he prepares supper while—

4. Arrival of night people—man, woman and child—preparing to spend night on the steps. They settle.

5. Emergence from shadows of the 5.

6. Confrontation of Brendel.

7. Statement of aims.

Progression: Brendel: from lonely, frightened old man to full stature: to revelation as Lang.
[Do you ever have people come here? No. Do you ever go out? No.]
[I heard that was all faked. B: it's not true!]

8. The 5's attitude to Lang— examination of the relics.

9. The actual time for action.

Cut in to all this the night people. Carry through this relations between 5.
Brendel observes.

10. Leading to moment of destruction.

Plaster mask: broken: Brendel's cry: coming of the night people.

END PART ONE

11. open with night people.

12. To: scene of absolute destruction in museum.

13. Question of Brendel's murder: put by Walter. The others' disgust and horror. Walter's insistence—contempt for Meyer. He believes he will fail to carry it through.

Brendel in his room with Peter and Elisabeth. Walter and Meyer in 1st Room: Jakob alone. Can only be done by one man.
Walter: otherwise, this will just look like the work of hooligans. Danger to ourselves.
Meyer insists that he must carry it out.

14. The breakup of the group.

Growing power of Brendel.

15. They go.

16. Meyer and Brendel alone.

Core of argument here.

17. Revelation of Brendel as Lang.

Story (Ironic—savage) 'within two days of my death they saw me as a different man. They saw me as *that*!' (the portrait).

Full stature of Brendel-Lang here. —matched by Meyer.

18. Departure of the night people.

(on way to harvesting in south? 'should have avoided town').

19. Brendel-Lang and Meyer come from the house into early light of summer morning. Conversation at top of steps.

20. Walter on steps. Murder of Brendel.

END OF PART TWO

ACT ONE

The action of the play takes place in and near a museum; and on the
   Taurian Steps.

The Taurian Steps are in the foreground. This public way goes down from
   sight and leads to the town. The wide stone steps are old and forbidding.
   They are marked by the weather.

A narrow street crosses the top of the steps, like a terrace. It is paved.
   There are some railings which lean, splay out. Among the iron bars there
   is faded gilt on an imperial shield. And there is a lamp-post.

Two houses stand on the street. The first, of which only part can be seen, is
   a derelict shell. All but one of its windows are boarded over. It is divided
   from the second house by an alley.

The second house is a museum. The interior can be seen.

From the front door on the street there is a way by a few steps through a
   passage to the first room. A second and smaller room adjoins this. The
   division is made by curtains. Both rooms form the museum and are
   dedicated to the memory of a man called LANG, and they contain the
   relics of his life. Steps go down from the second room to a door at the back
   of the house. This opens on to the alley.

There are glass cases in the museum rooms. They hold small personal belongings. The kind of things a man carries about his person at one time or
   another: perhaps accumulates on his desk. A tailor's dummy has a greatcoat round the shoulders and a cap on the faceless wooden head. There are
   several shelves of books. In the small room there is an old gramophone with
   a pile of records. A violin. Some walking sticks.

The walls of the rooms are covered with pictures, mostly photographs. There
   are some frames of letters and documents. The big room is dominated by
   one picture: a life-size portrait of LANG. It is a realistic painting in the
   revolutionary style of the 1920s. A greatcoat flung over his shoulder,
   LANG stands against a winter landscape with an arm stretched out in an
   embracing gesture of reconciliation. His proud bitter Jewish face stares
   beyond horizons. The artist in his love has over-reached himself. No man
   ever looked like this.

There is a stairway beyond the door of the larger room. It goes steeply up to a narrow landing and a third room. This is the curator's living room. It has the desolate, makeshift qualities of a solitary man. There is a bed with a table beside it. Clothes hang behind the door. There is a cooking pot on a stove. The walls are bare and discoloured. A ladder goes up from a corner of the room through an open trap to an attic. This can be seen. Rubbish lies about. A man could not stand upright in the place for rafters slope steeply across it. A small unclean window looks out over the town.

It is summer: late in the evening.

There are people in the museum. An old woman moves slowly from one object to another in the first room. Unseeing eyes: great weariness. In the second room a priest is bending over a glass case. A man of energy and decision. He carries pamphlets in his hand and a camera hangs from his neck.

The curator of the museum, BRENDEL, *stands by the door of the first room. He wears a blue jacket with brass buttons and a cap.*

The door to the street is open, propped back with a stone.

A group of schoolchildren stand at the top of the Taurian Steps. There are four boys and two girls. They have a schoolmaster with them. He uses his walking stick like a rod of office.

SCHOOLMASTER: What is the name of these steps?

1st BOY: The Taurian Steps.

SCHOOLMASTER: They have many historical associations, but are notable for one thing. What is that?

2nd BOY: The murder—

SCHOOLMASTER: The word is assassination.

2nd BOY: The assassination of Lang.

SCHOOLMASTER: When did it happen?

Silence: the children look at each other; the schoolmaster points his stick at a girl.

1st GIRL (*a whisper*): Fourteen years ago.

2nd GIRL: Sixteen years ago.

SCHOOLMASTER: Guesses! It was twenty-three years ago.

WALTER *comes up the steps. He is reading a tightly folded newspaper.*

He sits on the top step smoking a cigarette and continuing to read.

Twenty-three years. Remember that. Who killed Lang?

2nd BOY: His brother.

SCHOOLMASTER: Have you a brother?

2nd BOY: Yes, sir.

SCHOOLMASTER: Then you will understand this terrible thing. (*He points to a plaque let into the stones of the steps: the children gather round.*) Take your hats off. (*The boys do so.*) Read.

3rd BOY (*reading the inscription*): 'Lang died here. He loved mankind. Lang died here.'

SCHOOLMASTER: He died on that bitter winter morning. He was horribly murdered. They found him lying here on the steps. He was carried into the house. . . .

> The SCHOOLMASTER *begins to shepherd the group of children to the door of the house.* WALTER, *pushing the newspaper into his pocket, gets up and moves with them. Inside the house: the* OLD WOMAN *stands staring down at an armchair in the first room.*

OLD WOMAN: And is this where they put him?

BRENDEL: Yes. What was left of him.

OLD WOMAN: When did he breathe his last?

BRENDEL: He died at five twenty-three exactly.

OLD WOMAN: God rest him.

BRENDEL: Why, yes, indeed.

> *The children are clattering up the stairs into the room, followed by the* SCHOOLMASTER. WALTER *comes after them. He goes straight to the second room, and from sight. The children crowd round one of the museum cases.*

OLD WOMAN: Is there a picture of the corpse?

> *She turns the rack of postcards and pamphlets which is in the room.*

BRENDEL: No, there are some postcards of the tomb. Would that do?

> LEONIE *and* JACOB *come along the street. The girl carries a shopping basket. Inside the house: the* PRIEST *pushes his way through the crowd of children to* BRENDEL.

PRIEST: He had a great feeling, I believe, for minorities.

BRENDEL: Do you mean the less happy people?

PRIEST: Yes, I suppose I do. The less fortunate.

BRENDEL: He put it all in books. You can look at them, if you like.

> *He nods towards the shelves.*

PRIEST: Thank you. Am I allowed to take photographs?

BRENDEL: Yes.

PRIEST: I'm **from** another country, you know. I'm on a visit.

BRENDEL: There's not much of interest to photograph here, I'm afraid. Have you seen the tomb? That's very fine.

PRIEST: Yes, I've seen that. Look at that child's face. (*He means one of the boys who, alone, is staring up at* LANG'S *portrait.*) That's the meaning of this place. (*The* PRIEST *begins to unfasten his camera.*)

BRENDEL *goes across the room towards the stairs. He will go up the stairs and into his room. When he is there he will take a look into the cooking pot on the stove, straighten the covers of the unmade bed, and push some clothes which are lying on the floor under the bed with his foot.*

LEONIE *and* JACOB *have come into the house from the street and gone from sight through into the second room.*

The boy who stands in front of the portrait speaks to the SCHOOL-MASTER.

1ST BOY: Please, sir, is there a picture of the murderer?

SCHOOLMASTER: This house is a shrine, boy. And your question is disgusting.

The PRIEST *has approached the* SCHOOLMASTER.

PRIEST: I'd like to photograph the children.

SCHOOLMASTER: Why?

PRIEST: Well, I come from another country. I've been watching the children's faces in this house. Although their faith is secular I find it moving. This boy was looking at the portrait. I would like some record.

SCHOOLMASTER: All right.

The PRIEST *begins to arrange several of the children in front of the portrait. They are docile, tired, bored, with vacant faces.*

PETER *comes along the street. He turns into the house without hesitation and goes up into the first room. He glances at the* PRIEST *and the group of children and then at the* OLD WOMAN *who has sat in the armchair. She speaks to* PETER.

OLD WOMAN: This place isn't as comfortable as the Art Gallery. And it's not as interesting as the Railway Station. They ought to provide better amusements for old people.

PETER *smiles and after a moment will go through into the second room. The children have been arranged and a flashlight photograph is taken. The* PRIEST *steps back and speaks to the* SCHOOLMASTER.

PRIEST: Thank you.

SCHOOLMASTER: Don't use it for propaganda.

PRIEST: What do you mean?

SCHOOLMASTER: I know your sort in other countries. The things you make children believe. It's disgraceful. This man Lang lived. He didn't claim to be anything very much. His life isn't surrounded by mystery and superstition. . . .

PRIEST: Surely his death is.

SCHOOLMASTER: Perhaps. But his life was simple and good. A model for these children. Because we bring them up to believe in him is no reason for you to go back and show that photograph and say: See, this is the way they worship.

PRIEST: I don't mean to do that.

The children are wandering about the room looking at various objects. The SCHOOLMASTER *catches hold of one of the boys and holds him almost passionately to his side.*

SCHOOLMASTER: These children need a human being to love. Not someone divine masquerading as a man. They want to be able to touch his belongings and look upon his true face. Not a sentimental invention by besotted artists. They have to live and so they want truth. Lang gives them that.

MEYER *comes up the Taurian Steps. He hesitates at the top, looking back the way he has come. Then he goes quickly towards the door of the house. As* MEYER *enters the house . . .*

. . . BRENDEL, *in his room, has picked up a handbell and is sitting on his bed holding the bell and watching an alarm clock which is on the table.*

MEYER *comes up into the first room. The* PRIEST *has turned away from the* SCHOOLMASTER *and gone to the bookshelves. He takes down a book. Reads.*

The bell sounds through the house. BRENDEL *is coming from his room and down the stairs. He swings the bell as he walks. The people in the room shift and turn at the sound, and as* MEYER *passes them on his way to the second room.* BRENDEL *is approaching.*

SCHOOLMASTER: Form up in the street, please. We march to the station. (*To the* 1ST BOY): Take charge.

The children go down the stairs and into the street, where they begin to get into line. BRENDEL *has come down into the first room. He has stopped ringing the bell.*

BRENDEL: If you please, the museum is closing.

The clocks of the town are sounding the hour: ten o'clock. BRENDEL *speaks to the* SCHOOLMASTER.

Have the children got a long journey?

SCHOOLMASTER: Half an hour.

BRENDEL: I hope they've enjoyed themselves.

SCHOOLMASTER: Enjoyed? I don't know. It's part of their education.

The SCHOOLMASTER *goes towards the street door. The* PRIEST *looks up from the book at* BRENDEL.

PRIEST: You're an old man. Too old to have grown up under Lang's influence. What do you think?

BRENDEL: He was good.

PRIEST: No one doubts that. But was he . . .

BRENDEL: It's all in the books.

The PRIEST *smiles and puts the book back on the shelf. He gives some money to* BRENDEL.

PRIEST: Take this. It's not given with pride. I may come back.

BRENDEL: Everyone is welcome.

The PRIEST *goes out of the room. The children, directed by the boy, are formed in two lines in the street. The* SCHOOLMASTER *has come down to them and now marches them away. The* PRIEST *comes into the street and walks slowly away, enjoying the evening.*

Inside the house: the OLD WOMAN *is still sunk in the armchair.* BRENDEL *speaks to her.*

BRENDEL: Time to go home, dear.

OLD WOMAN: Who keeps the place clean?

BRENDEL: I do.

OLD WOMAN: All the brushing and dusting—

BRENDEL: And scrubbing. I do it all.

OLD WOMAN: Not much else to do.

BRENDEL: No.

A moment: the OLD WOMAN *is staring at the portrait.*

OLD WOMAN: I suppose he was a great man.

BRENDEL: Yes.

OLD WOMAN: I suppose we do owe him a lot.

BRENDEL: That's right.

OLD WOMAN: Did he give anything for old people?

BRENDEL: They say he loved everybody.

OLD WOMAN: Well, that's silly. Just talk. Like the dead always being good. Hoo!

BRENDEL *has been picking up rubbish from the floor. Now he stands looking at the* OLD WOMAN. *She pulls herself up from the chair.*

All right. I'm going.

She is on her feet and going to the door. BRENDEL *follows her down the few steps to the street. The* OLD WOMAN *comes out, and stands for a moment looking at the sky. Murmurs:*

I'll get a bus.

BRENDEL: Goodnight.

The OLD WOMAN *goes away down the street. She passes a man wheeling a bicycle. He puts on the gas street lamp and when he has done this he will lift his bicycle on to his shoulder and carry it down the steps.*

BRENDEL *has kicked away the stone and is locking and bolting the front door of the house. When he has done this he goes up through the first room and by way of the passage to the second room. There, out of sight, he locks and bolts the other outer door. This done, he comes back to the first room. He glances round, switches off the lights, and goes towards the stairs leading to his room. He is fumbling with and undoing the buttons of his coat.*

A MAN *and a* WOMAN *come up the steps. They are wretchedly dressed and drag bundles with them. They might be any age: shapeless clothes hide the years and almost the sex. The* MAN *throws down his bundle and sits on the steps.*

A MAN: Not going any more tonight. No.

Voice: thin and hoarse. The WOMAN *stares down at him: her lips move.* What you say? (*Shouts.*) What you say?

A WOMAN: We should've kept away from the town. Here. This—

A MAN: You would come!

A WOMAN: We should've kept to the country. Out there.

A MAN: You would do it!

A WOMAN: I know. I wanted to see the shops.

A MAN: Oh dear, well that's not much to ask. (*He finds it funny.*) To see the shops. They're full of things to make you happy. Food, clothes, fur, jewels, cars, food, drugs, gramophone records, flowers, hats, coats, food, furniture, silk, satin, tobacco. . . . (*Suddenly.*) I'm not going any more tonight!

A WOMAN: You can't be expected to. You're a sick man.

A MAN: I know. I'm very sorry for myself. I grieve.

The WOMAN *is sitting on the steps below the* MAN, *her bundle beside her.*

Inside the house: BRENDEL *has gone up to his room. He has taken off his buttoned jacket and his cap and hung them behind the door. He has taken down a woollen coat which he now puts on. In a moment he will go over to the stove and will stand stirring the cooking pot.*

The MAN *on the steps suddenly reaches forward and shakes the* WOMAN *by the shoulder.*

A MAN: Wake up!

A WOMAN: Yes!

A MAN: You can't sleep like that. Who do you think you are? An animal? Lie down.

A WOMAN: Here?

A MAN: Yes. They never move you if you're near a river. Or on steps. You would come through the town. Had to see the shops.

A WOMAN: It's not much to ask, you said.

A MAN: No. Whenever have I denied you the smallest luxury? (*The* MAN *has pulled a blanket from his bundle. The* WOMAN *does the same. They roughly cover themselves, leaning back against the bundles.*)

A WOMAN: Warm, isn't it?

A MAN: Might be worse. (*In a friendly way.*) Take your boots off, you dirty old lady. (*The* WOMAN *begins to do so: silence.*)

A WOMAN: The lights look pretty.

A MAN: What lights?

A WOMAN: Down there.

A MAN: Ah! I expect they're shops.

Inside the house: BRENDEL *has ladled some stew from the pot and taken it to the table beside the bed. He breaks a piece from a loaf of bread and puts it on the plate. He sits on the bed. He takes a book from under the pillow and props it up in front of him. He begins to eat, reading.*

The MAN *has been running his fingers over the plaque which is set into the steps beside him. He reads:*

A MAN: 'Lang died here. He lov - ed man - kind. Lang died here.'

A WOMAN: Lov - ed what?

A MAN: Mankind. You. Me.

A WOMAN: Well, that's nice, then.

After putting her boots on the step beside her the WOMAN *has been wrapping her feet in newspaper. Now she leans back against the bundle, pulling the blanket over her legs. The* MAN *is covered up to the neck: he stares down the steps.*

It is darker now. The street lamp throws little more than shadows. BRENDEL'S *room: harsh white light from an unshaded lamp.*

A MAN: Yes. If someone came this way . . . yes, and looked . . . and saw us. . .

A WOMAN: Whatever would he think?

A MAN: Rubbish. We must look as if we've been thrown down here

. . . left . . . forgotten and unwanted. Yet, wait. Cheer up. Do you re-member that old armchair which got the bugs in it? Remember how we tried to get rid of it. They wouldn't take it away. It wouldn't burn. Whatever I did to it nothing could make it stop being an armchair. Even when I dragged it from the house, down the road and across the fields in the middle of the night and threw it into a ditch, leaving it there, what did it look like? It looked like an arm-chair which had been left in a ditch. So I expect we still look like people.

A WOMAN: I expect so.

A MAN: Mind, armchairs have no right to be in ditches. And we have no right to be here.

A WOMAN: It's wrong.

Inside the house: BRENDEL *has finished eating and pushed the plate aside. He sits, his head in his hands, reading.*

Now figures can be seen emerging from the darkness of the passage which leads from the second room. Five people. They come silently forward and will soon be gathered together in the first room.

The words of the MAN *and* WOMAN *on the steps are broken, hesitant, until at last the voices pass into sleep.*

A WOMAN: I keep thinking. We should've afforded the railway fare.

A MAN: No. I wanted to walk home. It wasn't the money. I wanted to see the country. For the last time. When they say you're going to die you've got to believe them, you know. You can't go on in the old way.

A WOMAN: There's not much you can do.

A MAN: Not much more than we're doing. Pack up and go home.

A WOMAN: It'll all be changed. They say it's quite different now.

A MAN: Doesn't matter. I don't know why you ever leave a place. You're born there and it's all right.

A WOMAN: What took you away? You've never said.

A MAN: When I was a boy there was no work so I moved ten miles to find it. Then I moved another fifty miles to better myself. Then there was the war and they moved me three hundred miles. That's the way it goes. Nothing ever seems to take you back. So you have to wait until the day when they say, You've had it, you're no use, you'll be dead . . . then you can pack up and go home. Like we're doing.

Silence.

'Lang died here. He lov - ed mankind.'

A WOMAN: If he'd lived, I expect he'd have loved us.

A MAN: Small change we'd have got from it.

Silence.

In the house: BRENDEL *is turning the pages of the book.*

The five figures in the darkness have come forward into the first room. They are, MEYER, WALTER, JACOB, PETER *and the girl,* LEONIE. *Let us look at these people.*

MEYER *is twenty-six years old. The bone structure of his head is good, but there seems to be an overdevelopment of the brow. This clouds an otherwise handsome face. His pale eyes—perhaps he needs glasses—sometimes become hooded as if with tiredness. This is not likely to be affectation. His teeth are bad. His clothes show that he looks after himself, and his body is well exercised.*

The girl, LEONIE *is twenty. Her body is a little too fat to be pretty, but it is a matter of taste. The warm curves might suit a man very well, as they do* JACOB. *Her wide unpainted mouth is innocent. Her ears are too small. There is no effect in her clothes. She wears them as a covering, nothing more. When she speaks she does so like a provincial who can make a native language sound like a foreign tongue.*

WALTER *is forty-six, much older than the other four. His face and body seem to have fallen forward into a permanent attitude for the study of boring and abstruse documents. In fact, he is a librarian of no importance. His clothes have the shabby friendliness of a present day ecclesiastic. He sometimes picks at his face.*

JACOB *is a beautiful creature. Seen closely it is difficult to find any blemish of head or body, although on certain levels of society he might be faulted for an almost imperceptible animal smell. He is twenty-two.*

PETER, JACOB'S *brother, is a year older. He is greedy, and the effects are beginning to show in his face. Women like him, for his square tobacco-stained hands are expert, capable of rousing great expectation. But a lack of fulfilment, of decision, gives him a tension which quickly leads to anger. He wears thin cotton trousers which cling to his fat legs, and a leather jacket: like a mechanic.*

And BRENDEL *is apart in his room. He is sixty-three years old. His face is closely shaven and his hair cropped very short. His reading glasses sit squarely on his large nose. He has been seen preparing and eating his supper and his behaviour has all the small absurdities of an unobserved man: the close scrutiny of well-known objects, the exaggerated method in preparation for the meal, the audible self-reproach at some minor mishap. Now, however, he is still, quite concentrated on his reading of the book.*

The MAN *and* WOMAN *on the steps are asleep.*

In the first room: LEONIE *is with* JACOB. PETER *is sitting in the armchair, watching them.* WALTER *is running his hands over the surface of one of the glass cases: slightest of sound.* MEYER *is at the foot of the stairs. He looks round.* WALTER *nods his head.* MEYER *turns and goes up the stairs. He comes to the door of* BRENDEL'S *room. He hesitates. Then he puts out his hand and the movement of the latch is startlingly loud as the door is opened.* MEYER *goes into the room.* BRENDEL *stares at him: gets up.*

BRENDEL: The museum is shut.

MEYER: I know.

He is looking about the room: hardly even at BRENDEL.

BRENDEL: Who are you?

MEYER: Where does that go?

BRENDEL: To an attic.

MEYER: Come downstairs.

BRENDEL: There's nothing to steal here.

MEYER: Come with me, please.

BRENDEL, *with* MEYER, *comes out of the room and on to the stairs. He hesitates, looking down at the four people in the room below.*

BRENDEL: What do you want?

WALTER: Come down here.

BRENDEL *comes down into the first room.* MEYER *follows.*

BRENDEL: This is wrong. No one is allowed in . . .

MEYER: What's your name?

BRENDEL: Brendel. Arthur Brendel.

MEYER: Do you live here alone?

BRENDEL: Oh yes, quite alone.

WALTER: Do you ever have visitors?

BRENDEL: Well, this is a museum. People come all the time.

WALTER: I didn't mean that.

MEYER: He means, do your friends come here?

BRENDEL: I don't know anybody like that.

MEYER: So no one's likely to come tonight.

BRENDEL: No.

MEYER: What do you usually do with yourself now?

BRENDEL: After I've locked up?

MEYER: Yes.

BRENDEL: I go up to my room, have my supper, and read. Just as you found me.

MEYER: And then?

BRENDEL: Then I go to sleep.

MEYER: And in the morning?

BRENDEL: I get up . . .

MEYER: At what time?

BRENDEL: About six. And I clean the house.

MEYER: How do you manage about food?

BRENDEL: When I've done the house I go shopping.

MEYER: Just round about here?

BRENDEL: Oh, yes. Never very far away.

MEYER: And then you come back and open the museum.

BRENDEL: At ten o'clock. Yes.

MEYER: And do you do this every day?

BRENDEL: Every day.

> BRENDEL *is standing in the middle of the group. He has been looking from face to face as he answers the questions. Each person has stared back at him.*

MEYER: You've had a good look at us all. Now I want you to tell me something. What do you see?

BRENDEL: You're all young. Much the same age. Except him.

> *He means* WALTER, *who laughs.*

MEYER: His tragedy is no less because it came later in life.

WALTER: More touching, I think. I am a pathetic figure. Spit on me.

MEYER (*to* BRENDEL): You lied.

BRENDEL: No.

MEYER: You lied.

BRENDEL: I'm an old man. And I didn't tell a lie.

MEYER: You said you lived here alone.

BRENDEL: I do. Quite alone.

MEYER: No, you live here with Lang. Look around.

WALTER: He's right.

MEYER: Why did you tell me you're an old man?

BRENDEL: I don't want to be hurt.

MEYER: Why should being an old man stop you from getting hurt? Where do you think you're living? And when? Before we know where we are we shall start getting petitions for money from children and pregnant women, from the sick and insane.

BRENDEL: What do you want?

MEYER: You live here with Lang. Admit it.

BRENDEL: Lang's dead.

Silence. It is dark in the street now. Some light from the moon. Very deep shadows.

The MAN *and* WOMAN *lie like sacks on the steps.*

Inside the house MEYER *confronts* BRENDEL.

MEYER: Lang never died.

BRENDEL: He did. He did.

MEYER: Oh, the murder happened out there on the steps, that's certain. And Lang's body lies in that bloody great tomb. But the man is not dead. We've grown up with him in our head and our heart. You're young. That's what you said. And you smiled as if it was something pleasing and you could forgive us anything. Well, forgive us this. We were young. We could be young . . .

WALTER: Good morning, children.

'Good morning, sir,' say PETER, JACOB *and* LEONIE. *They turn to* WALTER *and the group makes a little class before him.* MEYER *will join the group in a moment.* WALTER, *standing, looks down on them and speaks:*

The subject, boys and girls, kiddies, you hope of the future, young citizens for whom nothing is good enough, the subject, my darlings, is history. A question. When did history begin?

PETER: Sir, history began with the emancipation of man.

WALTER: I hope you're using words you understand.

PETER: I hope so too, sir.

WALTER: Go on.

PETER: Man was set free, sir, by Mr Lang, sir.

WALTER: How?

PETER: For hundreds of years . . .

JACOB: Thousands of years . . .

LEONIE: Millions of years . . .

PETER: Well, anyway, for a very long time, they had believed in one way or another that they owed their existence to a superior being.

WALTER: You baffle me, boy. Explain.

PETER: It's not easy, sir. In the years since history began about 1923 much has been made clear and much has been obscured. I'm trying to answer your question, sir.

WALTER: Thank you.

PETER: I want to do so in simple terms.

WALTER: Thank you again.

PETER: So let me say this. In the years of pre-history men thought there might be a time before the womb and a time after the grave.

Lang's great achievement is that he snapped off these useless tag ends and revealed by its practical length life's true purpose.

WALTER: Were people grateful to him for showing them this?

PETER: Very grateful, sir. It did away with one of the most tiresome aspects of life. Silence and meditation.

WALTER: Thank you, Peter. Your homework has been well done.

MEYER *has now joined the group. He will sometimes turn to speak to* BRENDEL *outside the mockery of the proceedings of the classroom.* You're late, Meyer. Why?

MEYER: It was such a fine morning, sir. I stopped in the park. The band of the Tramway Workers' Guild was practising. The flowers were bursting like bombs. A breeze swept off the boating lake and carried the idiotic language of children. Birds were shitting on the public statues. Four park-keepers were hanging by their necks from the historic oaks. I stopped, sir, just for a moment to be happy. I'm ready for my punishment.

WALTER: Very well. The subject is history. Tell us all you know.

MEYER: He was born of humble parents, the lucky man. His mother was a cripple and his father was a fool. And he was called Lang. He had a brother. All of them lived in poverty. They had nothing but love. And it was love which made mother kick little Lang down the stairs with her twisted leg and hit his brother on the head with her crutch. It was love which made father get drunk a Friday night and fall forward on to the stove. When he rushed into the street blazing the children danced around him like a festival. It was from these simple good people that Lang began to understand the real meaning of his existence. (*Pause.*) Please, sir, I'm finding it hard to concentrate. Jacob and Leonie are doing funny things. They were doing funny things behind the bicycle shed yesterday, too.

WALTER (*gently*): Jacob and Leonie are in love, Meyer. People in love do funny things. Just don't look.

MEYER: Very well, sir.

WALTER: Go on with the lesson. What was the true meaning of Lang's life?

MEYER: The meaning of all our lives, sir. That we're all in the same boat. And adrift. There's nothing for it but to trust each other. And love each other. And believe.

WALTER: But that's an absurd proposition. Are you drunk boy?

MEYER: No, sir.

WALTER: Then I can't understand you. Do you mean that I am to trust—*you*?

MEYER: And I must trust and love you, sir.

WALTER (*he begins to laugh:* MEYER *is smiling*): And these others. They're all to love and trust?

MEYER (*now he is laughing with* WALTER): Yes, sir.

WALTER: And this old man . . . and out there . . . everyone . . . everyone . . .

MEYER: I'm only speaking my lesson, sir. That is what you've taught us to believe.

WALTER (*suddenly silent*): Yes, of course. And quite right. What are you grinning at, Meyer? What's funny about so noble an ideal?

MEYER: Everything, sir. Nothing, sir, I don't know, sir.

WALTER: You worthless boy! Sit down.

 MEYER *does so:* WALTER *turns to the girl.*

Leonie, take your hands out of Jacob's pockets and pay attention.

LEONIE: All right.

WALTER: Would you agree with the following? It was Lang's appeal to the rational man which began history. Do you agree with that?

LEONIE: If you want me to.

WALTER: I do.

LEONIE: All right, I will.

WALTER: Listen, my dear child, you stand there clothed in Lang's teaching. You are free. Nothing you do is touched with superstition as it was once. You are free to live and to love. You are the true individual at liberty to act entirely within your own instinct. Doesn't that make you feel good?

LEONIE: Fine.

WALTER: For hundreds of years the immortal soul of your kind of slut was threatened by your dirty sinful little ways. Not any more. All of you, my darlings, can live your beautiful free lives. Because of Lang. You can live your unconstrained span of years of pleasure and goodness and love and then you can rot in the earth for ever and ever and ever and ever. . .

MEYER (*shouting*): Shut up! Shut up!

 He turns to BRENDEL *and lifts his lowered face.*

That's how we were taught. That's what we were taught. And the children today. Who was this man?

BRENDEL He suffered for his ideas. He was persecuted.

MEYER: Persecuted! He should have been crucified. Who was he?

He snatches down one of the photographs from the wall and holds it out before him, staring down at it.

Look at this. Just an ugly little boy in a badly fitting suit and a hand on Papa's knee. Was it this that destroyed God? (*He throws the picture aside: takes down another.*) And this. A spotty student gripping a diploma. And this. A private soldier grinning like an imbecile against a canvas battlefield. How do we reach that ending—(*he means the big portrait*)—from these beginnings?

WALTER: Shall we go on with the lesson?

MEYER: The lesson is done! Shut up your books. We'll live all we've been taught. (*To* BRENDEL.) Open this.

He raps his fist on one of the glass cases.

BRENDEL: No! You musn't touch . . .

MEYER: Open!

Mute, BRENDEL *shakes his head.* MEYER *takes a wrench from his hip pocket and with the palm of his hand strikes down with it. The glass of the case is shattered.* BRENDEL *gives a cry and starts forward.* PETER *grips his arm and holds him back.* MEYER *has reached into the case and taken out a pair of plaster hands.* MEYER *holds them before him.*

How did this come about?

BRENDEL: They took a cast of his hands after his death. Let me have them.

MEYER: You're going to lose your occupation.

BRENDEL: What do you mean?

MEYER: He was taken prisoner in 1915.

BRENDEL: Yes. In France.

MEYER: They let him out in 1920 and he came home.

BRENDEL: Yes.

MEYER (*suddenly: to* JACOB): How long since you've seen that girl? A week, isn't it?

JACOB: Yes. Why?

MEYER: Give it another twelve hours, will you?

JACOB: All right.

He wanders across the room away from LEONIE.

MEYER (*to* BRENDEL): So he came home. 1920. Look, we just want to get it straight, that's all. We don't want to do . . . what we're going to do without having it straight.

BRENDEL: What do you want to know?

MEYER: What did he find? You were here then. What was it like?

BRENDEL: I can't remember. It's so long ago. I was a young man.

MEYER: Think. Forty years ago. Nothing to an old man.

BRENDEL: They came back by the trainload, stinking in their rotting uniforms. It was a beautiful springtime. The flowers covered the land in such a profusion that they might have been hiding a corpse. The strange feeling at that time was that there was nothing to do. Don't misunderstand. Not that there was nothing to be done in the idealistic sense. Just that there was nothing to do. We looked into each other's faces and hated what we saw. Men would go from house to house, begging. Not for want, but as if searching. I did it myself. It was to this kind of life that Lang came back.

MEYER: And what was the first thing he said? And where did he say it?

BRENDEL: I can't remember. It's all in the books.

MEYER: Forget the books. They always lie.

BRENDEL: How does a man spread an idea? I don't know. If it's something that is wanted then I suppose it gets about. If it's not wanted then it dies on the lips.

MEYER: And Lang's hateful ideas were wanted?

BRENDEL: Of course. For they were a message of comfort. You have been forsaken, he said. There has been treachery in high places. In the highest place a man can imagine. Everyone has been betrayed. The common people, the governors, the priests and the kings and queens. The gates have been shut for ever. There is no way out of the world.

MEYER: Jesus Christ!

BRENDEL: That is all *he* said, my dear boy. Others who came after him and loved him developed from this simple idea a way of life.

MEYER: Our way of life.

BRENDEL: I'm an old man. I've lived here for nearly twenty years. I don't know the way of the world. This world from which there is no escape.

MEYER: You should be happy to meet us. We are the people of that world. Look around you. Look at those two.

    JACOB *has now rejoined* LEONIE.

That's what is known as love. A state of mind and body highly praised by Lang, I believe.

LEONIE: Yes, he went on about it, didn't he? In the books. But why didn't he ever have a woman? That worries me.

    Laughter.

WALTER: It's the word, Leonie. It can mean man's highest duty to man or it can mean the beastly little act you're itching for with Jacob. It's the word, darling.

LEONIE: But Lang didn't want anything. A man's inclination seems to lie towards boys, beasts or bitches. . .

PETER: In your experience.

LEONIE: In my experience. But Lang . . . what did he have?

JACOB (*to* BRENDEL): Well, satisfy the lady. What did he have?

MEYER: The man who is speaking to you now . . . you must have known his kind in the old days. He's with us because he loves me. He'll follow me as men followed Lang. They never really know why, these silent holy fools. Unfortunately he's also a natural animal and has to have that—(*the girl*)—every so often. And Peter. He's the youngest. And he's Jacob's brother. You think that's a good reason for him to be with us? You're wrong. He hangs round Jacob and Leonie for the day when they break up, or the one day too long that Jacob has to be away. It may already have happened. Has it, Leonie?

The girl calmly and silently mouths an obscenity at MEYER, *who laughs.* Never mind.

WALTER: You're forgetting me.

MEYER: No, I was coming to you, Walter.

MEYER *puts an arm round* WALTER'S *shoulders.*

How could I forget you? Our theorist. The man who guides our principles. (*To* BRENDEL.) So, you see, we all have each other, as is taught. Each man a brother. What have you got?

BRENDEL: Nothing. Why are you here?

WALTER: Because one day I was sitting at my desk in the public library giving and getting the books as usual. I settled for the job ten years ago. People come to me and ask for books which will tell them how to paint the walls, make a table or a model railway train. I give out these books. A thousand and one ways to waste time, or How to Do for Yourself. That's all they want. Some guidance as to how to pass the time Lang gave us. He set an end and a beginning to it all: he never fitted in the middle. And so this dirty procession of men, women and children pass in front of my desk. Not one believes that he'll find anything more in the mass of print than a way of living. How to Bath the Baby, How to Make Love, How to Grow Roses. And stories about themselves. Stories of people bathing babies, making love and growing roses.

All unquestioned. This is it. They've been told so. Lang said so
and now the books say so. Therefore no questions. This is it.
Silence.
Then, one day, Meyer put down a pile of books in front of me.
He said:
MEYER: Isn't there anything better?
WALTER: I didn't answer. I was checking the books. Lang's 'The
Task Ahead', 'Letters from Geneva' and 'The New Gospels'. A
symposium called 'The Happy Humanist' and two volumes of
American poetry. Meyer spoke again:
MEYER: I asked you a question. Isn't there anything better?
WALTER: It was a question I'd waited a long time to hear.
MEYER: You sat back in your chair, pushed up your glasses and
looked at me. Finally you answered:
WALTER: No, there's nothing better. In the circumstances.
MEYER: Nothing?
WALTER: Nothing. Meyer walked away across the room. The fog
had got into the place that morning. I could hardly see him at the
door.
MEYER: I was outside on the steps. Walter came out putting on his
coat. He sort of ran up to me. Stared at me.
WALTER: Why did you ask that question?
MEYER: I didn't know what he was talking about. He looked like
a lunatic. Collar turned in, glasses crooked, steamed up. Stammer-
ing:
WALTER: Why did you ask that question?
MEYER: You're the librarian. I wanted to know.
WALTER: And now you do know?
MEYER: I can't remember what I did then. I must have turned
away...
WALTER: Yes, you went on down the steps. I followed you.
MEYER: I wanted to get away. I jumped on a tram. I'd asked an
innocent question. I wouldn't do it again. But did I get away?
WALTER: No. I had his address on the card at the library.
MEYER: Next morning. Sunday. The windows wanted cleaning and
the bedclothes were dirty. My clothes were in a heap where I'd
stepped out of them. But it was home. I was half awake and lay
playing about. Pastime.
WALTER: They said go up. Two floors. I waited. Then knocked on
the door.

MEYER: No answer.

WALTER: So I went in. The room smelled like a cage. Meyer was naked in bed.

MEYER: He didn't give me a moment, but began to talk. I was still asleep and whatever was in my mind wasn't this sort of thing.

WALTER: Why should you think there's something better? Why should you want something better? You're young. You can enjoy food and women. Have you ever heard of what they call the beauty of nature? There are the arts. There is science. Both hold some of man's highest achievements. Both offer a kind of faith badly needed by your sort.

MEYER: He went on talking while I got up and washed, picked up my clothes and dressed. He must have spoken of everything a man can do—decent or not—between being born and dying. It sounded very good. I was shown all I could be. At one moment I was sitting at my fireside with my beautiful satisfying wife: children, legally got, laughed with me: there were flowers in the garden: a radio played daylong music of an optimistic kind: all my possessions about me announced that they were earned by honest work.

WALTER: Meyer's face rose from the dirty water of the wash basin. It rejected this picture.

MEYER: And I rejected the next. Lonely, solitary, friendless, impossibly dedicated to some nonsense. It was one of Walter's poorer efforts, shamelessly borrowed from nineteenth-century fiction. I laughed that one out of existence.

WALTER: I insisted. There must be some known pattern of life which could apply. Meyer pulled his shirt over his head and answered:

MEYER: None.

WALTER: Out into the streets.

MEYER: Sunday morning. People enjoying themselves. Happiness. Leisure. Desolation.

WALTER: The river steamers were pulling away from the banks. Shouts and music from across the water. Buses were setting off for the countryside. Comic hats and packed food.

MEYER: We sat at a safe table. Everything was laid on to impress us with the urgent need to accept ourselves as we are. Lovers went past. Nothing much can be given to the old and the ugly but at least they had dignity that day. Children's voices were silver, uncorrupted. It was a beautiful morning. And the horror and the emptiness of that beauty, the forsaken sorrow of that free human activity has brought us here tonight.

BRENDEL: Why? How do you see yourself?

MEYER: As you see this place. There is everything here to make a man. His image and his work. His clothes—(*he is running his hands over the glass case*)—his watch, rings, gloves, spectacles, pocket book, pen and cigarette machine. Yes, everything is here. You would say this is a man. False. This is no man. He is dead. And in my filthy room at the other end of the town you'll find the same sort of thing. You'd look around and think . . . an animal smell, boots under the bed, best suit hanging from the picture rail, a gramophone, some dead flowers and fruit. Yes. And many small and useless things kept for a reason. An attempt to build a past of some substance. Reminders. There was a day. And from this you would say, Yes, here is a man. A man called Meyer. Wrong. This is no man. He is dead.

BRENDEL (*after silence: speaking to* JACOB): Do you believe this?

MEYER: It's not important.

BRENDEL: Surely.

MEYER: I believe it.

BRENDEL: But do they? Of themselves.

MEYER: Leave it!

BRENDEL: Why?

MEYER: They are with me. Now. That counts.

BRENDEL: I must do everything I can to stop you.

MEYER: I must

MEYER: Stop me?

BRENDEL: From doing this.

MEYER: Go on.

BRENDEL: You can't accept yourself. That's very sad. But what is the point of destroying something you don't believe in? That's what you mean to do.

MEYER: Yes.

> MEYER *is standing over the glass case. With a sudden movement he strikes down with his fists. The wood and glass of the case splinter and shatter.* MEYER *reaches into the case and takes out the plaster cast of a pair of hands. They are startlingly white. Blood runs on* MEYER'S *hands.* BRENDEL *has started forward.* PETER *grips his arms and holds him back.*

BRENDEL: But all this is nothing! You've said so. Why destroy it?

MEYER: The world sees a man in these things. This junk heap: they see Lang. My dirty little room: they see me.

MEYER is standing with the plaster hands extended.

The MAN on the steps suddenly starts up from his sleep. He gives a shout of despair. It is heard in the house.

A MAN (*then a whisper*): Oh my dear God!

The MAN covers his face with his hands. The WOMAN crawls up the steps to him.

A WOMAN: There, there. It's the middle of the night.

The people in the house are silent: BRENDEL speaks.

BRENDEL: Don't do it.

MEYER: Quiet. (*To WALTER.*) What was it?

WALTER: Somebody shouted in the street.

MEYER: Take him to his room. Keep him quiet.

MEYER goes from the room and along the passage to the door at the back of the house. He will unchain and unbolt this door and then go out.

WALTER and PETER take BRENDEL by the arms. He does not resist as they push him up the stairs and into his room. LEONIE and JACOB are left alone.

The WOMAN has her arms round the MAN. He looks up at her.

THE MAN: Nothing to hold to. That's the trouble. I was falling back. Nothing to hold to.

THE WOMAN: Now we've had this all before. And we made up our minds.

THE MAN: What did we decide? Tell me over again.

THE WOMAN: We weren't going to worry any more about what we were once. Used to be.

THE MAN: That's right, we weren't. I was an important man with my job in the bank.

THE WOMAN: Well, you had to give it up because of your illness. And we had our pretty little house . . .

THE MAN: Oh it was a pretty little house. You kept it beautiful.

THE WOMAN: You did the garden. That was a picture.

THE MAN: All gone. How dirty it got. You remember. We had to start throwing things away. And the garden overgrown. Take care of yourself, they said. Lift nothing. Rot. So we had to start throwing things away. And the garden . . .

THE WOMAN: So you see there's nothing to worry about. Nothing to be sad about. It had all gone before we set out.

THE MAN: But didn't it mean anything? All those years of work. The position I reached. They used to call me sir. The house. The garden. The fact that I paid my way. Did it all mean nothing at all?

THE WOMAN: Nothing at all. We decided. Remember? Now sleep.

Inside the house: WALTER *and* PETER *have taken* BRENDEL *to his room. He sits on the bed.* PETER *is looking up into the attic.* WALTER *has picked up the book from the table.*

In the first room: JACOB *and* LEONIE *have come together.*

LEONIE: Why do you go with Meyer?

JACOB: He doesn't care.

LEONIE: About other people? He's simple. He could find what he's looking for in a bed. It's all there, all, yes! Jacob, all there. The destruction and the shame. All in this little centre. You know. Come on, you know I know. It means something. Admit it.

JACOB: All right.

LEONIE: Look, we live now. Yes? All right? All this waiting till you're dead. What's all that about? It's now or never. You've got to take what you're given. You've got to say well Jesus Christ you haven't done such a good job with me. I'm not a very good example of Lang's mankindliness. There are mistakes in everything. Make the best of it. And the best can be very good. Let's go now.

JACOB: No.

LEONIE: Why not? What will you find here?

JACOB: I can't leave Meyer.

LEONIE: But what will you find here that we can't find down by the river, or back at your place? Why break up this old man's house? I don't want the taste of blood and dust in my mouth, I want the taste of your sex. Let Meyer get rid of his energy this way, but you come to me.

JACOB: I can't leave him.

JACOB *turns away:* LEONIE *stares after him.*

LEONIE: All right.

JACOB: You can go.

LEONIE: No. You love him.

JACOB: I hate Lang. That's enough.

MEYER *has come down the alley beside the house into the street. He sees the* MAN *and* WOMAN.

THE MAN: It was a dream. But what is a dream?

THE WOMAN: Don't speak of it. Forget. It's the best we can do. To forget.

THE MAN: Who is it?

THE WOMAN: I don't know.

MEYER *has approached them.*

MEYER: What are you doing here?

THE WOMAN: We're staying the night. We're on our way somewhere. How dare you? Who are you? He's a sick man. He must sleep.

MEYER: Did you shout just now? Did you cry out?

THE WOMAN: He had a dream.

THE MAN: Young man, will you tell me something?

MEYER: Yes.

THE MAN: Standing where you are now . . . look at me. What do you see?

Silence.

What do you see?

MEYER: A man. And a woman.

THE MAN (*he turns to the* WOMAN): There you are! It's all right. We can still be seen for what we are. It's all right. I can sleep now. Sleep till morning. (*To* MEYER.) Thank you.

MEYER: It's nothing.

THE MAN: How did you recognize us? Tell me. Why didn't you just see us as rubbish?

MEYER: By one thing. You're afraid. It shows in your face. Fear. You're a man all right.

MEYER *stares at them for a moment and then moves away down the street going from sight. Soon he will return, cross the street, go up the alley and come back into the house.*

THE MAN: He might have said he recognized me because I've a kind face. Because I've got a sort of twinkle in my eye. Or because my voice showed I was once a man of authority. He didn't say anything like that. He said: Because you're afraid. You get comfort. And it's taken away. By a word.

Inside the house: LEONIE *to* JACOB.

LEONIE: What's the matter with you? Are you trying to prove yourself superior to something?

No answer. In the upper room: WALTER, PETER *and* BRENDEL. WALTER *has picked up the book from the bed and has been looking at it.*

PETER: Walter, when you were a little boy did you smash up your
toys?

WALTER: Can't remember. I expect so.

PETER: I did. Remember very well. I deliberately broke them up.

WALTER: What are you talking about?

PETER: I used to get punishment every time. This made me think of
it. I used to get so scared. If I don't do it, I thought, things will go
on as they are. I shan't get hurt. But in the end I'd want to finish
it. Be done with it. That was a long time ago. You can take toys
away from children. But you can't take all this away from grown
men. Let's get on with it! Where's Meyer?

*This is where the second draft of the act ends. What follows is the
first draft, from the point where Meyer rejoins the others inside the room.*

MEYER *has come back down the street and after a glance at the* MAN
and WOMAN, *who are now settled again, has gone into the house and
bolted the main door behind him. Now he comes up into the first room.*

WALTER: What was it?

MEYER: There are some tramps sleeping on the steps out there.

WALTER: Did you move them?

MEYER: No. They're cattle. If I move them they'll set up complaints
which'll wake the town. Better leave them. Where are the others?

WALTER (*he nods towards the stairs*): Up there.

MEYER (*he smiles*): I hope they've found a bed. It's painful to watch
Jacob and the girl.

WALTER: Why did you bring them?

The tone of WALTER'S *voice turns* MEYER *to him. They stare at each
other for a moment.*

MEYER: Because they're part of our—

WALTER: Go on.

MEYER: Well, call it what you like. Group, movement, idea . . . I
don't know.

WALTER: They're no part of it.

MEYER: What do you mean?

WALTER: You and I could have done this job alone.

MEYER: Yes.

WALTER: Yet you had to bring the others. Why?

MEYER: You seem to know. Tell me.

WALTER: Because you can't see yourself as a leader unless you've

got someone to lead. I'm no good to you because I gave you the
ideas. You decided to put them into action, certainly. Something
that was beyond me. But you can't lead me because I'm a step
ahead. I know what should be done. You know how to do it.

MEYER (*he laughs*): Don't make excuses for yourself.

WALTER: I'm not. Don't be misled, that's all.

MEYER: How?

WALTER: Into thinking that Jacob, Peter and the girl can help in any
way except to provide a group on which you can base your self-
esteem. You believe that they follow you. Very well. That belief
isolates you. Which means that you must finally decide.

MEYER: Decide what?

WALTER: Really, Meyer. Do you think that when you've destroyed
this house that will be the end? There'll be more to come.

MEYER: You're wrong. We act as a group. It is the only way. You
say there'll be more to come. I don't quite see what you mean, but
whatever has to be done will be discussed and decided by all of us.
You despise the others.

WALTER: Not really. I let them exist in this because from the first I
saw that it was necessary for you. You must have someone to
explain to why you do certain things. You're a leader, Meyer.
You must have followers.

MEYER: I don't see myself in that way at all.

WALTER: I'm sorry. Then how do you see yourself?

MEYER: This will shock you.

WALTER: I doubt it.

MEYER: I believe I am a representative. It's not possible any more for
a man to lead, for one person to make absolute decisions. The
gamble's too great, The stakes too high. A man in my position
is not a leader. That's out of date. It's—

WALTER: Archaic.

MEYER: Yes. I must act on the opinion of others. In this case, our
group. If you had all been unable to reach a conclusion about
tonight I could have done nothing. We shouldn't have come here.

WALTER: Wouldn't you have come here alone?

MEYER: No.

WALTER: Yes, I'm very shocked. This isn't what I looked for in you,
Meyer. Not at all.
    Silence.

A chairman. A committee member. Dear me.

WALTER *suddenly reaches over and pulls* BRENDEL *upright.*
That's the way Lang thought, isn't it?
BRENDEL: What?
WALTER: Don't pretend you haven't been listening.
BRENDEL: Well, yes, I'd say Lang thought much the way Meyer—
is that his name?—does. Much the same way.
WALTER: And he died. He was murdered because of that.
BRENDEL Quite true.
MEYER: Because of it? What do you mean?
BRENDEL: I've always had the feeling that his death was a voluntary
act. A way out. Think of the circumstances.
    JACOB *has come down into the first room.*
JACOB: Meyer . . .
    MEYER *motions him to be quiet: speaks to* BRENDEL.
MEYER: Go on.
BRENDEL: Well, you know, there was this man Lang, and it was the
seventeenth day of March. He'd spent the morning at his desk.
From nine to two. There's nothing in the records to show any
out of the way happening. He was working on a report about the
proposed reform of the national theatre companies. It was not
a subject of importance, but he was interested. He drank coffee
and ate some fruit at midday. He sent out for some cigars. At two
o'clock he shut the files on the theatre organization and went
down into the street where a delegation of school children waited
for him. As usual when he was in a public place a crowd gathered.
Lang was without a hat or coat. It was a cold day. He was seen
to rub his hands together for warmth. He looked well. He was
laughing. He stayed with the children for half an hour. Their
cheers and a patriotic song followed him back to the office. He
was seen at the window for a moment. He waved. And then he
went from sight.
    PETER *has come down from the attic into* BRENDEL'S *room.*
ELIZABETH*, *who still sits on the bed, has picked up the book from the
table.* PETER *sits beside her on the bed, takes the book from her, and
shuts it. He whispers to her: some kind of obscenity.* ELIZABETH *laughs.
The laugh is heard by the men below in the first room. For a moment they
turn towards the sound, but* BRENDEL *goes on:*
Lang saw four people that afternoon. They were minor officials
from various ministries. The last was a woman. Lang questioned
* She becomes Leonie in the next draft.

her closely on the conduct of her department. He was not critical
and not unkind. The woman couldn't answer his questions. Lang
joked with her and suggested that she go back to her office and
bring him the files under discussion. She did this. Her office was
across the square and she was back within ten minutes. She
found Lang's room empty. She sat down and waited for half an
hour. Lang didn't return. The woman went down and spoke to
the guard at the door. No one had seen Lang leave the building.

Again ELIZABETH *laughs.* MEYER *does not look in the direction of
the sound, but speaks to* JACOB:

MEYER: Tell that bitch of yours to shut up. (JACOB *goes.*)

BRENDEL: Lang was next seen at half past nine that night. He was
sitting at a table outside Grossmann's Café. He was not alone. The
man with him was known later to be his brother, Oscar. They
were seen together at this place by a senior police officer who was
off duty, and with his wife and two children. It is probable that
this policeman was the only person to recognize Lang. It was
unknown for Lang to appear unaccompanied in a public place.
Even the policeman might have doubted whether it was really the
prime minister sitting there had Lang not looked up and smiled in
recognition. So the man introduced his wife. And Lang gave
the children some biscuits and nuts from the table. He made no
reference at all to his brother, or to the unusual circumstance that
he should be sitting in a public café. The policeman and his
family took their leave after some small talk. They were the last
people to see Lang alive.

JACOB *has come up into* BRENDEL'S *room.* PETER *and* ELIZABETH
are still sitting on the bed.

JACOB: Meyer says be quiet.

In the first room MEYER *turns* BRENDEL'S *face to him: a moment.*

MEYER: So they were the last people to see Lang alive.

BRENDEL: The rest . . . well, everybody's got their own ideas.
Nobody knows. Lang and his brother must have come back there
that night. The brother lived here. When they went through the
house it was squalid and filthy. Lang spent his last night here.
Christ knows what went on. But he came here of his own free will,
that's certain. He needn't have come. So he needn't have been
found dying on the steps.

MEYER: He was still alive.

BRENDEL: Yes. They were cleaning the streets. One of the hoses

washed his cap . . . there it is . . . (*the cap with the hat on the stand*)
. . . along a gutter. They came back and found the body.

MEYER: Why was the murder so brutal?

BRENDEL: Savage? Yes, it was. The spade was at the bottom of the
steps. Lang's left arm had almost been severed by one blow. An
eye hung on his cheek. It was like a big tear, they say. He never
spoke. They carried him in here and put him where I'm sitting
now. Then he died.

In the room above PETER, JACOB *and* ELIZABETH *speak in whispers.*

PETER: Let's go down.

JACOB: Can't we get on?

PETER: Does Meyer know what he's doing?

ELIZABETH: Do any of us?

JACOB: Does it matter?

PETER: No.

JACOB: Then let's get on with it.

They begin to come down towards the first room where BRENDEL *has
got up from the chair and now stands facing* MEYER *and* WALTER.

BRENDEL: He died. He died. Whatever you may say . . . he died!
He left what any man might leave. Look around you. Forget that
he was a famous man. And what does all this become? A junk
shop.

WALTER: Then why are you so concerned?

BRENDEL: Leave it. Let it alone. You can destroy this place. You
can, I know. All right. But you won't touch the man. Lang. He
doesn't exist here. So leave this place as it is. . . .

WALTER: Why are you so concerned?

MEYER: Because it will be his place we break up. He lives here. He
looks after it. He's responsible. Like a priest in a church. He's
responsible.

WALTER: He doesn't care about Lang. Do you mean that?

MEYER: Why should he? (*To* BRENDEL.) Why should you?

BRENDEL: I do care. I care very much.

JACOB, PETER *and the* GIRL *have come down into the room.*

PETER: Meyer, when do we start? It's late. I'm tired. I want to . . .

PETER *beats his fist down on the glass case.*

MEYER: Shut up!

BRENDEL: I care very much!

PETER: Let's get on.

BRENDEL: It seems such a senseless thing to do.

MEYER: That's it!

WALTER: For Christ's sake. . . !

MEYER: That's it! It's pure. All, beautiful . . .

PETER: What is he . . . ?

MEYER: I'd read the books. But I'd forgotten. A senseless thing. It seems such a senseless thing. A senseless thing to do. Walter, you read books and you get ideas and you get a feeling in your head or where? . . . here? . . . I don't know. But you feel. And you, Peter, you want a girl and you get a feeling in your . . . my God, know . . . and you, darling . . . (*the girl*) . . . you know . . . and when it's over there's something left . . . even then, there's something left Jacob. And Jacob, come here . . . you love me . . . and it's a feeling in your guts . . . because what I do seems right . . . and when I speak and act . . . when I do anything . . . it's good . . . because it's Meyer doing it . . . and it makes you feel all right yes all right . . . satisfied . . . good hell good . . . here.

He lightly punches JACOB *in the stomach. Then he stands back, his arms outstretched: an attitude to reveal.*

But this . . . it's a senseless thing . . . there's no feeling . . . even a motiveless, gratuitous act gives you something. But this. Nothing. Nothing.

He takes a deep breath: then very quietly:

So that's why we're here. That's why we're here. That's what it's all about.

Silence: stillness: then, with love and care, MEYER *reaches into the glass case and takes out a pair of white plaster hands. He holds them before him for a moment, and they make by their structure an impressive gesture. Then* MEYER *smashes them together and they fall in pieces.*

A bitter night wind is sweeping the steps. It stirs the MAN *and* WOMAN *as if they were paper.*

CURTAIN

THE NOMADS

A PLAY IN TWO ACTS

1963

January 1963: definitive draft

De tous les plaisirs, le voyage est le plus triste.

Montherlant

The utmost degree of coherence, of mutual relatedness of the single elements, being one of the chief artistic aims of Schoenberg and his followers, there was only one step from bringing the independently invented motives of a composition into close relationship to creating first a melodic prototype which would comprise the whole available material in a characteristic pattern, allowing the deviation of the individual motives from that pattern, in which their relatedness would be ascertained by their originating in a common matrix.

Ernst Krenek

GENERAL NOTES

1. An absolute scheme *must* be made before beginning the play. Remember writing 'The Devils'.
2. Total narrative. The necessity of 'the happening'.
3. Define the *poised* position of each person early. *What will they do?*
4. What is the matter of life and death (apart from the boy) which concerns me here. It must be found. *Story.*
5. The Nazi period. Caught in as inexorable a passion as that of sex. The excesses of destruction: impossibility of release from sex.
6. Political history of Robert, Frederic and Elisabeth (1st decade).

   Jessica and Bill   (2nd decade).

   Anderson's son   (3rd decade).

   Define with historical data.
   - 1st.   Have lived violent lives.
   - 2nd.   Have partly engaged.
   - 3rd.   Refused to engage. Totally withdrawn.
7. An atmosphere of wealth: arrogance.
8. Use of music. (Young Anderson sees *Tristan and Isolde* at Regententheater (steps of).)
9. Style. Harsh: direct, idiomatic: cut the plush.
10. Shifting society ('The Nomads'). Passion for technical objects. (Frederic's engineering), etc.
11. Rage. Conflict. Hate.
12. M: Sex. Sticking yourself into another person.

NOTES FOR 'THE NOMADS': 4 JUNE 1961

1. The idea of the city. Munich. A known and identifiable place. Use it.
2. The play is basically about the destruction of our ideal. Or at least, Western Europe's inability to come up to the ideal.
3. The idealist: young Anderson.
4. The pattern of society is formed by the others.
5. Their attitude: defined by their despair, their false values, impotence, sex, homosexuality, incest, money.
6. Particulars: Jessica and Bill: brother and sister.

   Jews.

   Rich.

   Once incestuous.

   Bill now homosexual (Frederic).

   Jessica—Robert.

Robert—photographer
Father of
Married to Englishwoman (not divorced)
Love affair with Jessica
Past love affair (before war) with
Elisabeth
Friend of Frederic

The old woman's love
affairs—no marriage.

Jessica's magpie atti-
tude about the past—
the mixed-up letters,
diaries, etc.

Robert to (Hanna) in Paris. There's a girl.
She's 20. They say she's pretty. She
cooks my meals and shares my bed.
Father French: Mother American. After
Jess I don't think of the word love any
more. But I wasn't going to be a fucking
monk.

Jessica—scene with
young novice priest.
Later—Mark scene in
wandering with him.

State funeral—famous
soldier? Watched by
Jessica, Robert, Fred-
eric and Mark.
R. and F. go. Beginning
of J. and M.?

CHARACTERS

ROBERT ANDERSON

Born 1917. England. Father: professional soldier, wounded 1918: invalid.

Mother: countrywoman: alive.

Robert's childhood in country. Shadow of war (as late as 1924 my father slept with a loaded pistol by his bed). Solitary life (his few childhood friends were all to be killed in 1939–45 war).

Nature: read Richard Jefferies (Does anyone read him now?) and Edward Thomas.

Loneliness: (I remember as a small boy staring at myself in a mirror and thinking: Well, you're ugly. Nobody's going to love you. So you'd better make your way by fame.) Childhood despair. (This is a terrible thing. People forget. Mercifully.)

Preparatory school in the country. Happiness.

A public school. Misery. Bullying. 1920 to early 30's. Unrest communicated?

Left school. (A failure. I was happy about it. No strings.)

Money left by grandfather (old radical, he was, in a hard black hat).

1934 (age 17). Robert took money and went to Europe. First France (historical facts) then Germany (I bought my first camera).

Germany 1934–38. (Historical fact.) Robert poor, made living by various
  means.
Meeting with Elisabeth and Frederic. Elisabeth two years older than
  Robert. Their love affair. Robert's uneasy friendship with Frederic.
  German society near Munich, and in Berlin, in middle and late 1930's.
Robert and Elisabeth (up to 21 and 23), their life together in France
  and Germany. The break (partly ideological) at the outbreak of war
  1939. Robert's return to England (good offices of Frederic and his
  father).
Robert in army 1939–45. Undistinguished career. Boredom.
Meeting with wife: London 1940. Marriage. (Legalized week-ends.)
Wife: Englishwoman. Same age.
End of war. (The great hiatus.)
1946. Birth of child.
Happiness with wife. Job. Settled. Dead.
Then revelation through violence.
Bedrooms: looking out on a floodlit abbey, a chestnut tree, across a lake,
  the roofs of Arles, many squares, a railway, the sea (thunder-
  storms), mountains.
Jess is one of those people who can't be happy (happily) in love.
Jessica and Mark's mockery of Tristan leading to love scene.
The mulish look on her face when she takes off her clothes for love.
Petit bourgeois! passionate regard for *people*—not for the person. (Tragedy
  is not that we die, but that we survive. So obsessed with death we have
  become that we make no plans to live.)
You can't do such violence to life, and not expect it to retaliate.
The sort of woman to whom one-night stands often mean more than
  prolonged affairs with their dwindling entanglements.
All over Europe these film gentlemen with wives who were once
  'beauties'.
Toutes les bonnes choses finissent pour recommencer.
Mon mari est un écrivain très connu.
She plays at life instead of living it. [strange, urgent little body]
Here we are, two sad little Jews out on a limb. Pity us.
('That's what you're always asking for)
What have you left to give, Jess?
J: Initiation?
M: Not really. There was a girl about six months ago. She smelt of soap.
J: Tell me.
M: I'm left on my own a lot, you know etc.
Terrible incapability of *showing* love: meeting at Geneva.
LACK OF FAITH. The tragedy of Jessica at 28: nothing left to give.
The impression presented to the world (our gay (little J)—

My father was very shocked by a social lapse. But he never seemed to mind if I behaved like a whore.

With no care for the past, and no love or hope for the future: living in the present becomes an obsessional intensity.

Such things wouldn't matter (would be unimportant) if you loved me. 'I *dare* not imagine.'

J: Do you always wear glasses?

M: No. I don't like to see too clearly. But my father shouts at me when I take them off.

J: I should wear them. I'm as blind as a bat.

M: Why don't you?

J: Same reason as you.

M: They think we're vain.

J: I know. Idiots (*She kisses him.*) Take those things off.

There have been those hopeless attempts to explain me in a rational way. By my family. My friends have tried. And my lovers. She's lonely, they said. She treats sex like a man. She's frustrated in the work she tries. All wrong. All hopelessly off the mark.

What is the truth!

Hanna: scene with Mark—he opts out.

Hanna and Robert: last scene.

MARK born 1946. Mother an English girl. She was drowned swimming off the South coast of England. The pram alone on the shore. (Mark's description of inquest evidence to Jessica.) The birds around the pram. I was laughing. The sea lapped the wheels. Her clothes blown away. (His own death.)

Bring Hanna into the action of the play.

Use of music?

HANNA: Frederic's in love. It's disturbing for all of us.

ROBERT: Who is he?

HANNA: An Englishman. A very plain boy indeed.

FREDERIC: He's a Jew.

ROBERT: What's his name?

FREDERIC: Gorski.

ROBERT: Bill?

FREDERIC: That's right.

ROBERT: He's got a sister.

FREDERIC: Jessica. Yes. I met them at an actor's party. . . .

Hanna's praise of romantic love (1 speech), Schumann—morning—car radio.

You're a wonderful woman! And an impossible person.

JESSICA *throws the book into the water. They stare at it.*

JESSICA: Down it goes.

BILL: Another?

JESSICA: Why not? (*She throws two more books into the water.*)

BILL: There's one more.

JESSICA: Have a go?

PLACES

1. Steps leading up from a river: a bridge nearby.
2. The railway yards.
3. Entrance to a theatre.
4. Bill and Jessica's rooms.
5. Frederic's house.
6. Streets.
7. Hotel rooms.
8. The airport.
9. An unrestored bombed building.
10. A museum: art gallery.
11. A library.

SCENARIO

1. Jessica and Bill	River		
2. Robert and Mark to	Street		
3. Hanna and Frederic/Robert and Mark	Room	Frederic comes to Hanna.
Mark to factory with Frederic		Robert and Mark in street. They come to H. and F. Frederic: I've been with Gorski. The usual tall arguments as to why we should, or should not, love each other.
4. Bill to	Street		

5. Frederic and Bill/   Mark and Frederic   Railway
   to
6. Elisabeth, Frederic and Bill
7. Jessica
   to
8. Robert and Jessica   Erotic element in meeting.
9. Robert, Jessica and Mark
10. Jessica and Mark
11. Robert and photographs
    Pistiorski. Mark assisting

PERSONS

JESSICA GORSKI

BILL GORSKI

ROBERT ANDERSON

MARK ANDERSON

HANNA FORSTER

FREDERIC FORSTER

*The action of the play takes place in
the city of Munich. The time is the
present day.*

ACT ONE

Munich. Morning.
Steps lead up from a river. There is a bridge nearby.
JESSICA GORSKI *comes this way. She carries some books. She wanders:*
hesitates: sits on the steps. After looking around, she opens a book. She
reads.
Some little time.
BILL GORSKI *comes to* JESSICA *by a different way.*

BILL: I got lost.
JESSICA: There now.
BILL: Have you been here long?
JESSICA: No.
BILL: You were late, too.
JESSICA: Yes.
BILL: Good. (*He sits by* JESSICA.) What have you got?
JESSICA: Reading matter.
BILL: Will these help?
JESSICA: They might. They might—
BILL: What?
JESSICA: —have a secret.
BILL: No, they'll just muddle you, darling. Muddle you until your
   head hurts. What are they, after all? Each man's view of a private
   mess. But not your mess.
JESSICA: All right. Throw them away.
BILL: Have you paid for them?
JESSICA: Not yet. Does it matter?
BILL: Not a bit. Poems. Verlaine.
JESSICA (*she takes the book: hesitates*): Will it float?
BILL: I don't know. Try.
   JESSICA *throws the book into the water. She stares at it.*
JESSICA: Down it goes.

BILL: Have another.

JESSICA: Why not?

BILL: 'A History of Modern Israel.' Another?

JESSICA: Yes, please.

BILL: Notebooks. Montherlant.

JESSICA: Thank you.

BILL: Such reading.

   JESSICA *throws two more books into the water.*

BILL: There's one more.

JESSICA: I know.

BILL: 'The Face of Europe': photographs by Robert Anderson. And no paper-back.

JESSICA: I'm in it.

BILL: Show me.

JESSICA: There.

BILL: It was marked. You cheat.

JESSICA: Always.

BILL: So there you are. Naked on a bed.

JESSICA: It was in London. June, would it be? I remember. Four o'clock in the afternoon.

BILL: Dirty pictures. Hm.

JESSICA: The sun was shining.

BILL: You were just going to sleep.

JESSICA: Yes. I remember.

BILL: Do you want it?

JESSICA (*a moment*): No. Your turn.

   BILL *kisses the book, and then throws it into the water.*

BILL: Now let's go home and burn that painting you bought yesterday.

JESSICA: All right. Then we'll sit at the opera tonight and whistle all the tunes.

   They do not move. Silence.

BILL: What shall we do?

JESSICA: I thought of buying some biscuits and going into the country.

BILL: It's miles.

JESSICA: Miles. Where have you been?

BILL: This morning?

JESSICA: Yes. What have you been doing?

BILL: I've been with Frederic.

JESSICA: Making love?

BILL: No.

JESSICA: Go on. Have you?

BILL: No. Not this morning. (*He takes a leaf from* JESSICA'S *coat, and crushes it in his hands.*)

JESSICA: Yes. It's late.

BILL: It'll be later up north.

JESSICA: It's cold, whenever it is.

BILL: Huddle up, little sister.

JESSICA: Billy, Billy. Why did you stay out all night? That place we have is not nice on my own. I couldn't sleep.

BILL: What was wrong?

JESSICA: There's nothing right, Billy. Not when a woman of nearly thirty, a good Jewish girl with money in the bank, has to wander in the kitchen at four in the morning, making tea, taking pills, five of them, and wanting her brother home. Her brother, Billy. Are you listening?

BILL: This town's got cemeteries all round it. No, I'm not listening to you.

JESSICA: Most towns have nowadays.

BILL: There's one to the north, south, east and west. It says so, on the map for the buses.

JESSICA: Shall we go back to London?

BILL: Let's not.

JESSICA: Then we'll go on. We'll go south.

BILL: No. I want to stay here.

JESSICA: Because of Frederic?

BILL: And other things.

JESSICA: Why does he love you? Turn round. You look like a bull. You're ugly.

BILL: Don't you love me?

JESSICA: Yes, Billy.

BILL: Why have you grown to look this way?

JESSICA: How do I look?

BILL: Beautiful. I think.

JESSICA: It's the light.

BILL: Don't laugh.

JESSICA: What, then? Cry?

BILL: No. Just hold my hand. Look, there it is.

JESSICA: Thank you very much.

ROBERT ANDERSON, *and his son,* MARK

ROBERT: What's the matter with you? Look at me. You've hardly said a word since we left the airport. Look at me. Oh, put your glasses on. You know you can't see a bloody thing without them. Better?

MARK: I suppose so.

ROBERT: Well? What can you see?

MARK: You. My father. And it looks as if it's going to rain. That car's a Porsche. That's a Thunderbird. That building over there's been burnt out—

ROBERT: Shut up. Wear them all the time. What stops you? Vanity? At sixteen? It's disgusting. Anybody would think you're a woman. Come on.

MARK: Where are we going?

ROBERT: To friends of mine.

MARK: Why not to the hotel?

ROBERT: Later.

MARK: I don't like this town.

ROBERT: What are you talking about?

MARK: This place. I don't like it.

ROBERT: It's the same as any city.

MARK: You've been here before.

ROBERT: I've been here a lot.

MARK: You've been everywhere.

ROBERT: I once lived here. What's that got to do with it?

MARK: I don't care for your past. I don't like going over the rotten ground again. It stinks. Why make me?

ROBERT (*after a moment*): Carry the bag.

MARK: All right. Is it far?

ROBERT: Ten minutes walk. Less.

    They go.

JESSICA *and* BILL

JESSICA: We should have been poor. You know: no money.

BILL: What difference would that have made?

JESSICA: You could have worked your fingers to the bone for some good woman.

BILL: I don't like women.

JESSICA: Except me. And I could have slaved for some good man.

On my feet all day, and on my back all night. Ah, darling, think
how happy we could have been.

BILL: Why didn't you marry him?

JESSICA: All we needed was less time to spend money. That's all.

BILL: Are we going to sit here all day?

JESSICA: I want to go and buy some clothes. Why didn't I marry
him?

BILL. I asked. Don't dress like a tart. We're cursed with bad taste.

JESSICA: I dress, if you'll forgive me, with what must be described
as perfect taste. Come and choose.

BILL: Anderson wanted to marry you. What went wrong?

JESSICA: I couldn't leave you, love. Perhaps you're right. About
the clothes. Yes, I was picked up by a waiter yesterday. A baby-
faced Aryan. Your type.

BILL: Did you go with him?

JESSICA: Not all the way. He lay on his bed, picking sausage from
his very good teeth, and suggested doing something so odd, I
laughed. I thought about it afterwards, and wondered if I could
play such games.

BILL: Could you?

JESSICA: Yes. I'm innocent.

BILL: No. You just won't learn.

They go.

HANNA FORSTER, *an old woman, alone.*

HANNA: I went walking the other day. Not such a usual thing now.
This is an old city, but not so old that it can't still breed the
young. There were girls in the streets with hands like claws.
There were young boys with bird faces lying in the gardens, and
the sunlight made them transparent, green. Do they wear black
glasses so that I shan't know their eyes have been torn out?
There's no war, no gunfire now. But they're still at it, I saw that.
They're looking for hatred, and crying when they can't find it.
Crying naked in their enemy's arms.

I've no courage to take a step forward. The continent is sinking
under our feet.

I was sixteen years old in the summer of 1898, and I was beautiful.
Were my hands like talons then? The steps down from the house
seemed long. A long way to go for such a young and unprepared

girl. It was to meet a king. He kissed me disgustingly, passed me to my father, and went in to his dinner. This was Bavaria. The little man had come to talk about war. The horses of the cavalry escort were fouling the yard. I imagined the lances entering my body. I wanted to live. I have lived. Too long. But something has died. What is it? That's a question. (FREDERIC FORSTER, *her son, comes to her*.) Freddy darling, are there still kings in the world? Do they reign?

FREDERIC: As best they can. Mother, why don't you go back to the house in the country?

HANNA: The way up to the house is too long for me now.

FREDERIC: What's happened to the woman who cleans for you?

HANNA: She's ill. Dying, they say.

FREDERIC: Can't you get another?

HANNA: I've not tried. Aren't you working today?

FREDERIC: I thought I'd stay in the city.

HANNA: To be near him?

FREDERIC: Yes.

HANNA: Are you afraid he'll leave?

FREDERIC: His sister is always wanting him to go.

HANNA: Where to?

FREDERIC: Some other place than where he is.

HANNA: Don't love him so much.

FREDERIC. You shouldn't live alone. He makes me happy.

HANNA: He's an ugly boy.

FREDERIC: I know. It touches me very much.

HANNA: Leave him:

FREDERIC: No.

BIBLIOGRAPHY OF WHITING'S
OTHER WRITINGS

Films

1952   Three Treatments for Group Three. *One Touch of Larceny, Love on Paper* and *The Golden Legend of Shults.*

1953   Dialogue for Kenwood Films. *Thanks for a Lovely Day.*
Treatment for Associated British. *These Are My Daughters.*

1954   Screenplay for *The Ship That Died of Shame* based on the story by Nicholas Monsarrat (Ealing).

1955   Screenplay for *Castle Minerva* (Ealing).

1956   Rewriting of screenplay *The Good Companions* for Associated British.
Screenplay of *The Golden Fool* for Associated British and *Talk of the Devil* for Rank.

1957   Screenplay of *Nya* for Associated British and (with Brian Forbes) of *The Captain's Table* for Rank.

1958   Screenplay of *The Reason Why* for Michael Powell and *The Gypsum Flower* for British Lion.

1959   Revisions of *Von Braun* for Columbia.

1960   Screenplay for *The Gentleman of China* for Columbia.
Screenplay for *Young Cassidy* for Sextant (M.G.M.).

He also did some revisions of *Cleopatra* for 20th-Century Fox and some work with Christopher Fry on *The Bible.* When he died he was writing notes for a film treatment of Ibsen's *The Lady from the Sea.*

Translations

Jean Anouilh   *Traveller Without Luggage*
                        Madame de . . .
André Obey   *Sacrifice to the Wind*

The Anouilh plays were produced as a double bill at the Arts Theatre by Peter Hall in January 1959 with Elizabeth Sellars, who was in both plays, and Denholm Elliott, who was Gaston in *Traveller Without Luggage*.

Both scripts are published by Samuel French, 1959.

The Obey play was televised in January 1954, with Margaretta Scott and Andrew Cruickshank, broadcast in April 1954 and staged at the Arts in March 1955. It is published by Heinemann Educational Books in *Three Dramatic Legends* edited by Elizabeth Haddon (1964).

Interviews

Writer as Gangster. An interview with the editors of *Encore*. *Encore* No. 29, Vol. 8, No. 1, January–February 1961.
This is reprinted in *Theatre at Work* edited by Charles Marowitz and Simon Trussler (Methuen, 1967).
Interview with Richard Findlater. *Time and Tide*, 9 March 1961.

Articles and Book Reviews

Writing for Actors, *The Adelphi*, second quarter 1952.
A Conversation, *Nimbus*, June–August 1953.
What the Theatre Means to Me, *Plays and Players*, August 1954.
In 'Six Opinions' (answer to John Gassner's *Modern Drama and Society*), World Theatre, Autumn 1955.
The Toll of Talent in a Timid Theatre, *Encore* No. 7, Summer 1956.
To the Plaguehouse to See the Smirching of Venus. *Act*. Autumn 1956.
Half Time at the Royal Court, *Truth*, 8 November 1957.
The Art of the Dramatist, *Plays and Players*, November 1957. (This is an excerpt of the lecture he gave at the Old Vic on 29 September 1957.)
At Ease in a Bright Red Tie, *Encore*, September–October 1959.
Book Review in *The London Magazine*, May 1960.
    on Beckett: *Krapp's Last Tape* and *Embers*.
        Tennessee Williams: *Orpheus Descending* and *Garden District*.
        Genet: *The Balcony*.
        Lorca: *Three Tragedies*.
Contribution to *The London Magazine*'s Symposium on 'A New English Theatre', July 1960.
Book Review in *The London Magazine*, November 1960.
    on Pinter: *The Birthday Party* and *The Caretaker*.

Ionesco: Plays, Volumes III and IV.
Genet: *The Blacks*.
Camus: *The Possessed*.
From My Diary, Twentieth Century, February 1961.
Book Review in *The Spectator*, 30 March 1962.
on Tennessee Williams: Five Plays.

These articles and reviews, together with the lecture *The Art of the Dramatist* and some fragments of fiction are collected in the volume *The Art of the Dramatist and Other Pieces by John Whiting* published by Alan Ross for London Magazine Editions (1969).

Play Reviews

From April 1961 till August 1962 he worked as drama critic for *The London Magazine*. The volume *John Whiting on Theatre* published by Alan Ross (1966) in the series London Magazine Editions includes reviews of Sartre's *Altona, Beyond the Fringe,* Wesker's *The Kitchen,* Osborne's *Luther,* Tynan's book *Curtains,* Fry's *Curtmantle,* the RSC production of *The Cherry Orchard,* Elaine Dundy's *My Place,* Brecht's *The Caucasian Chalk Circle,* Coward's *Sail Away* and articles headed *Some Notes on Acting* and *The Popular Theatre.*